Python Projects for Beginners

A Ten-Week Bootcamp Approach to Python Programming

Connor P. Milliken

Apress®

Python Projects for Beginners

Connor P. Milliken
Derry, NH, USA

ISBN-13 (pbk): 978-1-4842-5354-0   ISBN-13 (electronic): 978-1-4842-5355-7
https://doi.org/10.1007/978-1-4842-5355-7

Managing Director, Apress Media LLC: Welmoed Spahr
Acquisitions Editor: Nikhil Karkal
Development Editor: Rita Fernando
Coordinating Editor: Divya Modi

Cover designed by eStudioCalamar

Cover image designed by Pixabay

Distributed to the book trade worldwide by Springer Science+Business Media New York, 233 Spring Street, 6th Floor, New York, NY 10013. Phone 1-800-SPRINGER, fax (201) 348-4505, e-mail orders-ny@springer-sbm.com, or visit www.springeronline.com. Apress Media, LLC is a California LLC and the sole member (owner) is Springer Science + Business Media Finance Inc (SSBM Finance Inc). SSBM Finance Inc is a **Delaware** corporation.

For information on translations, please e-mail rights@apress.com, or visit http://www.apress.com/rights-permissions.

Apress titles may be purchased in bulk for academic, corporate, or promotional use. eBook versions and licenses are also available for most titles. For more information, reference our Print and eBook Bulk Sales web page at http://www.apress.com/bulk-sales.

Any source code or other supplementary material referenced by the author in this book is available to readers on GitHub via the book's product page, located at www.apress.com/978-1-4842-5354-0. For more detailed information, please visit http://www.apress.com/source-code.

Printed on acid-free paper

This book is dedicated to my girlfriend Jess.

Ever since we first met, you changed my life forever.

There's so much that I wish to tell you each day,
like how beautiful you are, how you inspire me, or how I would
give anything just to be with you every second of the day.

Your smile lights up my whole world and you make me so
unbelievably happy.

Anytime I have a bad day, I know you'll always be there for me.

I thought that I would only find you in my dreams, but here you are,
standing in front of me, looking beautiful as ever.

From the day I met you, I knew I wanted to give you everything.

You're smart, motivated, beautiful, and resemble all that is
right with this world.

If I only do one thing right in life, I'd like it to be you.

I promise to always push you to be better, always support
you in times of need, and always be there with a Werther's
candy to help you study.

Your dreams have become my dreams, and whatever you want in life,

I want to be there to celebrate and help guide you.

I will always love you, past forever, with all my heart and soul.

So I have only one question left for you…

(turn the page)

Will You Marry Me?

Table of Contents

About the Author

Connor P. Milliken Focused on helping others achieve their goals through education and technology, **Connor P. Milliken** brings a wealth of programming and business experience to his classes.

He graduated with a computer science degree from Daniel Webster College and is pursuing a master's in computer science with a focus in interactive intelligence from Georgia Tech.

Before becoming an instructor at Coding Temple, he was designing simulators in the video game industry for several years. During that time, he took on a vast number of roles from business to programming that he used to release a total of 11 different titles on PC and co-created an award-winning football card game called "Masters of the Gridiron."

Connor has experience in more than seven different languages and three frameworks. He focuses primarily in web development and data analytics using Python. When this book was written, he taught for a coding bootcamp in Boston, MA, where students can learn Python, web development, and data analytics over a 10-week full-time course. He is now a software engineer at Hubspot, Inc. in Cambridge, MA.

Github: *Connor-SM*

About the Technical Reviewer

 **Bharath Thiruveedula** currently works for a major telco service provider. He is core reviewer and key contributor to various OpenStack/ONAP projects. Bharath is passionate about open source technologies and is an evangelist who is focused on making his mark in the Cloud/Container domains. He has been working on distributed systems and machine learning for a significant amount of time.

Acknowledgments

I would like to thank the following people for their generosity and help:

Jessica Boucher, who has been my rock this whole time. Your love and support have continued to help me in all my endeavors. I'm truly blessed to have you in my life.

My family, who have supported and believed in me all my life. Without your guidance, none of this would be possible. To have parents and siblings like you all is nothing short of a miracle and I wouldn't have it any other way.

Clay and Dee Dreslough, who gave me an opportunity and mentored me. This book would not be possible without your guidance over the years. It was at Sports Mogul that I had realized my passion of computer programming, thanks to you both.

Derek Hawkins, who mentored and taught me a lot about teaching, programming, Python, and Ping Pong.

Kirsten Arnold, who created all the art within this book. The work you were able to create from my poor drawing skills was exactly what I had imagined.

Ripal Patel, who helped with the interview portion of Week 9. Your expertise in the hiring and interview process has been wonderful for not only me but the students.

My friends, who over the years have been there for me through it all. Whether it was watching my dog, going on adventures, or just hanging out… thank you. I will always make the drive for you all.

My coaches, who taught me about perseverance, hard work, commitment, and teamwork. Whether it was 6 AM practices or triple sessions in the middle of summer, you've played a big part in my life and for that I'm grateful.

The Coding Temple team, who gave me the opportunity and entrusted me to educate those wanting to pursue a career in tech.

The Apress team, who have helped me throughout this entire process with writing, formatting, reviewing, and more.

My students, who helped to show me why teaching is so rewarding.

CHAPTER 1

Getting Started

Hello there! Welcome to your first step toward becoming a Python developer. Exciting isn't it? Whether you're just beginning to learn how to program, or have experience in other languages, the lessons taught in this book will help to accelerate your goals. As a Python instructor, I can guarantee you that it's not about where you start, it's about how hard you're willing to work.

At the time of writing this book, my daily job is a coding bootcamp instructor where I teach students how to go from zero programming experience to professional developers in just ten weeks. This book was designed with the intent to bring a bootcamp-based approach to text. This book aims to help you learn subjects that are valuable to becoming a professional developer with Python.

Each subsequent chapter will have an overview and a brief description of what we'll cover that week. This week we'll be covering all the necessary basics to get us jump started. Following the age old saying, *"You must learn to walk before you can run,"* we must understand what our tools are and how to use them before we can begin coding.

Overview

- Understanding why and how this book works

- Installing Python and Anaconda

- Understanding how to use these new tools

- Understanding how to use the terminal

- Writing your first Python program

Without further ado, let's get started, shall we?

© Connor P. Milliken 2020
C. P. Milliken, *Python Projects for Beginners*, https://doi.org/10.1007/978-1-4842-5355-7_1

Monday: Introduction

Almost every programmer remembers that "Aha!" moment, when everything clicked for them. For me that was when I picked up Python. After years of computer science education, one of the best methods I found to learn was by building applications and applying the knowledge you learn. That's why this book will have you coding along rather than reading about the theory behind programming. Python makes it simple to pick up concepts otherwise difficult in other languages. This makes it a great language for breaking into the development industry!

You may have already noticed that the structure of this book is different than most. Instead of chapters, we have each topic separated by weeks or days. Notice the current header for the section. This is part of the bootcamp-based approach, so that you may set goals for each day. There will be two ways to follow along this book:

1. Over the course of ten weeks

2. Over the course of ten days

If you'd like to follow the 10-week approach, then think of each chapter as a weekly goal. All chapters are broken up further into daily segments Monday to Friday. The first four days, Monday through Thursday, will introduce new concepts to understand. Friday, or better known as Project Day, is where we will create a program together based on the lessons learned throughout the week. The focus is that you set aside 30–60 minutes each day to complete each daily task.

If you're eager enough to try the bootcamp style, where you learn all the material in ten days, then think of each chapter as a single day. Granted, you must know that in order to complete this book in ten days, you will need to dedicate around 8 hours per day, which is a typical day for coding bootcamp students. In bootcamps (*like the one I taught*), we go over several concepts daily, and each subsequent day we reiterate the topics learned from previous lessons. This helps to accelerate the process of learning each concept.

What Is Python?

Python is an **interpreted**, **high-level**, **general-purpose** programming language. To understand what each of these descriptions mean, let's make a few comparisons:

- **Low Level vs. High Level**: Refers to whether we program using instructions and data objects at the level of the machine or whether we program using more abstract operations that have been provided by the language designer. Low-level languages (like C, C++) require you to allocate and manage memory, whereas Python manages memory for us.

- **General Purpose vs. Targeted**: Refers to whether the operations of the programming language are widely applicable or are fine-tuned to a domain. For example, SQL is a targeted language that is designed to facilitate extracting information from relational databases, but you wouldn't want to use it to build an operating system.

- **Interpreted vs. Compiled**: Refers to whether the sequence of instructions written by the programmer, called "*source code*," is executed directly (*by an interpreter*) or whether it is first converted (*by a compiler*) into a sequence of machine-level primitive operations. Most applications designed with Python are run through the interpreter, so errors are found at runtime.

Python also emphasizes code readability and uses whitespace to separate snippets of code. We'll learn more about how whitespace in Python works as we get into our lessons, but for now just know that Python is a great first language to break into the computer science industry.

Why Python?

I could go on about why Python is so amazing, but a simple Google search would do that for me. Python is one of the easier languages to learn. Notice I said "*easier*" and not "*easy*"... that's because programming is still difficult, but Python reads closer to the English language than most other languages. This is one of the benefits of learning Python, because concepts that you learn from this book are still applicable to other languages. Python is also one of the most sought-after skills in the technology industry today, used by companies such as Google, Facebook, IBM, etc. It's been used to build applications like Instagram, Pinterest, Dropbox, and much more!

It's also one of the fastest growing languages in 2019, climbing to the top 3 languages to learn for the future.[1] How well does it pay though? According to Indeed.com, the average salary in 2018 was around **$117,000 USD**![2] That's a lot of monopoly money!

One of the biggest reasons for learning Python, though, must be the use of the language itself. It's used in several different industries: front-end development, back-end development, full-stack, testing, data analytics, data science, web design, etc., which makes it a useful language.

Why This Book?

Let's start with the main reason for wanting to read this book. The material taught throughout this book has a proven track record. I've personally used this exact organization approach to help get my students well-paying positions across a variety of industries. The structure of this curriculum has been repeatedly improved over the years to stick with current industry trends.

One of the next great strengths of this book vs. its competitors is how the concepts are taught. I won't bore you with details; instead we'll build small- and large-scale applications together throughout the course of this book. The best way to learn is often by doing! Especially when it comes to programming, one of the lessons I often tell students is to just try writing the code, and if it breaks, fix it. You won't be able to learn if you don't try to break things!

Lastly, this book will not only teach you how to program but how to think like a programmer. At the beginning of each week, I'll challenge you, and by the end of the lesson, you'll be able to understand the approach you need to take. You can always tell the difference between those who are only able to program and those that are proven developers.

Who This Book Is For?

It's always good to understand what you're getting into before you start reading the book. To want to read a book, you first must realize if the book itself is designed for you. If you can answer yes to any of the following questions, then this book is for you:

---

[1]www.tiobe.com/tiobe-index/

[2]www.indeed.com/salaries/Python-Developer-Salaries

- Do you have experience in other programming languages but want to pick up a high-level language?

- Have you never programmed before but are eager to learn?

- Did you take computer science courses previously, but they just didn't help you learn how to create applications?

- Do you want to make a career change?

- Have you tried to learn languages previously but couldn't because of the difficulty of the language?

- Have you programmed in Python before but want to improve your abilities and learn new tools?

This book is designed for a wide array of readers, no matter your background. The real question is on you, "**How hard are you willing to work**?" The concepts taught in this book can benefit anyone willing to learn. Even if you've programmed in Python before, this book can still help you become a stronger developer.

What You'll Learn

This book was created to be used for bootcamp classes designed in teaching Python. You can expect to cover necessary information that would be required of you on the job as a Python developer. These concepts will give you the ability to go forward with your education in programming. At the end of each chapter, we'll use the concepts covered to create a variety of real-world applications. After all, we're not just focused on Python here, we're trying to build you up to become a better developer.

Tomorrow, we'll find out how to install the necessary software that this book uses. If you already have Anaconda and Python on your machine, you can skip to Wednesday's lesson.

Tuesday: Setting Up Anaconda and Python

Today, we're going to get our software setup. Throughout this book we'll be using a software platform called **Anaconda**, an **integrated development environment (IDE)** called **Jupyter Notebook**, and the language of Python itself. This book will strictly cover Python 3; however, at times you may see me mention subtle differences between versions 2 and 3. Let's go ahead and download and install these first, then I'll get into what each of them are.

Cross-Platform Development

Python runs on all major operating systems, making it a cross-platform language. This means that you can write code on one operating system and work with someone that uses a completely different machine than you. If both machines have Python installed, they should both be able to run the program.

Installing Anaconda and Python for Windows

Most OS X and Linux operating systems already come with Python installed; however, you still need to download Anaconda. For Windows users, Python usually isn't included, but it gets installed with Anaconda. Use the following steps to install Anaconda properly:

1. Open your browser and type www.anaconda.com/distribution/.

2. Click the download button in the header (see Figure 1-1).

Figure 1-1. *Anaconda Download Page*

3. Once you are on the next page, make sure you select the proper operating system on the header at the top. Click that button (see Figure 1-2).

Figure 1-2. *Selecting an operating system*

4. Next, click the download button for the Python 3.7 (*or greater*) section (see Figure 1-3).

Figure 1-3. *Downloading Python 3.x version*

5. **This step is strictly for Windows users**... Once the installer fully downloads, go ahead and run it. Use all defaults except for one option. When you get to the page in Figure 1-4, make sure you click the "**add to path**" option. This will let us access Anaconda through our terminal.

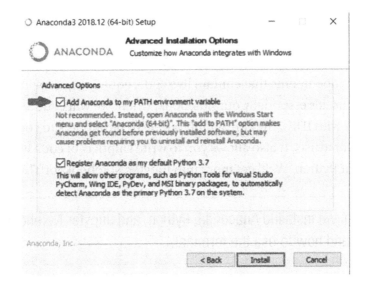

Figure 1-4. *Add to Path*

6. For all options (*besides step 5 for Windows users*), use default settings. Then go ahead and click the "Install" button and let Anaconda finish installing.

What Is Anaconda?

Anaconda is a Python and R distribution software. It aims to provide everything you need for Python "*out of the box*." Its primary use is for data analytics and data science; however, it's a superb tool for learning as well. Upon downloading, it includes

- The core Python language and libraries

- Jupyter Notebook

- Anaconda's own package manager

These are just a few features out of the many that Anaconda comes with; however, these are the ones we'll be using throughout the book. The first feature in this list is the Python language and included packages that Python has access to. Libraries are pre-written code by another developer that you can use for your own benefit. The second feature is talked about in the next section. Lastly, Anaconda has a way of managing environments for us. This is a complex topic that we'll get into in later weeks.

What Is Jupyter Notebook?

It is an open-source **integrated development environment (IDE)** that allows you to create and share documents that contain live code, equations, visualizations, and narrative text. For us, it's essentially our notebook, where we will code along together. If you're not familiar with IDEs, they are simply a tool for developers to code in. Think of them as a canvas for artists. It also allows you to write snippets of code without needing to know a lot about Python. We'll get more into Jupyter Notebook for Thursday's lesson.

In today's lesson, we installed Anaconda, Python, and Jupyter Notebook. Tomorrow, we'll learn why and how to use the terminal.

Wednesday: How to Use the Terminal

Depending on your operating system, you're going to be using the **Command Prompt** (*Windows*) or the **Terminal** (*Linux and OS X*). From this point forward, I'm going to refer to it as the "*terminal*," so just keep that in mind if you're on Windows. The terminal is a tool for users to be able to issue commands to the computer through basic text. For most of this book, we will use the terminal to either test our Python code or run Jupyter Notebook. Today we'll be learning basic commands and how to use the Python shell. To get started, let's open the terminal. As each operating system will look different, terminal sessions will be defined in code by the "**$**". Any text you see after that symbol will be what you need to write into the terminal yourself.

Changing Directories

While inside the terminal, you'll often want to move around from folder to folder. This gives you the power to navigate around your computer. It's important to understand how to do this, as it's always going to be what we do to start up Jupyter Notebook. In order to change directories, you need to type in "*cd*" followed by the folder name you wish to go to.

```
$ cd desktop
```

If you need to go backward, out of a folder, then you'll want to use two dots ("..").

```
$ cd ..
```

Often, throughout this book, you'll need to traverse through several directories to get into a project folder. When you use the "cd" command, you can go as far forward or backward as you select, you just need to specify the correct path to the folder you wish to go to. Take the following code, for instance...

```
$ cd desktop/../desktop
```

We're going into the desktop directory, but then going back out, only to go back into it. There's nothing wrong with this; however, this is just an example that the computer will follow the path that you specify. Normally we would just cd into the desktop and be done.

Checking the Directory

To check the directory that you're currently in, just look to the left of where you can write these lines of text. For Windows users, the directory you're currently in will be the ending URL that you're on, as marked in bold as follows:

C:\Users\name**desktop**>

The last folder name is the "*desktop*," which means that I'm currently in the directory for my desktop. If I were to create any files or folders, they would be created directly on there. To check which directory you're in for Linux, it will be the name just to the left of the "*$*":

user@user:~/**Desktop**$

For OS X users, it'll be to the left of your username (*who you're logged in as*):

User-Macbook-Pro:**Desktop** Name$

Making Directories

Though it's certainly okay to go into your file explorer, right-click, and select "*create new folder*," it's good to know how to create a new folder through the terminal session itself. Make sure that you're in the "*desktop*" directory that we "*cd*" into previously. Then write the following line:

```
$ mkdir python_bootcamp
```

This will create a new folder called "**python_bootcamp**" on your desktop. We'll be using this folder from here on out to store our lessons so that we stay organized.

Creating Files

Again, it's easier to create files by going into your file explorer. However, sometimes we need to create files in terminal depending on the file type. Before we create a new file, however, let's "*cd*" into our "*python_bootcamp*" folder that we created:

```
$ cd python_bootcamp
```

Now, for **Windows** users, we'll need to type the following:

```
$ echo.>example.txt
```

Or if you're on **Linux/OSX**:

```
$ touch example.txt
```

You should now be able to see the sample.txt file in file explorer.

Note   If you don't see the ".*txt*" extension, it's because you don't have "**extensions**" checked in your preferences within file explorer.

Checking a Version Number

The terminal is always a great way to check version numbers of certain software that we download. Since we already downloaded and installed Python, let's run the following code:

```
$ python --version
```

Clearing the Terminal Output

Sometimes the terminal gets full of useless output or just becomes tough to read. When you want to clear the output, you need to write the following line (*for Windows*):

```
$ cls
```

For Linux/OSX users, you'll need to type in the following:

```
$ clear
```

Using the Python Shell

Python is a language that requires what is called an *"interpreter"* to read and run the code we create. When the Python shell is activated, it acts as a local interpreter within the terminal session that is open. While it's open, we can write any Python that we wish to execute. This is generally great for practicing small snippets of code, so that you don't have to open an IDE and run an entire file. To start the Python shell up, while we are in the directory of *"python_bootcamp"*, simply type *"python"* and hit enter. The following will appear:

```
$ python
Python 3.7.0 (v3)
Type "help", "copyright", "credits" or "license" for more information
>>>
```

The output will show the Python version you're currently running. You'll notice the three arrows (>>>), this means that you're now working within the Python interpreter. While in the Python shell, everything you write is interpreted as the Python language. If for some reason you receive the following response:

```
$ python
'python' is not recongized as an internal or external command, operable
program or batch file.
```

This means that Anaconda and Python were not installed properly. I'd advise you to go back to yesterday's lesson and reinstall Anaconda following the step-by-step instructions given. You may need to restart your computer as well.

Writing Your First Line of Python

Up to this point, we haven't done any programming. Generally, I'm against not diving right into coding myself; however, these basic setup instructions are crucial to getting started as a developer. Although we haven't gone over any Python just yet, while the interpreter is still running, next to the arrows write the following code and hit enter:

```
>>> print("Hello, buddy!")
```

There you go! You've just written your first line of Python and should see the following output:

```
>>> print("Hello, buddy!")
Hello, buddy!
>>>
```

Exiting the Python Shell

Now, I'll get to explaining what you just wrote in a later lesson, but for now let's get out of the Python shell and finish today's lesson by writing the following line and hitting enter:

```
>>> exit( )
```

Today's lesson was all about operating and understanding the terminal. This is an important skill for several developer positions, especially those that use Linux operating systems. Tomorrow we'll discuss how to operate Jupyter Notebook!

Thursday: Using Jupyter Notebook

Jupyter Notebook is going to be where we spend most of our time throughout this book. It's a powerful tool that is used in the data science community and makes it easier for us to learn Python because we can solely focus on writing code. Today's lesson is all about how to use this tool, the cells, and how to open it.

Note   Each lesson will always ask you to open Jupyter Notebook, so keep this page handy in case you need to come back to it.

Opening Jupyter Notebook

Jupyter Notebook can be opened through the Anaconda program; however, I want you to start getting used to the terminal and how to operate it, so we're not going to open it through Anaconda. Instead, we're going to do this through the terminal. The two benefits to this are

- Jupyter Notebook will open in the same directory that our terminal is in

- Knowing how to use terminal will help you as a developer

If you still have the terminal session from yesterday open, skip the first step.

Step 1: Open Terminal

We need to open terminal and "*cd*" into our "*python_bootcamp*" directory:

```
$ cd desktop/python_bootcamp
```

Step 2: Writing the Jupyter Notebook Command

Opening Jupyter Notebook through the terminal is as simple as typing the name of the tool:

```
$ jupyter notebook
```

Be sure that you are in the proper directory before typing the code; otherwise it will open wherever your terminal directory is currently located. Often, this will open Jupyter Notebook up in your user folder. Jupyter Notebook will open in your browser.

Creating a Python File

Anytime we start a new week, we'll end up creating a new file to work from. To do so, it's simple; just click the "**New**" button on the right side of the screen when Jupyter Notebook first opens. Then select "*Python 3*" (see Figure 1-5).

Figure 1-5. *Creating a Python 3 notebook*

Once you click the "*Python 3*" option, a new tab will open as this file. Click the name at the top to rename it, and let's name this file "W*eek_01*" (see Figure 1-6).

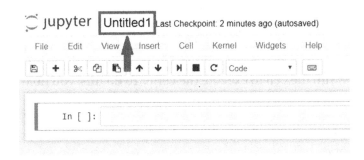

Figure 1-6. *Changing the file name*

Jupyter Notebook Cells

Now that we've opened up Jupyter Notebook and created a file that we can work with, let's talk about cells. I'm not talking about biology; rather, in this notebook you'll notice the empty white rectangle section below the tools (see Figure 1-7). These are known as "*cells.*"

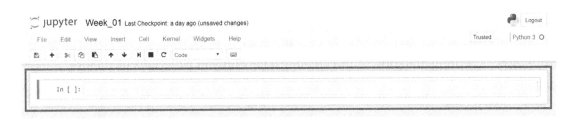

Figure 1-7. *Notebook cells highlighted in red*

Each cell is where we can write our code, or even use the **Markup** language. Let's write some markup to begin with.

1. Click in the first cell, so the surrounding area glows blue.

2. In the toolbar, you'll notice a drop-down menu that says "code." Click the drop-down, and select "markdown" instead.

3. Within the cell write the following:

```
# Week 01
```

> **Note**   When writing markup, the number of hashtags in a row relates to the size of the heading. Like HTML header tags.

4. Let's now run the cell to execute the code. To do this, you hold shift and press enter (*the cell must be selected*).

5. When you use shift + enter, a new cell will appear below the current one.

Within this newly created cell, let's go ahead and write a simple line of Python to see how the output works. Let's go ahead and write the following:

```
# this is python
print("Hello, buddy!")
```

Go ahead and run the cell. It will run all the code within the cell and output the result. Again, don't worry about the actual Python, this lesson is about how Jupyter Notebook cells run.

For the rest of this book, we'll be writing our code inside of Jupyter Notebook files. I'll be using markdown to specify certain sections, so be sure you're comfortable with running cells, writing markdown, and creating a new Jupyter Notebook file before moving on.

Today we learned how to use Jupyter Notebook and what we can do with cells. In tomorrow's lesson, we'll build our first Python application!

Friday: Creating Your First Program

Every Friday will be known as "**Project Day**," where we will build a small application or game together, which uses the concepts learned throughout the week. This week, however, I'm just going to have you write some code into a cell so that you can see the power of Python. Since we haven't gone over any Python just yet, I wanted you to be able to experience what we will learn over the upcoming weeks. The code your about to write will use concepts from weeks 2, 3, and 4. By the end of these weeks, you'll be able to fully understand each line of the following code and make your own tweaks to make the program more challenging.

We're going to be working from the Jupyter Notebook file from yesterday's lesson. If you had closed out of the program since coming back to this book, go ahead and reopen the file.

Note   If you forgot how to open Jupyter Notebook, go back to yesterday's lesson and redo the steps, except for creating a file.

Line Numbers Introduced

For larger projects, it becomes tough to follow along with books sometimes. For this project, and all other lessons going forward, I'll be implementing line numbers. This will make it easier for you to follow along and check if you wrote the code correctly:

```
1|  ←
```

Line numbers will now appear on the left side of all cells, as we will need to write all this code within a single cell. Be sure to pay attention to these numbers, as you may see them jump a couple lines:

```
1| # this is the first line in the cell
5| # this is the fifth line in the cell
```

This means that you should write the second line shown, on the 5th line.

Note   Turn lines on by pressing "L" after clicking the cell's side.

Creating the Program

The first thing that we need to do is create a new cell below the current cell in our file. In order to do that, simply follow these steps:

1. Click the last cell in the file.

2. While it is highlighted, go to the "**Insert**" tab in the menu bar, and click "**Insert Cell Below.**"

We now have a cell to work with for our project. If you'd like to create a markdown cell that says "**Guessing Game**" as the header, feel free to look back at the previous lesson and how we did it before. Within that new cell, let's go ahead and write the following code:

```
1|  # guessing game
2|  from random import randint
3|  from IPython.display import clear_output
5|  guessed = False
6|  number = randint(0, 100)
7|  guesses = 0
9|  while not guessed:
10|     ans = input("Try to guess the number I am thinking of!")
        # use tab to indent
12|     guesses += 1
14|     clear_output( )
16|     if int(ans) == number:
17|             print("Congrats! You guessed it correctly.")
                # use tab twice to indent twice
18|             print( "It took you { } guesses!".format(guesses) )
19|             break
20|     elif int(ans) > number:
```

```
21|            print("The number is lower than what you guessed.")
22|    elif int(ans) < number:
23|            print("The number is greater than what you guessed.")
```

This program is not perfect by any means, but it's certainly fun to try and guess the number that the computer is thinking of. Now, I know that this looks like a foreign language to you right now, but over the next couple of weeks, each line will begin to make sense. Eventually you'll even be able to make your own changes and improvements to the game! What I want you to do now is run the cell and play the game. Begin to think like a developer, and ask yourself these questions while you play:

- What improvements can I make?

- What makes the program crash?

- What would I do better?

Don't be afraid if you get an error, it's all part of the growth of becoming a developer! The fun part about testing the code that you write is that you try to break it. As we go forward, I'll challenge you with questions about why a line in the code works the way it does. When this happens, try to think about it for a couple minutes, even try to Google the answer. As a developer you'll find a lot of what you do is Googling a problem. This is what separates good developers from great ones... the ability to figure out problems on their own. With the rest of the lessons in this book, you'll be well on your way to figuring out problems without my help.

Final Output

All source code for each week will be located within the Github repository for this book. You may find the link to that repository in the front of the book. To find the specific code for this week, simply open or download the "**Week_01.ipynb**" file from the Github repository. If you ran into errors along the way, be sure to reference what you wrote with the code in this file to see where you went wrong.

Today we were able to see our first Python program in action. Granted you may not understand what is going on, I believe it's crucial that you see the power of Python. As we go forward, feel free to come back to this program and make your own improvements to it. After all the only way you get better is by doing!!!

Weekly Summary

I know this week was a bit slow, but it is a crucial week in the process. We covered how to download the necessary tools, how to use them, and how to use the terminal itself. These topics are important in understanding the content going forward and will help set you up for success.

At the end of this week, we ended up programming a fun guessing game together, that I hope you tried to break and play around with. As a developer it's important to want to break a program, so that you may improve it. In the upcoming week, the real fun begins. We'll start to learn the basics of Python and eventually write a small program together.

Weekly Challenges

Each week will have its own challenges at the end that you should certainly try. Completing them will help in improving your programming skills. As this week was mostly about setting up, the following challenges won't be about programming at all. All other weeks, however, will give you good examples to test your abilities.

1. **New File**: Create a new Jupyter Notebook file called "Week 1 – Challenges." You should now have two files within the main work folder.

2. **Writing Markdown**: Within the file from exercise 1, create a cell with markdown in it that says "Challenge 1." Try several different header sizes. Pick the one you like best.

3. **Exploring Python**: You should get used to Googling problems or topics that interest you. Try searching for Python topics that interest you, and keep them in mind as you begin to learn the language.

4. **Motivating Yourself**: Every programmer started from nothing. Each one became a great programmer from pushing themselves to learn the languages they were interested in. Figure out what motivates you to want to become a developer and write it down. Keep this in mind when you begin to struggle.

CHAPTER 2

Python Basics

No matter what famous programmer you think of, like Bill Gates or Guido van Rossum, they also started at a basic level at some point in their life. These basic concepts are a necessity to build a foundation on which you can learn any programming language. After all, you don't start building a house from the roof down, you need to have a foundation to work from. That's where this week comes in to play.

The focus this week will be on **data types** and **variables**. These are core concepts in just about any programming language. The beauty of learning a single language is that it allows you to pick up other languages easily. This is due in part that all languages follow the same core concepts. By the end of this week, you'll be able to understand how to write simple programs on your own. A program such as the one that we'll build together, where we will print information out to the user in a nicely formatted receipt.

This week I also introduce your first *challenge question*. These questions are to ensure that you begin to "**think like a developer.**" Some questions may not have definitive answers, but rather they'll push you to create solutions and **problem-solve**. It's important that you spend some time thinking about each question, so that you can begin to train your problem-solving skills. After all, it's the most sought-after skill in every development industry.

Overview

- Understanding data types

- How to use variables

- Seeing what you can do with strings

- How to manipulate a string

- Coding a program that prints receipts

21

© Connor P. Milliken 2020
C. P. Milliken, *Python Projects for Beginners*, https://doi.org/10.1007/978-1-4842-5355-7_2

CHALLENGE QUESTION

In programming, we have a concept called "**algorithms**." An algorithm is simply just a set of steps. Whether you know it or not, you've used algorithms throughout your life. A common algorithm is a recipe that you follow to make food.

To think like a developer, you must begin to understand how a computer reads code. A computer is only as smart as the program that it's supposed to execute. This means that even the smartest computers can fail if the steps aren't correct. Let's use a recipe to bake a cake, for instance. If we miss a single step or leave the cake in the oven for too long, then we fail, as would a computer that is missing a crucial step.

Now, I'd like you to think about the steps for making a peanut butter and jelly sandwich. Write down your steps on a piece of paper. Try to think like a computer when you write them out and understand that you need to be as precise as possible. The answer will be at the end of this chapter.

Monday: Comments and Basic Data Types

Today marks your first lesson of the Python language! The two concepts taught today will help build that foundation that we're striving for. To follow along with the content for today, let's open up Jupyter Notebook from our "*python_bootcamp*" folder. If needed, go back to last week's lesson on how to open up Jupyter Notebook. Once it's open, create a new file, and rename it to "*Week_02*." Next, make the first cell markdown, with the following code:

```
# Comments & Basic Data Types
```

What Are Comments and Why Use Them?

Comments are like notes that you leave behind, either for yourself or someone else to read. They are not read in by the interpreter, meaning that you can write whatever you want, and the computer will ignore it. A good comment will be short, easy to read, and to the point. Putting a comment on every line is tedious, but not putting any comments at all is bad practice. As you program, you'll begin to understand what that happy medium looks like.

When you begin to write larger programs, you'll want to leave notes for yourself. Too often have I created a program, stopped working on it for three weeks, and when I came back, I forget what I was working on. Leaving comments isn't only good for yourself but also for others who will read your code. Think of comments as breadcrumbs that help you understand what's going on.

Writing Comments

In Python, we can write comments using the **hash** (#) symbol. Any text that follows this symbol will be commented out. In the cell below our markdown header, let's write our first comment:

```
# this is a comment
```

Let's go ahead and run the cell. Notice that nothing happens. This is because the computer completely ignores any comments. For the most part, we'll write comments on their own line; however, in certain instances you may see comments written in line with code. In the same cell as the previous comment, let's add the following line:

```
print("Hello")        # this is also a comment
```

The first portion of this line will run and output **"Hello",** but the second part will be ignored because of the hash symbol.

Note   Markdown uses hash characters for headers, like Python comments. Make sure you know what type your cell is set to *"markdown/cell."*

To write multiline comments so that you may write more descriptive paragraphs for larger portions of code, we would need to use three opening and closing double quotes:

```
"""
    This is a multi-Line comment
"""
print("Hello")        # this is also a comment
```

Go ahead and run the cell. Notice that the text within the multiline comment gets ignored. These types of comments are great for adding descriptive paragraphs about your code. Be sure not to overuse them, however, as you can certainly make a mess of a program by using too many of them.

What Are Data Types?

Almost all languages use data types, they are essential to every program. **Data types** are how we define values, likes words or numbers. If I were to ask you what a sentence is made up of, you would probably reply with *"words or characters."* Well, in programming, we call them strings. Just the same as we refer to numbers as their own data type as well. Data types define what we can do and how these values are stored in memory on the computer. In Table 2-1, you'll find that each row displays a data type, a sample value, and a description for each. Read each section for a longer explanation for each type. You can find the four basic types that we cover this week within the table.

Table 2-1. *Data type examples*

Data Types	Sample Value	Description
Integer	5	Whole numbers
Float	5.7	Decimal numbers
Boolean	True	True or False values
String	"Hello"	Characters within quotes

The Print Statement

Before we go any further, I just want to touch on the **print statement**. In almost every language, you need the ability to output information to the user; within Python we're able to do this through the print statement. Now I don't want to get too far in depth, but the print statement is what we call a **function** in Python. We will cover functions during the entire fifth week. For now, though, just know that the print statement allows us to output information to the user. The way it works is by writing the keyword *"print"* followed by parenthesis. Whatever is inside of the parenthesis will be output for the user to see.

Integers

These data types are often called **integers** or **ints**. They are positive or negative **WHOLE** numbers with no decimal point. Integers are used for a variety of reasons, between math calculations and indexing (*which we'll get into later*); they are a main data type in any language. Let's go ahead and print a couple examples out in the next cell of our file:

```
# the following are all integers
print(2)
print(10)
```

Go ahead and run the cell. The resulted output should be a series of numbers **2** and **10**.

Floats

Anytime a number has a decimal point on it, they're known as floating point data types. It doesn't matter if it has 1 digit, or 20, it's still a **float**. The primary use of floats is in math calculations, although they have other uses as well. Let's check out an example:

```
# the following are all floats
print(10.953)
print(8.0)        # even this number is a float
```

Go ahead and run the cell. The output should be a series of numbers **10.953** and **8.0**.

Note   The number "8.0" is considered a float, because it includes a decimal point.

Booleans

The **boolean** data type is either a True or False value. Think of it like a switch, where it's either off or on. It can't be assigned any other value except for True or False. Booleans are a key data type, as they provide several uses. One of the most common is for tracking whether something occurred. For instance, if you took a video game and wanted to know if a player was alive, when the player spawned initially, you would set a boolean to "**True**". When the player lost all their lives, you would set the boolean to "**False**". This way you can simply check the boolean to see if the player is alive or not. This makes for a quicker program rather than calculating lives each time. Let's go ahead and run the following:

```python
# the following are booleans
print(True)
print(False)
```

Go ahead and run that cell. The output should be the words **True** and **False**, respectively.

Strings

Also known as "*String Literals,*" these data types are the most complex of the four that we go over today. The actual definition of a string is

Strings in Python are arrays of bytes representing unicode characters.

To most beginners, that's just going to sound like a bunch of nonsense, so let's break it down into something simple that we can understand. Strings are nothing more than a set of ***characters, symbols, numbers, whitespace, and even empty space between two sets of quotation marks***. In Python we can use either single or double quotes to create a string. Most of the time it's personal preference, unless you want to include quotes within a string (*see line 3 in the next block*). Whatever is wrapped inside of the quotation marks will be considered a string, even if it's a number. Let's go ahead and write some examples in the next cell for strings:

```python
# the following are strings
print(" ")
print("There's a snake in my boot!")
print('True')
```

The output will include an empty line at the top, as we print out nothing in the first statement.

MONDAY EXERCISES

1. **Output**: Print out your name.

2. **Type Checking**: Try checking the type of a value by using the type() method. This will always print out what kind of data type you're checking. This is useful to check data types when you're unsure. As an example:

```
>>> type(int) # will output <class 'int'>
```

Today, we focused on the four essential data types in Python. Understanding the difference between each is key as we move forward. In tomorrow's lesson, we will begin to understand how to save these data types to be used later in the program.

Tuesday: Variables

Variables are one of the most important beginner-level concepts in programming. They allow us to save values into memory using a name that we assign. This lets us use those values later in the program. Yesterday's lesson covered different data types, but what if you wanted to save one of those data types to use later? This works like how we store information in our brain, variables are stored in computer memory, and we can access them later by referencing the name we used. I won't go into the theory behind how Python stores information, as we're focusing more on the application of programming, but it's worth noting that Python automatically handles memory storage and **garbage collection** for us.

To follow along with this lesson, let's continue from our previous notebook file "*Week_02*" and simply add a markdown cell at the bottom that says "**Variables.**"

How They Work

We declare a name on the left side of the **equals operator** ("="), and on the right side, we assign the value that we want to save to use later. Take the following example (*no need to write this*):

```
>>> first_name = "John"
```

When you create a variable, the line where you assign the value is a step called **declaration**. We've just declared a variable with a name of "*first_name*" and assigned it the value of the string data type "*John*". This string is now stored in memory, and we're able to access it by calling the variable name "*first_name*".

Note   Variable names can contain only letters, underscores, and numbers; however, they cannot start with a number.

Handling Naming Errors

All programmers make mistakes, so it's not a problem if you run into errors. It just comes with the job. Let's look at a common mistake that occurs with variables (*no need to write this*):

```
>>> Sport = 'baseball'      # capital 'S'
>>> print(sport)            # lowercase 'S'
```

If we try to run this code, we'll get the following error/output:

```
NameError: name 'sport' is not defined
```

This is because the names are completely different. We referenced a variable with a lowercase "s" but declared one with capital "S." To fix this we would capitalize the "s" in sport within print.

Integer and Float Variables

To store an integer or float in a variable, we give a name to the left of the operator and write a number on the right side. In the next cell, let's go ahead and write the following code:

```
num1 = 5              # storing an integer into a variable
num2 = 8.4            # storing a float into a variable
print(num1, num2)     # you can print multiple items using commas
```

Go ahead and run that cell. Notice the output is **5 and 8.4**, even though we print out "*num1*" and "*num2*." We're printing out the value that is stored in those variables.

Boolean Variables

Remember that booleans are **True** or **False** values, so storing them is as simple as typing in one of those two words. Let's write the following:

```
# storing a boolean into a variable
switch = True
print(switch)
```

Go ahead and run that cell. The resulted output is "**True**". Notice that in Jupyter Notebook, the value of True or False will glow green. This is a good indication if we wrote it correctly.

String Variables

Strings are as easy to store as the previous three data types. Just keep in mind that the use of single or double quotes matters. Let's go ahead and write the following code in a new cell:

```
# storing strings into a variable
name = 'John Smith'
fav_number = '9'
print(name, fav_number)            # will print 9 next to the name
```

Go ahead and run that. Remember that the string "**9**" is not the same as the integer 9. These two data types act differently, even though the output looks similar.

Using Multiple Variables

In almost any program you'll write, you're going to need to perform some calculations or manipulation on variables. In the following code, we access the values from previously declared variables and add them together to create a sum. Make sure that the previous cells have been run before running this cell. Let's go ahead and put this in a new cell:

```
# using two variables to create another variable
result = num1 + num2
print(result)
```

After running this cell, you'll notice that it added **5** and **8.4** together to output **13.4**.

Note   If you get an error saying that a variable doesn't exist, try running the cell where that variable is declared first.

Using Operators on Numerical Variables

Think of Python as a calculator, where we can alter any variables we want. In the following code, we alter the "*result*" variable defined previously:

```
# adding, deleting, multiplying, dividing from a variable
result += 1    # same as saying result = result + 1
print(result)
result *= num1    # same as saying result = result * num1
print(result)
```

Go ahead and run the cell. In the first line, we added 1 to the result, then later we multiplied it by the value of "*num1*," which is 5. All the while, the computer saved the result variable so we could continue to edit it. Then we print the result, which comes out to **72.0**.

Overwriting Previously Created Variables

Python makes it easy for us to change the value of a variable, by simply re-declaring it. In some languages you would have to define the data type, but Python handles all of that for us. We've seen this occur with the preceding result variable, but it's worth noting in its own cell:

```
# defining a variable and overwriting it's value
name = 'John'
print(name)
name = 'Sam'
print(name)
```

Go ahead and run that in a new cell. You'll notice that the output shows **"John"** and **"Sam"**. The location of when you access or re-declare your variables matter; keep that in mind.

Whitespace

Whitespace just means characters which are used for spacing and have an *"empty"* representation. In the context of python, it means tabs and spaces. For example:

```
>>> name = 'John Smith'
```

There's whitespace to the left and right of the equals operator. It's not required, but it makes reading the code easier. The computer simply ignores whitespace when compiling the code. Within the string, however, the space is **NOT** whitespace, this is simply a "spacing" character.

TUESDAY EXERCISES

1. **Variable Output**: Store the value 3 in a variable called "x" and the value 10 in a variable called "y". Save the result of x * y into a separate variable called "result". Finally, output the information so it shows like the following:

   ```
   >>> 3 + 10 = 13
   ```

2. **Area Calculation**: Calculate the area of a 245.54" x 13.66" rectangle. Print out the result. HINT: Area is width multiplied by height.

Variables are used everywhere, and Python makes it easy for us to incorporate them. Being able to store information is a key part of any program. Tomorrow we'll look at how we can manipulate strings.

Wednesday: Working with Strings

It's important to understand what you can do with string data types. The next two days cover **working with** and **manipulating** strings so that we may build a receipt printing program at the end of the week. We won't worry about taking in user input but rather how to format strings, what a string index is, etc.

To follow along with this lesson, let's continue from our previous notebook file "*Week_02*" and simply add a markdown cell at the bottom that says, "**Working with Strings.**"

String Concatenation

When we talk about concatenating strings, I mean that we want to add one string to the end of another. This concept is just one of many ways to add string variables together to complete a larger string. For the first example, let's add three separate strings together:

```
# using the addition operator without variables
name = "John" + " " + "Smith"
print(name)
```

Go ahead and run that cell below the markdown cell. The output we get is "**John Smith**". We ended up adding two strings that were names and separated them with the use of a string with a space inside. Let's go ahead and try to store the two names into variables first:

```
# using the addition operator with variables
first_name = "John"
last_name = "Smith"
full_name = first_name + " " + last_name
print(full_name)
```

Go ahead and run that cell. We get the exact same output as the previous cell; however, we used variables to store the information this time.

Formatting Strings

Earlier we created a full name by adding multiple strings together to create a larger string. While this is perfectly fine to use, for larger strings it becomes tough to read. Imagine that you had to create a sentence that used 10 variables. Appending all ten variables into a sentence is tough to keep track of, not to mention read. We'll need to use a concept called string formatting. This will allow us to write an entire string and inject the variables we want to use in the proper locations.

.format( )

The format method works by putting a period directly after the ending string quotation, followed by the keyword *"format"*. Within the parenthesis after the keyword are the variables that will be injected into the string. No matter what data type it is, it will insert it into the string in the proper location, which brings up the question, how does it know where to put it? That's where the curly brackets come in to play. The order of the curly brackets is the same order for the variables within the format parenthesis. To include multiple variables in one format string, you simply separate each by a comma. Let's check out some examples:

```python
# injecting variables using the format method
name = "John"
print( "Hello { }".format(name) )
print( "Hello { }, you are { } years old!".format(name, 28) )
```

Go ahead and run that cell. We'll see that the output in the first line is "**Hello John**" and the second "**Hello John, you are 28 years old**". Keep in mind that the format function will inject variables and even data types themselves. In this instance, we injected the integer value 28.

f Strings (New in Python 3.6)

The new way to inject variables into a string in Python is by using what we call **f strings**. By putting the letter "**f**" in front of a string, you're able to inject a variable into a string directly in line. This is important, as it makes the string easier to read when it gets longer, making this the preferred method to format a string. Just keep in mind you need Python 3.6 to use this; otherwise you'll receive an error. To inject a variable in a string, simply wrap curly brackets around the name of the variable. Let's look at an example:

```python
# using the new f strings
name = "John"
print( f"Hello {name}" )
```

Go ahead and run the cell. We get the same output that we had gotten with the *.format()* method; however, it's much easier to read the code this time.

Note   Throughout this book, we'll be using the .format() method.

Formatting in Python 2

Python 2 doesn't include the .format() method; instead you would use **percent operators** to mark the location of the variable being injected. The following is an example to inject the variable "*name*" into the location of "**%s**". The letter after the percent operator signifies the data type. For integers, you would use "**%d**" for digit. After the string closes, you would place a percent operator, followed by the variables you would like to use. Let's look at an example:

```
# one major difference between versions 2 & 3
name = 'John'
print('Hello, %s' % name)
```

Go ahead and run that cell. You'll notice that we get the same output as the previous methods. If you wanted to format a string in Python 2 with multiple variables, then you would need to write the following:

```
# python 2 multiple variable formatting
first_name = "John"
last_name = "Smith"
print( "Hello, %s %s" % (first_name, last_name) )
        # surround the variables in parenthesis
```

Go ahead and run the cell. We'll get the output "Hello, John Smith". When passing multiple variables, you need to surround the variable names within parenthesis and separate each by a comma. Notice there are also two symbols within the string that represent the location of each respective variable in order from left to right.

String Index

One other key concept that we need to understand about strings is how they are stored. When a computer saves a string into memory, each character within the string is assigned what we call an "**index.**" An index is essentially a location in memory. Think of an index as a position in a line that you're waiting in at the mall. If you were at the front of the line, you would be given an index number of zero. The person behind you would be given index position one. The person behind them would be given index position two and so on.

Note   Indexing in most languages, including Python, starts at 0 not 1.

The same is true for Python strings. If we take a string like *"Hello"* and break down their indexes (see Figure 2-1), we can see that the letter *"H"* is located at index zero. Let's try an example:

```
# using indexes to print each element
word = "Hello"
print( word[ 0 ] )          # will output 'H'
print( word[ 1 ] )          # will output 'e'
print( word[ -1 ] )         # will output 'o'
```

In order to index a specific element, you use square brackets to the right of the variable name. Within those **square brackets**, you put the index location you wish to access. In the preceding case, we're accessing the first two elements in the string **"Hello"** stored in the variable **"word"**. The last line accesses the element in the last position. Using negative index numbers will result in trying to access information from the back, such that -4 would result in the output of the letter "e".

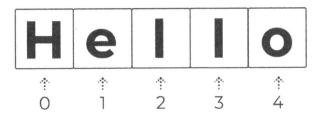

Figure 2-1. *Index locations for a string*

Be very careful when working with indexes. An index is a specific location in memory. If you try to access a location that is out of range, you will crash your program because it's trying to access a place in memory that does not exist. For example, if we tried to access index 5 on the *"Hello"*.

String Slicing

I want to just quickly introduce the topic of slicing. Slicing is used mostly with Python lists; however, you can use it on strings as well. Slicing is essentially when you only want a piece of the variable, such that if I only wanted "He" from the word "Hello", we would write the following:

```
print( word[ 0 : 2 ] )            # will output 'He'
```

The first number in the bracket is the starting index; the second is the stopping index. We will touch on this concept in a later week; however, feel free to mess around with slicing. Before the day ends though, I'd like to quickly cover the start, stop, and step arguments when slicing. The syntax for slicing is always

```
>>> variable_name[ start : stop : step ]
```

In the previous cell, we only included the start and stop because the step is optional and defaults to incrementing by one each time. However, what if we wanted to print every other letter:

```
print( word[ 0 : 5 : 2 ] )          # will output 'Hlo'
```

Go ahead and run the cell. By passing the step as the number two, it increments the index by two each time instead of one. We will cover this more in depth in a later chapter; for now let this be an introduction into slicing with all three arguments.

WEDNESDAY EXERCISES

1. **Variable Injection**: Create a print statement that injects an integer, float, boolean, and string all into one line. The output should look like "*23 4.5 False John*".

2. **Fill in the Blanks**: Using the format method, fill in the following blanks by assigning your name and favorite activities into variables:

   ```
   "{ }'s favorite sports is { }."
   "{ } is working on { } programming!"
   ```

We covered some key concepts when working with strings today, formatting and indexing. Tomorrow we'll use other methods that will help us manipulate strings.

Thursday: String Manipulation

In many programs that you'll build, you're going to want to **alter** strings in one way or another. String manipulation just means that we want to alter what the current string is. Luckily, Python has plenty of **methods** that we can use to alter string data types.

To follow along, let's continue from our previous notebook file "*Week_02*" and simply add a markdown cell at the bottom that says, "**Manipulating Strings.**"

.title()

Often, you'll run into words that aren't capitalized that should be usually names. The title method capitalizes all first letters in each word of a string. Try the following:

```
# using the title method to capitalize a string
name = "john smith"
print( name.title( ) )
```

Go ahead and run that cell. The output we get is a "**John Smith**" with capital letters on each word. This **method** is great for formatting names correctly.

Note   Try using name.lower() and name.upper() and see what happens.

.replace()

The replace method works like a find and replace tool. It takes in two values within its parenthesis, one that it searches for and the other that it replaces the searched value with:

```
# replacing an exclamation point with a period
words = "Hello there!"
print( words.replace( "!", "." ) )
```

Go ahead and run that cell. This will result in an output of "**Hello there**".

Note   For the replace to be stored properly afterward, we would have to re-declare our words variable: **words = words.replace('!', '.').**

.find( )

The find method will search for any string we ask it to. In this example, we try to search for an entire word, but we could search for anything including a character or a full sentence:

```
# finding the starting index of our searched term
s = "Look over that way"
print( s.find("over") )
```

Go ahead and run that cell. You'll notice that we got an output of **5**. Find returns the starting index position of the match. If you count where the word "**over**" begins, the "**o**" is at index location 5. This is important when you want to access a specific index on a search.

.strip( )

In cases where you want to get rid of a certain character on the left and right side of a string, you would use the strip method. By default, it will remove spaces. Let's try running the following:

```
# removing white space with strip
name = "   john   "
print( name.strip( ) )
```

The output will produce "**john**" because we've removed all the spaces on the left and right side.

Note   Try .lstrip( ) and .rstrip( ) and see what happens.

.split( )

I won't go into too much detail with split simply because what it returns is a list and we haven't covered those quite yet; however, I wanted you to see how to use this method. What it does is separate the words in the sentence into a group of words, stored within a list. Now don't worry about lists just yet, we'll get there. For now, let's just see how this method works:

```
# converting a string into a list of words
s = "These words are separated by spaces"
print( s.split(" ") )
```

Go ahead and run the cell. The output results in a list of words "['**These**', '**words**', '**are**', '**separated**', '**by**', '**spaces**']". We'll come back to this method and why it's important.

THURSDAY EXERCISES

1. **Uppercasing**: Try manipulating the string "uppercase" so it prints out as all uppercase letters. You'll need to look up a new method.

2. **Strip Symbols**: Strip all the dollar signs from the left side of this string "$$John Smith". Try it with .lstrip( ) and .strip( ). To see a description on how to use the strip method further, try using the help function in Python by typing the following:

   ```
   >>> help(" ".strip)
   ```

Today you learned a handful of manipulation methods, but there are many more. Try experimenting with others that you find on the Web.

Friday: Creating a Receipt Printing Program

Welcome to your first project! We'll be creating a very basic receipt printing program. For this week, as we've learned about variables, operators, and string manipulation, we'll be using these skills in order to create this program.

To follow along, let's continue from our "*Week_02*" notebook and simply add a markdown cell at the bottom that says, "**Friday Project: Printing Receipts.**"

Final Design

It's always good to picture the design of what you're trying to build. For larger projects, you'll want to create a flow chart or some sort of design document that will keep you on track. This way you don't sway from the intended result. For us, we'll be building a small receipt printing program with the concepts we've learned, in which the output will look like Figure 2-2.

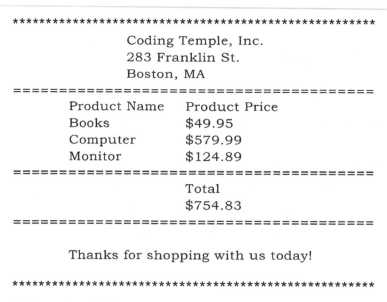

Figure 2-2. *End result of Friday project*

Let's begin, shall we!

Initial Process

Whenever you begin a project, you must always understand where to start. No matter the size of the project, there are certain dependencies. Like building a house, you must have a foundation before you can put the roof on. Now, this program will be around 50 lines and have little to no dependencies, so we'll start with the top border and work our way down to the bottom.

Defining Our Variables

In the cell below our markdown header, let's begin to define the variables that we'll be working with throughout this program:

```
1| # create a product and price for three items
2| p1_name, p1_price = "Books", 49.95
3| p2_name, p2_price = "Computer", 579.99
4| p3_name, p3_price = "Monitor", 124.89
```

I always like to introduce new concepts while building out these Friday projects, as it's good to implement good coding techniques. The technique introduced within this block is the ability to declare multiple variables on the same line. To do so, we simply separate the variable names and their associated values by a comma. Looking at the first two variables declared, the value of "**Books**" will be saved into the variable name "**p1_name**", and the value "**49.95**" will be saved into the variable name "**p1_price**". Rather than writing six lines, we've reduced our program by half already. The less lines we use the better (*most times*). Variables such as x and y, or in our case, a name and price, are good examples of declaring variables associated together in one line.

Next, let's define the variables we'll be using for the company at the top of the receipt. All the code for this project may be done in a single cell, or you can separate the cells. It's up to you. I've provided line numbers in case you follow along on a single cell:

```
6| # create a company name and information
7| company_name = "coding temple, inc."
8| company_address = "283 Franklin St."
9| company_city = "Boston, MA"
```

As an example, we've left the company name all lowercase so that we can use a string manipulation method to fix this issue.

Lastly, let's declare the message that we'll output to the user at the bottom of the receipt:

```
11| # declare ending message
12| message = "Thanks for shopping with us today!"
```

Go ahead and run the cell. Now that we've defined all our variables, we can move on.

Creating the Top Border

As we can see from the design that we've laid out at the beginning of this project, we'll need to print out a border on the top and bottom. Let's start with the top border:

```
14| # create a top border
15| print( "*" * 50 )
```

Go ahead and run the cell. There's a new concept being applied here, where we write "*****" * **50**. All we're trying to do is print out 50 stars in a row for a top border, and rather than making 50 print statements, we can simply multiply the string by the number we want. This way we get our top border while keeping our code slim and easy to read. Readability of code is always key.

Displaying the Company Info

We've already defined our variables for the company in the preceding lines, so let's display them:

```
17| # print company information first, using format
18| print( "\t\t{ }".format( company_name.title( ) ) )
19| print( "\t\t{ }".format(company_address) )
20| print( "\t\t{ }".format(company_city) )
```

Go ahead and run the cell. These print statements may seem a little hard to understand at first; however, I'm introducing an escape character to you. Escape characters are read in by the defining backslash "****" character. Whatever comes after that backslash is what the computer will interpret. In the three print statements, we use "**\t**" for a tab indentation. Another popular escape character you may see is "**\n**" which means newline and acts as if you hit the enter key. We use two escaping characters in a row to center it within our output. Let's create a divider:

```
22| # print a line between sections
23| print( "=" * 50 )
```

Go ahead and run the cell. Like how we printed out our top border, we'll multiply the equal symbol by 50 to create the same width line. This will give the appearance of separate sections.

Displaying the Product Info

Looking at our original design, we want to create a header before we list out each product's name and price. This can be done simply by using our escaping characters for indenting:

```
25| # print out header for section of items
26| print("\tProduct Name\tProduct Price")
```

Go ahead and run the cell. Due to the size of the header names, we only need to use a single tab before each header. Now we can go ahead and output a row for each products' information:

```
28| # create a print statement for each product
29| print( "\t{ }\t\t${ }".format(p1_name.title( ), p1_price) )
30| print( "\t{ }\t\t${ }".format(p2_name.title( ), p2_price) )
31| print( "\t{ }\t\t${ }".format(p3_name.title( ), p3_price) )
```

Go ahead and run the cell. We're using similar styles as the previous print statements in order to center each product's title and price under their respective headers. Try not to get too confused by all the symbols within the print string; you can simply break them down to a tab, followed by the first variable being formatted into the string, followed by two tabs, followed by a dollar sign (*in order to make the price look like currency*), and followed by the second variable being formatted into the string. This completes the section for our items, so let's put in another section divider:

```
33| # print a line between sections
34| print('=' * 50)
```

Go ahead and run the cell. This will set us up for our next section to display the total.

Displaying the Total

Like the products section, we want to create a header for our total, but we want to also center it underneath the price column of the products section. To do so, we'll use three tabs:

```
36| # print out header for section of total
37| print("\t\t\tTotal")
```

Go ahead and run the cell. Now that we have our total header aligned with the price column in products, we can output our total on the next line. Before we can print out a total, however, we must first calculate the total, which is the sum of all our products. Let's define a variable called total and then print it out:

```
39| # calculate total price and print out
40| total = p1_price + p2_price + p3_price
41| print( "\t\t\t${ }".format(total) )
```

Go ahead and run the cell. Again, we've gone ahead and added three tabs, plus a dollar sign to make the total value appear as currency. Let's now add a section border:

```
43| # print a line between sections
44| print( "=" * 50)
```

Go ahead and run the cell to make sure it looks like the desired output so far.

Displaying the Ending Message

To display the final thank you message, our design has it spaced out slightly more than any other section, so we'll need to add a couple of newlines to give it some extra spacing:

```
46| # output thank you message
47| print( "\n\t{ }\n".format(message) )
```

Go ahead and run the cell. Our message is now centered, and we're ready to move on.

Displaying the Bottom Border

To finish off this simple printing program, we need to throw in a bottom border for aesthetics:

```
49| # create a bottom border
50| print( "*" * 50 )
```

Go ahead and run the cell one last time.

Congratulations! As simple as it may be, it's a huge milestone. After learning more material, try coming back here to improve it.

Weekly Summary

This week we went over some very important foundational concepts in programming with variables and working with strings. You must always keep in mind that variables need to be declared before you can use them and that the name associated is saved in memory with the value on the right side of the equals operator. Strings are easy to work with in Python, as the language has a variety of methods that we can call in order to do the work for us. At the end of the week, we were able to build a simple receipt printing program. Try breaking the program! I always encourage students to try and break programs because it will teach you how to fix it.

Challenge Question Solution

There isn't a definitive solution to making a PB&J sandwich, but I want you to go back and see if you weren't specific enough. **Computers are only as smart as we program them to be**, so if you said to put the peanut butter on the bread, it may just interpret it as putting the entire jar on the bread instead. As a developer you need to be specific with your descriptions. Even try rewriting a new algorithm with improved steps.

Weekly Challenges

To test out your skills, try these challenges:

1. **Side Borders**: In the Friday project, we ended up creating borders above and below the information printed out. Try adding a star border on the sides as well now.

2. **Researching Methods**: We've gone over a few of the string manipulation methods that are widely used; however, there are many more; try looking up some and implementing them.

3. **Reverse**: Declare a variable equal to "Hello". Reverse the string using slicing. Try looking it up if you struggle.

Tip   You can define a start, stop, and step when slicing.

CHAPTER 3

User Input and Conditionals

Welcome to Week 3! This week we'll be introducing how to work with user input and making decisions within our programs. These "*decisions*" are known as **branching statements or conditionals**. If you think of your life every day, you make decisions based on specific conditions without knowing, such as when to get up in the morning, what to have for lunch, when to eat, etc. These are known as branching statements. The same applies in programming, where we need to have the computer make decisions.

Overview

- Working with user input

- How to use "if" statements to make decisions

- How to use "elif" statements to make multiple decisions

- How to use "else" statements to make decisions no matter what

- Building a calculator with decision-making and user input

CHALLENGE QUESTION

This week's challenge is to test your ability to read code. I want you to read the code block and think about whether it will work or not. If you believe it will not work, I want you to make a note of why it won't. It's important to be able to both read and write:

```
>>> print('{} is my favorite sport'.format(element))
>>> element = 'Football'
```

After you've written down your answer, go ahead and run the code within a cell. If your answer was incorrect, try to analyze where you why. The answer will be at the end of this chapter.

© Connor P. Milliken 2020
C. P. Milliken, *Python Projects for Beginners*, https://doi.org/10.1007/978-1-4842-5355-7_3

Monday: User Input and Type Converting

In today's lesson we'll introduce the ability to interact with the user and a concept called type conversion. These will be necessary to understand how to build the calculator at the end of the week.

To follow along with the content for today, let's open up Jupyter Notebook from our *"python_bootcamp"* folder. Once it's open, create a new file, and rename it to *"Week_03."* Next, make the first cell markdown that has a header saying: "**User Input & Type Converting.**" We'll begin working underneath that cell.

Accepting User Input

In many programs we'll be creating, you'll need to accept user input. To do so, we need to use the **input()** function. Like the print function, input will print the string inside of the parenthesis, but it will also create a box for the user to enter information. Let's look at an example:

```
# accepting and outputting user input
print( input("What is your name? ") )
```

Go ahead and run that cell. You'll notice that the cell will output whatever you write within the box. When the interpreter comes across the **input** function, it will pause until enter is pressed.

Note   Information entered is taken into the program as a string.

Storing User Input

In the previous cell, we simply printed out the input that the user put in. However, in order to work with the data that they enter, we need to store it into a variable:

```
# saving what the user inputs
ans = input("What is your name? ")
print("Hello { }!".format(ans) )
```

Go ahead and run that cell. Storing the information that the user puts in our program is as easy as storing it into a variable. This way we can work with the data they input at any point.

What Is Type Converting?

Python defines **type conversion** functions to directly convert one data type to another which is useful in day-to-day and competitive programming. In some situations, the data you're working with may not be the correct type. The most obvious example is user input because no matter what the user types in, the input is taken as a string. If you are expecting a number to be input, you'll need to convert the input to an integer data type, so that you're able to work with it.

Checking the Type

Before we go over how to type convert, I'd like to touch on an important function that Python has which allows us to check the type of any given variable:

```
# how to check the data type of a variable
num = 5
print( type(num) )
```

Go ahead and run that cell. The output here will be "**<class 'int'>**". Don't worry about the class portion here, we'll get into classes another week. Focus on the second part where it outputs the type as an integer. This allows us to check what data type where working with.

Converting Data Types

Python gives us the ability to type convert easily from one type to another simply by wrapping the type around the variable. Let's check out an example of converting a **string** to an **int**:

```
# converting a variable from one data type to another
num = "9"
num = int(num)      # re-declaring num to store an integer
print( type(num) )   # checking type to make sure conversion worked
```

Go ahead and run that cell. We've just converted the string of "9" to an integer. Now we can use the variable num in any calculations. For the conversion to process correctly, we used the **int()** type conversion. Whatever data type is put inside of the parenthesis is converted into an int. Check Table 3-1 for how to convert from one data type to another.

Table 3-1. *Converting data types*

Current Type	Data Value	Converting to	Proper Code	Output
Integer	9	String	str(9)	'9'
Integer	5	Float	float(5)	5.0
Float	5.6	Integer	int(5.6)	5
String	'9'	Integer	int('9')	9
String	'True'	Boolean	bool('True')	True
Boolean	True	Integer	int(True)	1

As you can see, there are several ways to **type convert**; you just need to use the keyword for each defining data type. The boolean type of True converts to an integer of 1 because the True and False values represent 1 and 0, respectively. Also, converting a float to an integer will just truncate the decimal, as well as any numbers to the right of the decimal.

Note   Not all data types can be converted properly. There are limits.

Converting User Input

Let's try working with a user's input in order to add 100 to whatever they type:

```
# working with user input to perform calculations
ans = input("Type a number to add: ")
print( type(ans) )    # default type is string, must convert
result = 100 + int(ans)
print( "100 + { } = { }".format(ans, result) )
```

Go ahead and run that cell. Inputting the number "**9**" will give us a proper result; however, this conversion would not work well with the word **"nine"** because the default return type for input is a string as noted by the first print statement in this cell.

Handling Errors

In the last cell, we convert the user input to an integer; however, what if they put in a word instead? The program would break right away. As a developer, we must assume that the user won't put the proper information that we expect them to. To handle this issue, we're going to introduce **try and except** blocks. Try and except are used to catch errors. It works by trying to run what is inside the try block; if it doesn't produce an error, then it continues without hitting the except block; however, if an error occurs, then the code in the except block runs. This is to make sure your program doesn't stop running if an error pops up. This is a generic way to handle errors; there are many other methods like using the functions *isalpha()* and *isalnum()*. Let's look at an example using the try and except blocks:

```
# using the try and except blocks, use tab to indent where necessary
try:
    ans = float( input("Type a number to add: ") )
    print( "100 + { } = { }".format(ans, 100 + ans) )
except:
    print("You did not put in a valid number!")
# without try/except print statement would not get hit if error occurs
print("The program did not break!")
```

Go ahead and run that cell. Try inputting different answers including non-numbers. You'll notice that our nonvalid print statement will output if you don't input a number. If we didn't have the try and except in place, the program would break, and the last print statement wouldn't occur.

Code Blocks and Indentation

In most other programming languages, indentation is used only to help make the code look pretty. For Python though, it is required for indicating a block of code. Let's take our previous code from the "*Handling Errors*" section. The two lines after our try statement are indented and are known as **blocks of code**. These lines belong to the try statement because they are directly indented after the statement. The same goes for our other print statement within the except block. It's the reason that our nonvalid print statement only runs if the except block runs. All blocks of code need to be connected to a statement; you can't indent a section randomly.

Note The indents must be consistent. It does not always need to be four spaces; however, a tab is four spaces, so it's usually easier to indent with tabs.

MONDAY EXERCISES

1. **Converting**: Try converting a string of "*True*" to a boolean, and then output its type to make sure it converted properly.

2. **Sum of Inputs**: Create two input statements, and ask the user to enter two numbers. Print the sum of these numbers out.

3. **Car Information**: Ask the user to input the year, make, model, and color of their car, and print a nicely formatted statement like "2018 Blue Chevrolet Silverado."

Today was an important step in covering user input, how to convert from one data type to another, and how to handle errors.

Tuesday: If Statements

Today we'll learn all about how to make decisions in our code. This will give us the ability to have our programs decide what lines of code to run, depending on what the user inputs, calculations, etc. This is the most important lesson of this week. Be sure to spend a good amount of time going on today's lesson.

To follow along with this lesson, let's continue from our previous notebook file "*Week_03*" and simply add a markdown cell at the bottom that says, "**If Statements.**"

How They Work

Every day you make hundreds of decisions. These decisions define what you do with your day. In programming these are known as **branching statements** or **"if statements."** An if statement works the same way that a decision is made. You check a condition, and if that condition is true, you perform the task, and if it's not true, then you move on without performing that task:

> *"Am I hungry?"*
>
> *"Yes, so I should make some food."*
>
> ✳✳✳ *proceeds to cook food* ✳✳✳

The same decision-making process can be implemented in programming using an if statement.

Writing Your First If Statement

All branching statements begin the same way, with the keyword "**if**". Following the keyword is what is known as a **condition**. Lastly, there will always be an ending colon at the end of the statement. The *if statement* checks to see if the given condition is **True** or **False**. If the condition is True, then the code block runs. If it is False, then the program continues without running any of the code indented directly after the if statement. Let's try it out:

```
# using an if statement to only run code if the condition is met
x, y = 5, 10
if x < y:
    print("x is less than y")
```

Go ahead and run that cell. Notice here that the output is **"x is less than y"**. This is because we originally declared x equal to 5 and y equal to 10 and then used an if statement to check if x was less than y, which it was. If x was equal to 15, then the print statement indented after the **"if"** would have never ran, because the condition would have been False.

Comparison Operators

Before we continue with branching statements, we need to go over comparison operators. So far, we've used **arithmetic operators** for adding and subtracting values and **assignment operators** for declaring variables, and with the introduction of the *"if statement,"* we've now seen **comparison operators**. There are several comparisons that you're able to make. Most comparison operators that you'll use, however, are shown in Table 3-2.

Table 3-2. *Comparison operators*

Operator	Condition	Functionality	Example
==	Equality	if x == y:	if x is equal to y ...
!=	Inequality	if x != y:	if x does not equal y...
>	Greater than	if x > y:	if x is greater than y...
<	Less than	if x < y:	if x is less than y...
>=	Greater or equal	if x >= y:	if x is greater or equal to y...
<=	Less or equal	if x <= y:	if x is less or equal to y...

Note   w3 Schools[1] has great reference material for additional information on the many different types of operators.

Checking User Input

A great use for our newly learned **conditional statement** is for checking user input. Let's try:

```
# checking user input
ans = int( input("What is 5 + 5? ") )
if ans == 10:
    print("You got it right!")
```

---

[1]www.w3schools.com/python/python_operators.asp

Go ahead and run that cell. Our conditional statement checks to see if the user's input is **equal** to the integer 10. If it is, then the indented print statement will run. Notice in line two that we ask for user input and immediately convert their answer to an integer. As we did not use a **try** and **except**, inputting a non-number would result in an error.

Logical Operators

Logical operators are used to combine conditional statements. You can write as many conditions on a single "if statement" as you'd like. Depending on the logical operators used, the if statement may or may not run due. Let's look at the three logical operators we can use.

Logical Operator "and"

The **"and"** logical operator is to ensure that, when you check multiple conditions, **both sides** of the condition are True. This means that if either the condition to the left or right of the **"and"** is False, then the code will not run the block of code. Let's try an example:

```
# using the keyword 'and' in an 'if statement'
x, y, z = 5, 10, 5
if x < y and x == z:
    print("Both statements were true")
```

Go ahead and run that cell. The output will result in **"Both statements were true"** because x is less than y and the same value as z.

Note   You can have as many conditions in one line as you'd like.

Logical Operator "or"

The **"or"** logical operator is used to check for **one or both** conditions to be true. Such that if the condition to the left is False and the condition to the right is True, the block of code will still run because at least one condition was True. The only time an *"if block"* will not run using an *"or"* operator is when both conditions are False. Let's check out an example:

```
# using the keyword 'or' in an 'if statement'
x, y, z = 5, 10, 5
if x < y or x != z:
    print("One or both statements were true")
```

Go ahead and run that cell. Notice that we get an output of **"One or both statements were true"**. This worked even though our second condition is False, since x is equal to z and we we're checking if it was not equal to it; however, since the condition on the left is True, it runs.

Logical Operator "not"

In certain instances, you'll want to check for the opposite of a value. The **"not"** operator is used for just that. It essentially returns the opposite of whatever the current value is. Let's try it out:

```
# using the keyword 'not' within an 'if statement'
flag = False
if not flag:                   # same as saying if not true
    print("Flag is False")
```

Go ahead and run that cell. You'll notice that the resulting output is **"Flag is False"**. This is due to the *"not"* operator, which took the opposite value of False and made the condition return True.

Note   We get the same result if we write "*if flag == False:*".

Membership Operators

Membership operators are used to test if a sequence appears in an object. There are two keywords that we can use to check if a value exists in an object or not. Let's check them out.

Membership Operator "in"

When you want to check if a given object has a value appear in it, you use the **"in"** operator. The best use case is checking for a certain value within strings. Let's check out an example:

```
# using the keyword 'in' within an 'if statement'
word = "Baseball"
if "b" in word:
        print( "{ } contains the character b".format(word) )
```

Go ahead and run that cell. The resulted output is **"Baseball contains the character b"**. This is case sensitive, but lucky for us the word Baseball has one lowercase and one uppercase b.

Membership Operator "not in"

Likewise, if you want to check to see if an object doesn't include a specific value, you would use the **"not in"** operator. This is essentially just checking the opposite of the *"in"* operator. Let's see:

```
# using the keyword 'not in' within an 'if statement'
word = "Baseball"
if "x" not in word:
        print( "{ } does not contain the character x".format(word) )
```

Go ahead and run that cell. The resulting output is **"Baseball does not contain the character x"**. It simply checks to see if the character x is not included in the string value of our word variable.

TUESDAY EXERCISES

---

1. **Checking Inclusion – Part 1:** Ask the user for input, and check to see if what they wrote includes an "*es*".

2. **Checking Inclusion – Part 2**: Ask the user for input, and check to see if what they wrote has an "*ing*" at the end. **Hint**: Use slicing.

3. **Checking Equality**: Ask the user to input two words, and write a conditional statement to check if both words are the same. Make it case insensitive so that capitals do not matter.

4. **Returning Exponents**: Ask for the user to input a number, and return that number squared if it is lower than 10. **Hint**: Investigate arithmetic expressions for exponents.

Today was an important lesson on conditional statements. Having the ability to let the computer make decisions and perform an action based off them is an important key to any program.

Wednesday: Elif Statements

Conditional statements give us the power to make decisions in our program, but so far, we've only seen a glimpse of the capabilities that we have with them. Today, we'll be learning all about **elif statements**. They give us the ability to run separate blocks of code depending on the condition. They are also known as "**else if statements.**"

To follow along with this lesson, let's continue from our previous notebook file "*Week_03*" and add a markdown cell at the bottom that says, "**Elif Statements.**"

How They Work

As we saw in the previous lesson, conditional statements give us the ability to make decisions within our program; however, how would you handle making multiple decisions? In Python, we use the **elif statement** to declare another decision based on a given condition. *Elif statements* must be associated with an *if statement*, meaning that you cannot create an **elif** without an **if**. Python works in top to bottom order, so it checks the first *if statement*; if that statement is False, it continues to the first *elif statement* and checks that condition. If that condition returns False as well, it continues to the next conditional statement until there are no more to check. However, once a single conditional statement returns True, all other conditionals are skipped, even if they are True. It works so that the first conditional to return True is the only block of code that runs.

Writing Your First Elif Statement

Creating an *elif statement* is identical to an *if statement*, with one difference, you use the **elif** keyword instead. You're able to have multiple conditions for each **elif** as well. Let's try it:

```
# using the elif conditional statement
x, y = 5, 10
if x > y:
    print("x is greater")
elif x < y:
    print("x is less")
```

Go ahead and run that cell. Notice that the output is **"x is less"**. It checked the initial *if statement*, but since that returned False, it moved on to the *elif conditional statement*. That statement returned True and the block of code within it ran.

Checking Multiple Elif Conditions

Having the ability to write multiple decisions based on a single variable is a necessity, which is why elif statements were built. Take the following code, for instance:

```
# checking more than one elif conditional statement
x, y = 5, 10
if x > y:
    print("x is greater")
elif (x + 10) < y:                 # checking if 15 is less than 10
    print("x is less")
elif (x + 5) == y:                 # checking if 10 is equal to 10
    print("equal")
```

Go ahead and run that cell. The resulting output is **"equal"**. The first *if* and *elif statements* both returned False, but the second *elif statement* returned True, which is why that block of code ran. You can have as many **elifs** as you want, but they must be associated with an *if statement*.

59

> **Note**   Within the conditional, we perform addition, but we wrap it within
> parenthesis so that it executes the math operation first.

Conditionals Within Conditionals

We've gone over how Python uses indentation to separate blocks of code. So far, we've
only seen one indentation level, but what if we added an *if statement* within an *if
statement*?

```
# writing multiple conditionals within each other - multiple block levels
x, y, z = 5, 10, 5
if x > y:
    print("greater")
elif x <= y:
    if x == z:
            print("x is equal to z")       # resulting output
    elif x != z:
            print("x is not equal to z")   # won't get hit
```

Go ahead and run that cell. The output results in **"x is equal to z"**. To break it down,
the initial *if statement* returns False, and the next *elif statement* returns True, so it runs
that block. Now inside of that block is another conditional statement, so it checks the
first *if statement*, which returns True, and runs the block of code inside that.

If Statements vs. Elif Statements

A major difference that you'll need to understand going forward is the use for *elif
statements* against using multiple *if statements*. All *elif statements* are connected to one
original *if statement*, so that once a single conditional is True, the rest do not run. Let's
see an example:

```
# testing output of two if statements in a row that are both true
x, y, z = 5, 10, 5
if x < y:
```

```
        print("x is less")
if x == z:
        print("x is equal")
```

Go ahead and run that cell. Notice that the resulting output is both print statements here. This is due in part to having two *if statements*. These *if statements* are not related to each other; they are separate conditional statements, whereas an *elif* is always connected to an *if*.

```
# testing output of an if and elif statement that are both true
x, y, z = 5, 10, 5
if x < y:
        print("x is less")
elif x == z:
        print("x is equal to z")
```

Go ahead and run that cell. Notice that the output here is only **"x is less"** and doesn't include the second print statement. That's because an *elif* is attached to an *if statement*, and once one of the conditionals returns True, all others will not be checked even if they are True themselves.

WEDNESDAY EXERCISES

1. **Higher/Lower**: Ask the user to input a number. Type convert that number, and use an if/elif statement to print whether it's higher or lower than 100.

2. **Find the Solution**: Given the following code, fix any/all errors in order to make it output "lower":

```
x, y = 5, 10
  if x > y:
        print("greater")
  try x < y:
      print("lower")
```

Today was the next step into creating a program that will make decisions for us, not just one decision, but multiple.

Thursday: Else Statements

The third and final part of any good decision is what to do by default. In Python, we know them to be **else statements**. Today's lesson will be quite short, but necessary in understanding conditional statements further.

To follow along with this lesson, let's continue from our previous notebook file "*Week_03*" and add a markdown cell at the bottom that says, "**Else Statements.**"

How They Work

Else conditional statements are the **end all be all** of the *if statement*. Sometimes you're not able to create a condition for every decision you want to make, so that's where the *else statement* is useful. The *else statement* will cover all other possibilities not covered and will always run the code if the program gets to it. This means that if an *elif or if statement* were to return True, then it would never run the **else**; however, if they all return False, then the *else clause* would run no matter what every time. Again, it's always easier to see it in code; let's try!

Writing Your First Else Statement

Like an *elif statement*, the *else clause* needs to always be associated with an original *if statement*. The *else clause* covers all other possibilities, so you don't need to write a condition at all; you just need to provide the keyword **"else"** followed by an ending colon. Remember that an else clause will run the code inside of it if the program reaches the statement. Try the following:

```
# using an else statement
name = "John"
if name == "Jacob":
      print("Hello Jacob!")
else:
      print("Hello { }!".format(name) )
```

Go ahead and run that cell. Notice the output here is **"Hello John"**. The first *if statement* returned False, so as soon as it reached the *else clause,* it ran the print statement inside of it.

Complete Conditional Statement

Now that we've covered all three parts of a conditional statement, let's go ahead and try using all three together in one statement:

```
# writing a full conditional statement with if, elif, else
name = "John"
if name[0] == "A":
    print("Name starts with an A")
elif name[0] == "B":
    print("Name starts with a B")
elif name[0] == "J":
    print("Name starts with a J")
else:                                   # covers all other possibilities
    print( "Name starts with a { }".format( name[0] ) )
```

Go ahead and run that cell. The resulting output is **"Name starts with a J"**, which was output by the second *elif statement*. The first *if and elif statements* returned False, so their blocks of code didn't run. Once the second *elif statement* returned True and ran its own code, the *else statement* will be skipped over and not run. Remember that **indexing** starts at **0**, so by using the bracket notation after the name variable was accessing the first element within the string.

Note   Be sure to go back and check out the section on string indexing if you're having trouble understanding the bracket notation.

THURSDAY EXERCISES
---

1. **Fix the Errors**: Given the following code, fix any/all errors so that it outputs *"Hello John"* correctly:

```
>>> name = "John"
>>> if name == "Jack":
>>>             print("Hello Jack")
>>> elif:
>>>>             print("Hello John")
```

2. **User Input**: Ask the user to input the time of day in military time without a colon (1100 = 11:00 AM). Write a conditional statement so that it outputs the following:

    a. "*Good Morning*" if less than 1200

    b. "*Good Afternoon*" if between 1200 and 1700

    c. "*Good Evening*" if equal or above 1700

Today we learned all about else statements. You're now able to build programs that can generate code given a condition.

Friday: Creating a Calculator

Last week we built a receipt printing program together. With the lessons learned from this week, we're going to be building a simple calculator that accepts user input and outputs the proper result.

To follow along with this lesson, let's continue from our previous notebook file "*Week_03*" and add a markdown cell at the bottom that says, "**Friday Project: Creating a Calculator.**"

Final Design

For each week we always want to lay out the final design. As this week is based around the logic rather than how it looks, we'll lay out the steps necessary to build our calculator:

1. Ask the user for the calculation they would like to perform.

2. Ask the user for the numbers they would like to run the operation on.

3. Set up try/except clause for mathematical operation.

    a. Convert numbers input to floats.

    b. Perform operation and print result.

    c. If an exception is hit, print error.

Step #1: Ask User for Calculation to Be Performed

For each one of these steps, let's put the code in separate cells. This will allow us to section of the specific steps for our project, making it easier to test each step. The first step is to ask the user to input the mathematical operation to be performed (add, subtract, etc.):

```
# step 1: ask user for calculation to be performed
operation = input("Would you like to add/subtract/multiply/divide? ").lower( )
print( "You chose { }.".format(operation) )   # for testing purposes
```

Go ahead and run that cell. Depending on what the user inputs, your output will print what they chose. You'll notice that on the line where we accept the input, we also convert it to lowercase right away. This is to avoid case-sensitive issues later. Our print statement is simply for testing purposes on this cell only and will be removed later.

Step #2: Ask for Numbers, Alert Order Matters

In the cell below step #1, we'll need to create the next step of our logic. Here, we ask the user to input a couple of numbers and output those numbers for testing purposes:

```
# step 2: ask for numbers, alert order matters for subtracting and dividing
if operation == "subtract" or operation == "divide":
    print( "You chose { }.".format(operation) )
    print("Please keep in mind that the order of your numbers matter.")
num1 = input("What is the first number? ")
num2 = input("What is the second number? ")
print( "First Number: { }".format(num1) )   # for testing purposes
print( "Second Number: { }".format(num2) )   # for testing purposes
```

Go ahead and run that cell. Notice that we put in a print statement alerting the user that if they chose subtraction or division, the order of numbers matters. This is important as *num1* will always be on the left side of the operator (*in our program*), which makes a huge difference.

Note   Rerun the previous cell if you get an error for undefined.

Step #3: Set Up Try/Except for Mathematical Operation

The third, and final step, is to try performing the operation. The reason for setting up a **try/except** block here is because we must convert the user's input to floating data types. We must assume that they may not enter the proper input. Let's see how this cell will work:

```
# step 3: setup try/except for mathematical operation
try:
        # step 3a: immediately try to convert numbers input to floats
        num1, num2 = float(num1), float(num2)
        # step 3b: perform operation and print result
        if operation == "add":
                result = num1 + num2
```

```
        print( "{ } + { } = { }".format(num1, num2, result) )
    elif operation == "subtract":
        result = num1 - num2
        print( "{ } - { } = { }".format(num1, num2, result) )
    elif operation == "multiply":
        result = num1 * num2
        print( "{ } * { } = { }".format(num1, num2, result) )
    elif operation == "divide":
        result = num1 / num2
        print( "{ } / { } = { }".format(num1, num2, result) )
    else:
        # else will be hit if they didn't chose an option correctly
        print("Sorry, but '{ }' is not an option.".format(operation) )
except:
    # steb 3c: print error
    print("Error: Improper numbers used. Please try again.")
```

Go ahead and run that cell. There's a lot going on here so let's start from the top. We set up a *try* block and immediately convert the user's input to floats. If this causes an error, the *except* clause will be hit and output that an error occurred rather than the program breaking. If the input can be converted, then we set up an *if/elif/else* statement to perform the calculation and output the proper result. If they didn't input a proper operation, then we let them know. This cell is dependent on the previous two. If you're getting errors, rerun the previous cells.

Final Output

Now that we've created the logic for our program in three separate cells, we can now put it all together in one. Let's remove all the testing print statements. You can essentially take all the code from the three cells and paste them into one cell, resulting in the following:

```
# step 1: ask user for calculation to be performed
operation = input("Would you like to add/subtract/multiply/divide? ").
lower( )
# step 2: ask for numbers, alert order matters for subtracting and dividing
if operation == "subtract" or operation == "divide":
     print( "You chose { }.".format(operation) )
     print("Please keep in mind that the order of your numbers matter.")
num1 = input("What is the first number? ")
num2 = input("What is the second number? ")
# step 3: setup try/except for mathematical operation
try:
     # step 3a: immediately try to convert numbers input to floats
     num1, num2 = float(num1), float(num2)
     # step 3b: perform operation and print result
     if operation == "add":
          result = num1 + num2
          print( "{ } + { } = { }".format(num1, num2, result) )
     elif operation == "subtract":
          result = num1 - num2
          print( "{ } - { } = { }".format(num1, num2, result) )
     elif operation == "multiply":
          result = num1 * num2
          print( "{ } * { } = { }".format(num1, num2, result) )
     elif operation == "divide":
          result = num1 / num2
          print( "{ } / { } = { }".format(num1, num2, result) )
     else:
          # else will be hit if they didn't chose an option correctly
          print("Sorry, but '{ }' is not an option.".format(operation) )
except:
     # steb 3c: print error
     print("Error: Improper numbers used. Please try again.")
```

Go ahead and run that cell. Now you're able to run a single cell to get our program to work from start to finish. It's not perfect, but it gives you the ability to perform simple calculations. As always, try to break the program, change a line around, and make it your own.

Congratulations on finishing another project! As simple as this calculator may be, we have shown the ability to use logic, take user input and convert it, and check for errors.

Weekly Summary

What a week! We've just seen how we can interact with our user and be able to perform branching statements. This will allow us to build projects with logic, which will perform specific code based on information that the program is using. The biggest concepts to remember here are our conditional statements and try/except blocks. It's important to know the difference between catching an error and an error causing your program to crash. We always want to catch errors when possible to sure up our program. Next week we'll learn about loops and how we can continuously run blocks of code over and over until we no longer want to.

Challenge Question Solution

If you were to run the code block for the challenge question, you would find that it produces an error. This is because we try to access our "element" variable before it's declared. If you were to reverse these two lines, the program would work as desired.

Weekly Challenges

To test out your skills, try these challenges:

1. **Reversing Numbers**: Alter the calculator project so that the order of the numbers doesn't matter. There are a few ways to get the same result; one way is to ask the user if they'd like to reverse the placement of the numbers.

2. **Age Group**: Ask the user to input their age. Depending on their input, output one of the following groups:

   a. Between 0 and 12 = "Kid"

   b. Between 13 and 19 = "Teenager"

   c. Between 20 and 30 = "Young Adult"

   d. Between 31 and 64 = "Adult"

   e. 65 or above = "Senior"

3. **Text-Based RPG**: This is an open-ended exercise. Create a text-based RPG with a story line. You take user input and give them a couple choices, and depending on what they choose, they can go down a different path. You'll use several branching statements depending on the length of the story.

CHAPTER 4

Lists and Loops

Throughout this week, I'll be introducing a new data type called "**lists**" and a new concept called "**loops**." Lists will give us the ability to store large sets of data, while loops will allow us to rerun sections of our code.

These two topics are being introduced together because lists work well with loops. Even though lists are one of the most important data types in Python, we needed to understand the basics of data types and branching statements before introducing them. By the end of the week, we'll have the tools necessary to build a small-scale hangman game. We'll use all the concepts that we've learned from previous weeks and this week.

Through application and repetition, you'll be able to understand each concept further each time it's introduced. If you don't get a concept just yet, it's important to keep pushing through and try not to get stuck on a single lesson.

Overview

- Understanding list data types

- How and why to use for loops

- How and why to use while loops

- Understanding how to work with lists

- Creating Hangman together

CHALLENGE QUESTION

Imagine that you're the mayor of a major city. For this example, let's assume that the major city is Boston, MA. You've just been alerted that you need to evacuate the city. What do you do first?

© Connor P. Milliken 2020
C. P. Milliken, *Python Projects for Beginners*, https://doi.org/10.1007/978-1-4842-5355-7_4

Monday: Lists

Today we'll be introducing one of the most important data types in Python, the **list**. In other languages, they are also known as *"arrays"* and have similar characteristics. This is the first **data collection** that you learn. We'll see other data collection types in later weeks.

To follow along with the content for today, let's open up Jupyter Notebook from our *"python_bootcamp"* folder. Once it's open, create a new file, and rename it to *"Week_04."* Next, make the first cell markdown that has a header saying: "**Lists**." We'll begin working underneath that cell.

What Are Lists?

A **list** is a data structure in Python that is a **mutable**, **ordered sequence** of elements. Mutable means that you can change the items inside, while ordered sequence is in reference to index location. The first element in a list will always be located at *index 0.* Each element or value that is inside of a list is called an *item.* Just as strings are defined as characters between quotes, lists are defined by having different data types between square brackets **[ ]**. Also, like strings, each item within a list is assigned an **index**, or location, for where that item is saved in memory. Lists are also known as a **data collection**. Data collections are simply data types that can store multiple items. We'll see other data collections, like dictionaries and tuples, in later chapters.

Declaring a List of Numbers

For our first **list**, we're going to create a list filled with only numbers. Defining a **list** is like any other data type; on the left of the operator is the name of the variable, and on the right is the value. The difference here is that the value is a set of items declared between square brackets. This is useful for storing similar information, as you can easily pass around one variable name that stores several elements. To separate each item within a **list**, we simply use commas. Let's try:

```
# declaring a list of numbers
nums = [5, 10, 15.2, 20]
print(nums)
```

Go ahead and run that cell. You'll get an output of **[5, 10, 15.2, 20]**. When a list is output, it includes the brackets with it. This current list is made up of three integers and one float.

Accessing Elements Within a List

Now that we know how to define a list, we need to take the next step and understand how to access items within them. In order to access a specific element within a list, you use an **index**. When we declare our list variable, each item is given an index. Remember that indexing in Python starts at zero and is used with brackets. Wednesday of Week 2 also covers indexing:

```
# accessing elements within a list
print( nums[1] )        # will output the value at index 1 = 10
num = nums[2]           # saves index value 2 into num
print(num)             # prints value assigned to num
```

Go ahead and run that cell. We'll get two values output here, **10** and **15.2**. The first value is output because we're accessing the index location of 1 in our *nums* list, which has an integer of 10 stored there. The second value was printed out after we created a new variable called *num*, which was set to the value stored at index 2 within our *nums* list.

Declaring a List of Mixed Data Types

Lists can hold any data type, even other lists. Let's check out an example of several data types:

```
# declaring a list of mixed data types
num = 4.3
data = [num, "word", True]          # the power of data collection
print(data)
```

Go ahead and run that cell. This will output **[4.3, 'word', True]**. It outputs *4.3* as the first item because when the list is defined, it stores the value of *num*, not the variable itself.

Lists Within Lists

Let's get a little more complex and see how lists can be stored within another list:

```
# understanding lists within lists
data = [5, "book", [ 34, "hello" ], True]      # lists can hold any type
print(data)
print( data[2] )
```

Go ahead and run that cell. This will output **[5, 'book', [34, 'hello'], True]** and **[34, 'hello']**. The first output is the entire *data* variable's value, which stores an integer, a string, a list, and a boolean data type. The second output is the list stored inside of our *data* variable, which is located at index 2 and includes an integer and string data type.

Accessing Lists Within Lists

In the last cell, we saw how to output the list stored within the data variable. Now, we'll see how we can access the items within the inner list. To access items within a list normally, we simply use bracket notation and the index location. When that item is another list, you simply add a second set of brackets after the first set. Let's check out an example and come back to it:

```
# using double bracket notation to access lists within lists
print( data[2][0] )       # will output 34
inner_list = data[2]      # inner list will equal [34, 'hello']
print( inner_list[1] )    # will output 'hello'
```

Go ahead and run that cell. The first output will be **34**. This is because our first index location is accessing the second index in *data*, which is a list. Then the second index location specified is accessing the value in that *list* at location zero, which results in the integer of 34. The second output is **"hello"**. We get this result because we declared a variable to store the value at index 2 of our *data* variable, which happens to be a list. Our *inner_list* variable is now equal to *[34, 'hello']* and we access the value at index 1, which is the string **"hello"**. To get a little bit more understanding of how multi-indexing works, check out Table 4-1.

Table 4-1. *Multi-indexing values*

Index Location	Value at Location	Data Type	Can Be Indexed Again
0	5	Integer	No
1	'book'	String	Yes
2	[34, 'hello']	List	Yes
3	True	Boolean	No

Notice that strings can also be index further. If you wanted to only print out the "b" in "book," you would simply write the following:

```
>>> print( data[ 1 ][ 0 ] )    # will output 'b'
```

Changing Values in a List

When you work with lists you need to be able to alter the value of the items within the list. It's like re-declaring a normal variable to a different value, except you access the index first:

```
# changing values in a list through index
data = [5, 10, 15, 20]
print(data)
data[0] = 100            # change the value at index 0 - (5 to 100)
print(data)
```

Go ahead and run that cell. Before we altered the value at index 0, it outputs **[5, 10, 15, 20]**. Once we accessed the zero index and changed its value to *100*, however, the list ended up changing to **[100, 10, 15, 20]**.

Variable Storage

When variables are declared, the value assigned is put into a location in memory. These locations have a specific reference ID. It's not often you'll need to check the ID of a variable, but for educational purposes, it's good to know how storage works. We would use the **id()** function to check the storage location in memory for a variable:

```
>>> a = [ 5, 10 ]
>>> print( id(a) )      # large number represents location in memory
```

When a list is stored in memory, each item is given its own location. Changing the value using index notation will change the value stored within that memory block. Now, if a variable's value is another variable, like so:

```
>>> a = [5, 10]
>>> b = a
```

Changing the value at a specific index will change the value for both lists. Let's see an example:

```
# understanding how lists are stored
a = [5, 10]
b = a
print( "a: { }\t b: { }".format(a, b) )
print( "Location a[0]: { }\t Location b[0]: { }".format( id(a[0]), id(b[0]) ) )
a[0] = 20                  # re-declaring the value of a[0] also changes b[0]
print( "a: { }\t b: { }".format(a, b) )
```

Go ahead and run that cell. We're going to get several outputs here. The first is printing out the values of both list variables to show that they have the same values. The second print statement will output the location in memory for each list's first item. Then lastly, after we change the value of the first item within our "a" list, the value in our "b" list also changes. This is because they share the same memory location.

Copying a List

So how do you create a similar list without altering the original? You copy it! Let's see how:

```
# using [:] to copy a list
data = [5, 10, 15, 20]
data_copy = data[ : ]          # a single colon copies the list
data[0] = 50
print( "data: { }\t data_copy: { }".format(data, data_copy) )
```

Go ahead and run that cell. The output this time will result in only our *data* variable having the first item set to **50**. As *data_copy* was merely a copy of the list, now we're able to always keep the original list in tact if we need to use it again.

Note   You can also use the method .copy( ).

```
                        MONDAY EXERCISES
```

1. **Sports**: Define a list of strings, where each string is a sport. Then output each sport with the following line "I like to play {}"...

2. **First Character**: For the following list, print out each item's first letter. *(output should be 'J', 'A', 'S', 'K')*

   names = ['John', 'Abraham', 'Sam', 'Kelly']

Today was all about our first data collection type, the list. There was a lot to cover, but it's important to understand how to define, change values, and make copies of lists.

Tuesday: For Loops

Today will be spent covering a crucial concept in programming, **loops**. In most applications, you're going to need the ability to run the same code more than once. Rather than writing the same lines of code several times, we use loops. In Python there are two types of loops, today's lesson will be on "**For Loops**."

To follow along with this lesson, let's continue from our previous notebook file "*Week_04*" and simply add a markdown cell at the bottom that says "**For Loops**."

How Loops Work

Loops are how programmers rerun the same lines of code several times. Loops will always run until a condition is met. Take a first-person shooter, the game will continue to run until either you've won, or your health reaches zero. Once either of those conditions occur, the game ends.

Note   It's always important to condense your code down to as few lines as possible, as it is more efficient for the program.

Whether you know it or not, loops are everywhere in life. Every day we wake up, go to work, and go to bed, we know it as a routine, but it's simply a loop. We repeat the same process each day until we reach the weekend. The same concept is applied to the loops in our programs.

Writing a For Loop

For loops are primarily used to loop a set number of times. Take Figure 4-1, for instance, this syntax suggests that the loop will run five times. Let's break this down further. Every for loop begins with the keyword "**for**". Then you define a temporary variable, sometimes known as a *counter* or *index*. Next is the "**in**" keyword, followed by the range function (which will be explained later). Lastly, we have a colon to end the statement. All for loops will follow this exact structure of keyword, variable, keyword, function, and colon.

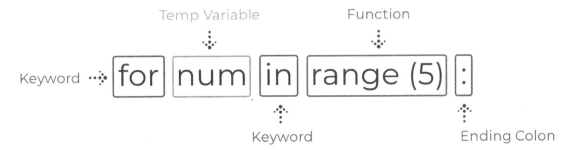

Figure 4-1. *For loop syntax*

Now that we've talked about the structure of writing a for loop, let's write one:

```
# writing your first for loop using range
for num in range(5):
    print( "Value: { }".format(num) )
```

Go ahead and run that cell. This will output "**0, 1, 2, 3, 4**" for our values. This loop is essentially counting to five and printing out each number. So how does it print out each number? When the for loop is created, the range function begins at zero by default and assigns the value of zero into our temporary variable *num*. Each time through the loop is what we call an *iteration*. For each iteration, once all the code within the block runs, the current iteration is finished, and the loop starts over again at the top. Except this time, it increments the value of *num*, which by default is **1**. Our temporary variable is assigned the value of **1** and continues to run the lines of code inside the for loop, which is simply printing out the value of *num*. It will continue to do this until we reach the number 5. To give you an idea of the values assigned for each iteration, reference Table 4-2.

Table 4-2. *Values assigned for each iteration using range( )*

Loop Iteration	Value of Num	Output
1	0	Value: 0
2	1	Value: 1
3	2	Value: 2
4	3	Value: 3
5	4	Value: 4

Note   The value 5 is not output because range( ) counts up to but not including

Range( )

Range allows us to count from one number to another while being able to define where to **start** and **end** and how much we **increment** or **decrement** by. Meaning that we could count every other number or every fifth number if we wanted to. When used with a for loop, it gives us the ability to loop a certain number of times. In the previous example, we saw that a range of 5 printed out five numbers. This is because range defaults to starting at 0 and increments by 1 each time. Let's see another example:

```
# providing the start, stop, and step for the range function
for num in range(2, 10, 2):
    print( "Value: { }".format(num) )  # will print all evens between 2
    and 10
```

Go ahead and run that cell. This time we've specified our program to start the loop at the value of 2 and count to 10 but increment by 2. The output for our values becomes "**2, 4, 6, 8**".

Looping by Element

When working with data types that are *iterable*, meaning they have a collection of elements that can be looped over, we can write the for loop differently:

```
# printing all characters in a name using the 'in' keyword
name = "John Smith"
for letter in name:
    print( "Value: { }".format(letter) )
```

Go ahead and run that cell. The output will be each letter printed out one at a time. Remember that strings can be indexed and are a collection of characters or symbols, which makes them *iterable*. This for loop will iterate over each character and run the code within the block with that character/symbol. Table 4-3 goes over the first few iterations of this loop.

Table 4-3. *Iteration values for looping over strings with range*

Loop Iteration	Value of Letter	Output
1	J	Value: J
2	o	Value: o
3	h	Value: h
4	n	Value: n
5	space symbol	Value:
6	S	Value: S

Continue Statement

Now that we've seen how a loop works, let's talk about a few important statements that we can use with loops. The first is the **continue** statement. Once a continue statement is hit, the current iteration stops and goes back to the top of the loop. Let's see an example:

```
# using the continue statement within a foor loop
for num in range(5):
    if num == 3:
        continue
    print(num)
```

Go ahead and run that cell. The output will result in "**0, 1, 2, 4**" because the *continue* statement is only read when *num* is equal to the value of **3**. Once the statement is hit, it stops the current iteration and goes back to the top to continue looping on the next iteration. This completely stops the code below *continue* from being interpreted, so it doesn't hit the print statement.

Break Statement

One of the most important statements we can use is the break statement. It allows us to break out of a loop at any point in time. Let's see an example:

```
# breaking out of a loop using the 'break' keyword
for num in range(5):
    if num == 3:
            break
    print(num)
```

Go ahead and run that cell. The output will result in "**0, 1, 2**" because we broke the loop completely when *num* was equal to **3**. Once a *break* is read, the loop completely stops, and no more code within the loop is run. These are useful for stopping a loop when a condition is met.

Note   If you use a double loop, the break statement will only break out of the loop that the statement is within. Meaning, it will not break out of both loops if the break statement is used within the inner loop.

Pass Statement

The last of these three statements is pass. The pass statement is simply just a placeholder so that the program doesn't break. Let's see an example:

```
# setting a placeholder using the 'pass' keyword
for i in range(5):
    # TODO: add code to print number
    pass
```

Go ahead and run that cell. Nothing happens, but that's a good thing. If you take the pass statement out completely, the program will break because there needs to be some sort of code within the block.

It's simply there so that we don't have to write code within the loop just yet. It's useful for framing out a program.

Note   Using "*TODO*" is general practice for setting a reminder.

┌───┐
│   **TUESDAY EXERCISES**   │
└───┘

1. **Divisible by Three**: Write a for loop that prints out all numbers from 1 to 100 that are divisible by three.

2. **Only Vowels**: Ask for user input, and write a for loop that will output all the vowels within it. For example:

   ```
   >>> "Hello" → "eo"
   ```

Today was spent learning all about for loops and how they work. Looping allows us to run the same lines of code several times.

Wednesday: While Loops

We'll be going over the other type of loop today, the **while** loop. Yesterday we saw how loops work, and why we would use a for loop. A **while** loop is generally used when you need to loop based on a condition rather than counting. Today will be all about condition-based looping.

To follow along with this lesson, let's continue from our previous notebook file "*Week_04*" and simply add a markdown cell at the bottom that says, "**While Loops**."

Writing a While Loop

Like a for loop, the while loop starts out with the keyword **"while"**. Following that, we have a conditional like we would use to write an *if statement*. Let's see an example:

```
# writing your first while loop
health = 10
while health > 0:
    print(health)
    health -= 1    # forgetting this line will result in infinite loop
```

Go ahead and run that cell. This will continue to print out the value of *health* until the condition is met. In this case, once *health* is no longer greater than zero, the loop stops running. On the last line, we decrement *health* by one, so each iteration reduces *health* closer to zero. If we didn't decrement *health* at any point in time, this would become an infinite loop (*which is bad*).

While vs. For

I've explained a few times now why we would use each loop; however, it's always good to reiterate concepts. For loops are generally used when you need to count or iterate over a collection of elements. While loops are generally used when doing condition-based looping. When using a while loop, often you'll use boolean variables. Each loop has their use cases; in most cases it's personal preference, but the general rule of thumb is counting with for loops, conditions with while loops.

Note   The pass, break, and continue statements all work the same way for while loops as well.

Infinite Loops

In a previous cell, I mentioned that infinite loops were bad. An infinite loop will continue to run until the program breaks, the computer is shut down, or until time stops. Knowing this, stay away from creating infinite loops. Here is an example of an infinite loop:

```
>>> game_over = False
>>> while not game_over:
>>>          print(game_over)
```

If you were to run this within a cell, eventually you would have to shut down Jupyter Notebook and restart it (*or at least the kernel*). This is because the *game_over* variable never becomes **True**, and the condition is running until *game_over* becomes **True**. Always make sure you have a way to exit your loops, whether it be by a *break* or by a condition.

Nested Loops

The concept of a loop within a loop is what we call a **nested loop**. The concepts of a loop still apply. When using nested loops, the inner loop must always finish running, before the outer loop can continue. Let's see an example:

```
# using two or more loops together is called a nested loop
for i in range(2):     # outside loop
    for j in range(3):     # inside loop
        print( i, j )
```

Go ahead and run that cell. At first, this may seem a bit confusing, since there's a lot going on here. Let's break the output down with Table 4-4.

Table 4-4. *Tracking nested loop values*

Iteration	Value of i	Value of j	Inner Loop Count	Outer Loop Count
1	0	0	1	1
2	0	1	2	1
3	0	2	3	1
4	1	0	4	2
5	1	1	5	2
6	1	2	6	2

In total we can see that the inner loop runs six times and the outer loop runs twice. The value of *i* only increments when the outer loop runs, which doesn't occur until the inner loop finishes. The inner loop must count from 0 to 3 each time to run the next iteration on the outer loop.

WEDNESDAY EXERCISES

1. **User Input**: Write a while loop that continues to ask for user input and runs until they type "quit".

2. **Double Loop**: Write a for loop within a while loop that will count from 0 to 5, but when it reaches 3, it sets a *game_over* variable to *True* and *breaks* out of the loop. The while loop should continue to loop until *game_over* is *True*. The output should only be **0, 1, 2**.

Today was a bit of a shorter day, as the concept of loops is the same whether it's a while or for. Remember that a while loop is used for conditional looping, while we use a for loop for counting/iterating.

Thursday: Working with Lists

Now that we've learned what lists are and how to use loops, we're going to go over how to work with lists today. Lists are an important key to any program in Python, so we need to understand our capabilities when using them.

To follow along with this lesson, let's continue from our previous notebook file "*Week_04*" and simply add a markdown cell at the bottom that says, "**Working with Lists**."

Checking Length

Often, we'll need to know how many items are within a list. To do so, we use the **len()** function:

```
# checking the number of items within a list
nums = [5, 10, 15]
length = len(nums)          # len() returns an integer
print(length)
```

Go ahead and run that cell. This will output **3**. We use the length function for several uses, whether it's checking for an empty list or using it within the range function to loop a list.

Slicing Lists

A few weeks back we talked about slicing a string. Lists work the same way so that you're able to access specific items. Slicing follows the same arguments as the *range* function **start, stop, step**:

```
# accessing specific items of a list with slices
print( nums[ 1 : 3 ] )      # will output items in index 1 and 2
print( nums[ : 2 ] )        # will output items in index 0 and 1
print( nums[ : : 2 ] )      # will print every other index - 0, 2, 4, etc.
print( nums[ -2 : ] )       # will output the last two items in list
```

Go ahead and run that cell. The outputs are shown in the comments next to each statement. We use bracket notation as if we're accessing an index; however, we separate the other values via a colon. The order is always **[start : stop : step]**. By default, start is zero and step is one. You have the option to leave those values out if you'd like to keep the defaults. Using a negative number for the step position will result in slicing backward. If you use a negative number in the start or stop positions, then the slice will either start or stop further from the back. Meaning that if you state -5 as the stop position, it will slice from the start of the list all the way to five elements before the list ends.

Adding Items

When you need to add items to your lists, Python has two different methods for doing so.

.append( )

Append will always add the value within the parenthesis to the back of the list. Let's see:

```
# adding an item to the back of a list using append
nums = [10, 20]
nums.append(5)
print(nums)              # outputs [10, 20, 5]
```

Go ahead and run that cell. We declared a list with two items in it to start and then added the integer value of 5 to the back of the list.

.insert( )

The second method to add items to a list is using insert. This method requires an index to insert a value into a specific location. Let's see an example:

```
# adding a value to the beginning of the list
words = [ "ball", "base" ]
nums.insert(0, "glove")   # first number is the index, second is the value
```

Go ahead and run that cell. The output will result in **['glove', 'ball', 'basex']**. Glove is in the zero index now because we specified that index within our insert method.

Removing Items

There are several ways to remove items from a list, the following are the main two methods.

.pop( )

By default, the *pop* method removes the last item in the list; however, you can specify an index to remove as well. This method is also widely used to save the removed item too. When *pop* is used, it not only removes the item but also returns it. This allows us to save that value into a variable to be used later:

```
# using pop to remove items and saving to a variable to use later
items = [5, "ball", True]
items.pop( )                      # by default removes the last item
removed_item = items.pop(0)    # removes 5 and saves it into the variable
print(removed_item, "\n", items)
```

Go ahead and run that cell. Using *pop*, we can see that it removed the **True** item first, then the element in index zero, which happens to be the integer **5**. While popping it out of the list, we saved it into a variable, which we later output along with the new list.

.remove( )

The remove method allows us to remove items from a list based on their given value:

```
# using the remove method with a try and except
sports = [ "baseball", "soccer", "football", "hockey" ]
try:
      sports.remove("soccer")
except:
      print("That item does not exist in the list")
print(sports)
```

Go ahead and run that cell. Here we'll see that the output is our *sports* list without **soccer** because we were able to remove it correctly. Now the reason why we use a *try and except* with the removal is because if **"soccer"** didn't exist in the list, then the program would crash.

Working with Numerical List Data

Python provides a few functions for us to use on lists of numerical data, such as min, max, and sum. There are several more that we can use, though these are used most frequently:

```
# using min, max, and sum
nums = [5, 3, 9]
print( min(nums) )   # will find the lowest number in the list
print( max(nums) )   # will find the highest number in the list
print( sum(nums) )   # will add all numbers in the list and return the sum
```

Go ahead and run that cell. The output will result in **3, 9, and 17**. As their names state, they'll find the minimum and maximum number. The *sum* function will simply add all the numbers up.

Sorting a List

Often, you'll need to work with a sorted list. There are a couple methods for doing so, but they are very different. One will change the original list, while the other returns a copy.

sorted( )

The *sorted* function will work on either numerical or alphabetical lists, but not one that is mixed. Sorted also returns a copy of the list, so it doesn't alter the original. Usually if you need to keep the original intact, be sure to use this function:

```
# using sorted on lists for numerical and alphabetical data
nums = [5, 8, 0, 2]
sorted_nums = sorted(nums)       # save to a new variable to use later
print(nums, sorted_nums)         # the original list is in tact
```

Go ahead and run that cell. You'll notice the output of our *nums* list is still in the original order when we declared it. To use the new sorted list, we simply save it to a new variable.

.sort( )

The sort method is used for the same purpose that our previous sorted function is used for; however, it will change the original list directly:

```
# sorting a list with .sort() in-place
nums = [5, 0, 8, 3]
nums.sort( )              # alters the original variable directly
print(nums)
```

Go ahead and run that cell. The resulted output will be a properly sorted list. Just remember that the *nums* variable is now changed, as **.sort()** changes the value directly.

Conditionals and Lists

When working with lists, often you'll need to check if values exist. Now we'll introduce how to run conditional statements on a list. There are many reasons to run a conditional on a list; these are simply a couple examples.

Using "in" and "not in" Keywords

We've seen the use of these keywords already, when we covered conditional statements last week. When working with lists, they serve a purpose to find values within the list quickly:

```
# using conditional statements on a list
names = [ "Jack", "Robert", "Mary" ]
if "Mary" in names:
        print("found")          # will run since Mary is in the list
if "Jimmy" not in names:
        print("not found")      # will run since Jimmy is not in the list
```

Go ahead and run that cell. The output results in **"found"** and **"not found"**. On the first statement, we were trying to see if *"Mary"* existed in the list, which it does. The second conditional statement checked to see if *"Jimmy"* did not exist, which is also true, so it too runs.

Checking an Empty List

There are so many reasons to need to check for an empty list. It's usually to ensure you don't cause any errors in your program, so let's see how we can check:

```
# using conditionals to see if a list is empty
nums = [ ]
if not nums:              # could also say 'if nums == []'
     print("empty")
```

Go ahead and run that cell. This will output **"empty"**. It's mentioned in the comment, but we could have also checked to see if it were equal to empty brackets. Here, I wanted to show you how to use the *"not"* keyword. To check for a list with items, you would write the following:

```
>>> if nums:
```

Loops and Lists

You can use both the for and while loops to iterate over the items within a list.

Using For Loops

When iterating over a list with a for loop, the syntax looks like when we used the range function previously; however, this time we use a temporary variable, the in keyword, and the name of the list. For each iteration, the temporary variable is assigned the item's value. Let's try it out:

```
# using a for loop to print all items in a list
sports = [ "Baseball", "Hockey", "Football", "Basketball" ]
for sport in sports:
     print(sport)
```

Go ahead and run that cell. Here we can see that this cell will output each item within the list. During the first iteration, the temporary variable *"sport"* is assigned *"Baseball,"* and once it prints it out, it moves on to the next item.

Using While Loops

While loops are always used for conditional looping. One great use case for a while loop with lists is removing an item. There are so many uses, this is just one of them:

```python
# using the while loop to remove a certain value
names = [ "Bob", "Jack", "Rob", "Bob", "Robert" ]
while "Bob" in names:
        names.remove("Bob")     # removes all instances of 'Bob'
print(names)
```

Go ahead and run that cell. The output will be our names list without *"Bob"* in the list. We used the combination of the while loop with a conditional to check for our *"Bob"* value in the list and then continued to remove it until our condition was no longer true.

THURSDAY EXERCISES

1. **Remove Duplicates**: Remove all duplicates from the list below. Hint: Use the *.count()* method. The output should be *['Bob', 'Kenny', 'Amanda']*

   ```
   >>> names = ['Bob', 'Kenny', 'Amanda', 'Bob', 'Kenny']
   ```

2. **User Input**: Use a while loop to continually ask the user to input a word, until they type "*quit*". Once they type a word in, add it to a list. Once they quit the loop, use a for loop to output all items within the list.

Today was important so that we could understand how to work with lists, whether it be a conditional statement or a loop. There are many methods out there that lists can use; we'll go over more of them throughout the rest of this book.

Friday: Creating Hangman

As the weeks go on, the projects will generally get longer. Today we're going to be building Hangman with the use of all the concepts learned from the past four weeks. As usual, new concepts will be introduced as we code along. Today's goal is to have a fully functioning Hangman game, where we can guess, lose a life, and win or lose the game. We won't be adding graphics, although after we complete the project together, feel free to add them yourself.

To follow along with this lesson, let's continue from our previous notebook file "*Week_04*" and add a markdown cell at the bottom that says, "**Friday Project: Creating Hangman**."

Final Design

As always, we want to lay out our final design before we begin coding. This week will not be based around graphics, like last week, so we'll focus on the logic and the steps necessary to run the program. Luckily for us, the logic is essentially the steps needed to play the game:

1. Select a word to play with.

2. Ask user for input.

3. Check if guess is correct.

    a. If it is, show the letter in the proper place.

    b. If it isn't, lose a life.

4. Continue steps 2 and 3 until one of the following occurs:

    a. The user guesses the word correctly.

    b. The user loses all their lives.

This is the main game play functionality. There are several other steps we need to perform before actually running the game, like declaring game variables; however, this is the primary functionality that we needed to lay out before we begin coding. Knowing this structure will allow us to stay on track with our program.

Previous Line Symbols Introduced

Like how we added line numbers back in Week 1, we're going to introduce the concept of line symbols for this project and all others going forward. With the need to edit previously written lines, or even add code in the middle of the project, we'll be introducing the concept of line symbols. These symbols will be shown by the use of three empty squares and will represent previously written code. You can see an example here:

```
1| if num > 1:   □□□
3|               # new code will go here
5|               print(   □□□
```

When we add lines in between previously written code, I will use these three squares to signify which line should be above and below the code we're writing. It also means that you should leave the line unaltered. When we need to overwrite a previous line, I will let you know. Be sure to pay attention to line numbers when you see those three squares, as that will help to let you know if you missed a line or not.

Note   Turn lines on by pressing "L" after clicking the cell's side

---

Adding Imports

We'll be writing this program in one cell, and it will be around 50 lines long. The first step is to import a few additional functions that we need:

```
1| # import additional functions
2| from random import choice
3| from IPython.display import clear_output
```

The second line is importing a function called **"choice"** which will select a random item from a list. We'll use this to randomize the word chosen. The third line is importing a Jupyter Notebook specific function which clears the output. When using a loop, if we don't clear output, it will continue to output on top of each other.

Declaring Game Variables

The next step is to understand what variables we need to run the game and declare them. If you think about Hangman and what we need to keep track of, we need to track the user's lives, the word they are trying to guess, a list of words to choose from, and whether the game is over:

```
5| # declare game variables
6| words = [ "tree", "basket", "chair", "paper", "python" ]
7| word = choice(words)      # randomly chooses a word from words list
8| guessed, lives, game_over = [ ], 7, False    # multi variable assignment
```

Line seven declares a variable called *word*, which will select a random item from our *words* list. The eighth line is where we declare three variables together; *guessed* will be given the value of an **empty list**, *lives* will be set to **7**, and *game_over* will be declared to **False**.

Note   As we code along, feel free to write print statements to check the value of each variable. It helps to see what we're declaring.

Generating the Hidden Word

During the game, we want the user to be able to see how many letters are within the word. To do this, we can create a list of strings, where each string is an underscore. The number of items in the list will be set to the same length of the word chosen:

```
10| # create a list of underscores to the length of the word
11| guesses = [ "_ " ] * len(word)
```

On line 11 we're declaring a variable called *guesses*, which is set to a list of underscores. We get the proper length by multiplying the list by the length of the word.

Creating the Game Loop

Every game has a main loop no matter the size of the program. Our main loop will perform the logic that we defined in our **Final Design** section. Rather than writing it all out at once, let's take small steps. The first step is to be able to accept user input and stop playing the game:

```
13| # create main game loop
14| while not game_over:
15|         ans = input("Type quit or guess a letter: ").lower( )
17|         if ans == "quit":
18|             print("Thanks for playing.")
19|             game_over = True
```

Go ahead and run the cell. If you type *"quit"*, the program should stop as we are looping until *game_over* is set to **True**, which only occurs when we input *"quit"*.

Note   Always make sure the cell is done running before moving on.

Outputting Game Information

The next step is to start outputting information to the user. Let's output their lives and the word that they're trying to guess in a nicely formatted statement:

```
14| while not game_over:    □□□
15|         # output game information
16|         hidden_word = "".join(guesses)
17|         print( "Word to guess: { }".format(hidden_word) )
18|         print( "Lives: { }".format(lives) )
20|         ans = input(    □□□
```

Go ahead and run the cell. Depending on the word chosen, you'll get a different output. If the word chosen was four letters, we'll get an output of "**Word to guess: _ _ _ _**" and "**Lives: 7**". The format is nothing new, but what about line 16? The reason we're able to create a string of underscores to output in line 17 is because of the join method. It states that we want to join all the items within the guesses list together with no spaces in between. For example:

```
>>> chars = ['h', 'e', 'l', 'l', 'o']
>>> print('-'.join(chars))
```

The preceding two lines would output "**h-e-l-l-o**". This is a simple way to display our list as a string.

Checking a Guess

The next step is to check and see if the user's input was a correct guess. We won't alter any letters just yet, as we first want to make sure we can identify a correct guess and either output that they guessed correctly or remove a life:

```
24|          game_over = True   □□□
25|          elif ans in word:        # check if letter in word
26|          print("You guessed correctly!")
27|          else:                    # otherwise lose life
28|          lives -= 1
29|          print("Incorrect, you lost a life.")
```

Go ahead and run the cell. If you continue to guess incorrectly, you'll notice the lives will go below zero. Be sure to guess a correct letter and incorrect letter to know that this works.

Clearing Output

Now that we're getting further with our program, we can see that the loop is continually outputting information below previous outputs. Let's begin to clear the output:

```
20|     ans = input(   □□□
22|     clear_output( )          # clear all previous output
24|     if ans == 'quit':   □□□
```

Go ahead and run the cell. You'll notice that it properly clears the previous information displayed no matter how long we play. This is a Jupyter Notebook specific function.

Creating the Losing Condition

The next logical operation would be creating a way to lose, since our lives can go below zero:

```
31|         print('Incorrect,  □□□
33|         if lives <= 0:
34|             print("You lost all your lives, you lost!")
35|             game_over = True
```

Go ahead and run the cell. Now if you lose all your lives, the game will stop running and tell you that you lost. Remember that the loop is only running until *game_over* is **True**, which is what we set it to once the variable of *lives* drops to **zero**.

Handling Correct Guesses

Now that we can lose, we need the ability to see correct guesses. To understand how to alter the letters shown, we first need to remember what's being output. Our *guesses* list is being turned into a string and output. This means that when the user has guessed correctly, we need to change the items within our *guesses* list in their corresponding positions. The list is the same length of the word we chose at the beginning of the cell, so each underscore represents a letters position. If the word was **"sport"**, then the first underscore in "_ _ _ _" would represent the **"s"**. We simply need to replace the proper underscore in the list with the letter guessed. We can do this by using a for loop and keeping track of the index:

```
28|         print('You guessed correctly!')   □□□
30|         # create a loop to change underscore to proper letter
31|         for i in range( len(word) ):
32|                 if word[ i ] == ans:      # comapares
                                              values at indexes
33|                         guesses[ i ] = ans
34|         else:   □□□
```

Go ahead and run that cell. Now when guessing a correct letter, it will output the change. The for loop is looping to the length of the word, and we're using the variable "*i*" to keep track of the index. We then check if each character is equal to the letter guessed. If it is, then we change the item from an underscore to the letter guessed at that index. Check out Table 4-5 for an example on the process. Let's use **"pop"** for our word and "**p**" for the guess.

Table 4-5. *Tacking index value to check guess*

Value of ans	Value of i	Value of word[i]	Condition Value	Value of guesses after change
'p'	0	'p'	True	['p', '_', '_']
'p'	1	'o'	False	['p', '_', '_']
'p'	2	'p'	True	['p', '_', 'p']

Creating a Winning Condition

One of the last steps to completing this project is building the winning condition. To win, the user needs to guess all the letters within the random word chosen. We're already keeping track of the word as they guess correctly, so we just need to check that against the random word:

```
40|        game_over = True    □□□
41|        elif word == "".join(guesses):
42|        print("Congratulations, you guessed it correctly!")
43|        game_over = True
```

Go ahead and run the cell. Now the user can officially win if they guess all the letters correctly. We use the same join method from earlier that turns our list into a string, so that if any underscores remain in the list, the joined string will not be equal to the random word. We then print out a congratulations and change our *game_over* variable to True to end the loop.

Outputting Guessed Letters

Although our game is now complete and we can win or lose, we should add one more key functionality to it, which is handling previously guessed letters. Whenever a user guesses a previous letter, they shouldn't be penalized for it, but they should also be able to see the previous guesses. At the beginning of this project, we created a variable called *guessed* that we haven't used until now. This variable has remained an empty list thus far, so let's implement it. Before we add to the list, let's make sure we can print out the information properly:

```
16|      hidden_word =    □□□
17|      print("Your guessed letters: { }".format(guessed) )
18|      print("Word to guess    □□□
```

Go ahead and run the cell. At the top of where we output information, we're now printing out the full list of guessed letters. It's perfectly fine to leave this in list form. Even when you guess, it'll still show an empty list because we haven't added that functionality yet.

Adding Guessed Letters

Let's now add the functionality to append the user's guess to our *guesses* list:

```
37|      print("Incorrect,    □□□
39|      if ans not in guessed:
40||     guessed.append(ans)        # add ans to guessed list
42|      if lives <= 0:    □□□
```

Go ahead and run the cell. Now the *guesses* list will update as the user plays the game.

Handling Previous Guesses

The very last order of business is making sure that when they guess the same letter again, that they don't have a life taken away, but rather they are alerted that it's been guessed. We'll need to rewrite the entire conditional statement for checking if the letter is in the word though:

```
27||            game_over = True   □□□
28|             elif ans in word and ans not in guessed:
29||            print("You guessed correctly!")   □□□
34|                                 guesses[ i ] = ans   □□□
35|             elif ans in guessed:
36||            print("You already guessed that. Try again.")
37|             else:   □□□
```

Go ahead and run the cell. We had to change the *elif statement* for line *28* because we also needed to check that the letter was not added to the *guessed* list yet. On line *35* we add a second *elif statement* that will check if the letter is specifically in the *guessed* list. Remember that once an *if/elif statement* runs, the following statements will not. If neither of those conditionals are **True**, then it means that they haven't guessed the letter yet, and it's not in the random word. The game is now complete with full functionality.

Final Output

Congratulations on completing this project! Due to the size of the project, the full code will not be written here. Instead, you may find the completed version of the code where this book's resource files are located on *Github.* You can find the link in the front of the book. All resource files for each week are located within that link. To find the specific code for this project, simply open or download the "**Week_04.ipynb**" file. If you ran into errors along the way, be sure to cross-reference your code with the code in this file and see where you may have gone wrong. The final code output for all future projects can also be found in the same location, so be sure to bookmark this page.

What a day! We were able to use the concept of looping, along with the power of lists to create a fun game. Try adding your own flare, or breaking it, to understand further what may or may not work.

Weekly Summary

This was certainly one of the longer weeks, filled with a ton of information. Be sure to take some time to practice these concepts, either on your own or by completing the end of week exercises. We covered why lists are so important in Python and how to use them within our program. Also covered were the two loops that Python offers, for loops and while loops. Using loops, we can rerun code as many times as necessary, or to iterate over data collections like lists. If you feel overwhelmed with all the information, rest assured that we use loops and lists in everything that we do. This will give you a lot of practice and repetition.

Challenge Question Solution

Even though there is a specific answer we're looking for, this was a bit of a trick question. If your first action was turning around and asking, *"what is the problem?"* or *"why am I evacuating the city?"*, then you answered correctly. The reason we need to ask this question first is because different problems require different solutions. If you began writing an evacuation plan that required using cars, what if the problem was that all the streets were flooded. It wouldn't be very wise to advise people to drive out of the city. Sometimes the answer to a question is a question itself. One other lesson to take away from this is that you should always take a step back and think through each problem. Never assume you know the solution right away; it's okay to ask questions.

Weekly Challenges

To test out your skills, try these challenges:

1. **Pyramids**: Use a for loop to build a pyramid of x's. It should be modular so that if you loop to 5 or 50, it still creates evenly spaced rows. **Hint**: *Multiply the string "x" by the row.* For example, if you loop to the range of 4, it should produce the following result:

   ```
   >>>     x
   >>>    x x
   >>>   x x x
   ```

2. **Output Names**: Write a loop that will iterate over a list of items and only output items which have letters inside of a string. Take the following list, for example, only **"John"** and **"Amanda"** should be output:

   ```
   >>> names = ['John', '  ', 'Amanda', 5]
   ```

3. **Convert Celsius**: Given a list of temperatures that are in Celsius, write a loop that iterates over the list and outputs the temperature converted into Fahrenheit. Hint: The conversion is "F = (9/5) ∗ C + 32":

   ```
   >>> temps = [32, 12, 44, 29]
   Output would be [89.6, 53.6, 111.2, 84.2]
   ```

CHAPTER 5

Functions

This week begins the topic of **functions**. Along with loops, functions can be one of the tougher topics to understand. For this reason, this entire week has been dedicated to covering functions only. This is also one of the more important topics in programming. Knowing how to use a function will greatly improve your programming skills.

Functions give us the ability to make our programs much more powerful and clean while also saving us time. We'll go over how they work on the first day, but the reason we use functions is because of the ability to write once and call repeatedly.

Many of the programs that we've already built can benefit from the use of functions, especially games like Hangman. At the end of the week, we'll build a program that resembles a shopping cart list. We'll see why it's important to separate tasks such as adding, removing, and displaying into separate functions.

Overview

- How to use functions and what they are

- Passing data around using parameters

- Returning data from functions

- Understanding scope and its importance

- Creating a shopping cart program

CHALLENGE QUESTION

Remember that an algorithm is nothing more than a set of step-by-step instructions. If we were to write an algorithm for changing a light bulb, what would it look like? What problems do you have to consider? How many steps are necessary? What is the most efficient method? Using the following algorithm, what problems may occur?

105

© Connor P. Milliken 2020
C. P. Milliken, *Python Projects for Beginners*, https://doi.org/10.1007/978-1-4842-5355-7_5

1.   Retrieve spare bulb.

2.   Turn off switch powering current bulb.

3.   Unscrew current bulb.

4.   Screw in spare bulb.

5.   Turn on switch powering new bulb.

6.   If spare bulb does not turn on, repeat steps 1 through 5.

Monday: Creating and Calling Functions

Today's lesson is all about understanding what functions are, the stages of a function, and how to write a function. We'll find out why they are so important in programs and how they'll make our lives easier.

To follow along with the content for today, let's open up Jupyter Notebook from our "*python_bootcamp*" folder. Once it's open, create a new file, and rename it to "*Week_05.*" Next, make the first cell markdown that has a header saying: "**Creating & Calling Functions.**" We'll begin working underneath that cell.

What Are Functions?

One of the best reference materials for programming is **w3schools**.[1] They even have Python tutorials. Their official documentation describes functions as the following:

A function is a block of code which only runs when it is called.

You can pass data, known as parameters, into a function.

A function can return data as a result.[2]

Programs will often need to run the same code repeatedly, and although loops help with that, we don't want to write the same loop many times throughout our program. The solution to the issue is using a function. They essentially store code that will only run when called upon.

---

[1]www.w3schools.com/python/
[2]www.w3schools.com/python/python_functions.asp

All functions are generally associated with a single task or procedure. This makes it easier for us to break down our program into functions. If you build a program that needs to repeatedly print five lines of information, and you need to output it in five different places, you would need to write 25 lines of code. Using a function, you would store the five lines in a block and call the function whenever you need it, resulting in five lines for the information to output and five lines for calling the function, for a grand total of ten lines. This results in a much more efficient program.

Function Syntax

Like loops, functions follow an exact pattern for every functioned created. They all begin with the keyword "**def**", followed by the **name** of the function. This name is arbitrary and can be anything except for Python keywords and previously defined functions. Directly following the name is the **parenthesis**, and within those are **parameters**. We won't cover parameters until tomorrow so just know that parameters are optional, but parenthesis is required. Lastly, we need an ending **colon** like any other Python statement. See Figure 5-1 for an example.

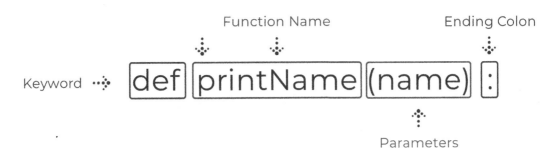

Figure 5-1. *Function syntax*

Writing Your First Function

Now that we know what the syntactical structure looks like, let's go ahead and write our own:

```
# writing your first function
def printInfo( ):                     # defines what the function does when called
     print("Name: John Smith")
     print("Age: 45")
printInfo( )                      # calls the function to run
printInfo( )                      # calls the function again
```

Go ahead and run the cell. We define a function called printInfo, which prints two lines of information each time it's called. Below that we call the function twice, which outputs the information two times. It may not seem like a more efficient program, but imagine you needed to output that exact information 20 times in a program. It's concise and efficient.

Function Stages

In Python there are two stages to each function. The first stage is the *function definition*. This is where you DEFINE the name of the function, any parameters it's supposed to accept, and what it's supposed to do in the block of code associated with it. See Figure 5-2.

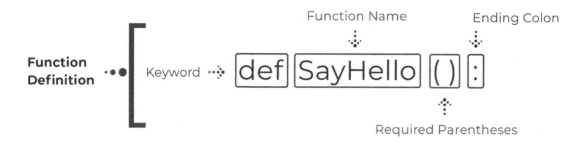

Figure 5-2. The two steps of a function life cycle (definition and call)

The second stage is known as the *function call*. Functions will never run until called, so you can define as many functions as you'd like, but if you never call one of them, then nothing will happen. When you call a function, it will run the block of code within the definition.

UDF vs. Built-in

Without even knowing it, you've been using functions this whole time. Functions such as range, print, len, etc., are all known as "**built-in**" functions. They are included in Python because they serve a specific purpose to help build our applications. Now that we're learning about functions, we can begin to create our own known as **UDFs** or "**user-defined functions**."

Performing a Calculation

Let's check out one more example of a basic function, but this time do more than just print inside of the block:

```
# performing a calculation in a function
def calc( ):
    x, y = 5, 10
    print(x + y)
calc( )                 # will run the block of code within calc and output 15
```

Go ahead and run the cell. We'll get an output of **15** every time we call the calc function here.

MONDAY EXERCISES

---

1. **Print Name**: Define a function called *myName*, and have it print out your name when called.

2. **Pizza Toppings**: Define a function that prints out all your favorite pizza toppings called pizzaToppings. Call the function three times.

Although there wasn't much coding today, it was important to understand the value of functions. Now we can separate our code into blocks, which will make the program easier to read and run.

Tuesday: Parameters

One of the main reasons we use functions is so that we can make our code modular. Today is all about understanding how to use parameters within functions and what they are.

To follow along with this lesson, let's continue from our previous notebook file "*Week_05*" and simply add a markdown cell at the bottom that says, "**Parameters**."

What Are Parameters?

Parameters are temporary variables declared on the function definition. While the functions we've written so far perform a specific task, they aren't modular because they will always print out the same response for every call. When you want to call a function with different values, you need to use **parameters**. Within the parenthesis of the function definition is where you would state a parameter name. This is an arbitrary variable name that you use to reference the value within the function block; however, you usually want it to be relevant to the data that you're working with. When calling the function, you would pass in the necessary value to run the block of code with. Take Figure 5-3.

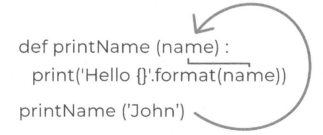

Figure 5-3. *Accepting parameters into a function*

Note   Arguments are the values passed into the function call. In the preceding figure, line 3 is passing the argument "John" into the printName function, where it will the value will be passed into the parameter name

The function is defined with a parameter of "*name*" within the parenthesis. Again, this could be called anything, but we're expecting a person's name to be passed in. The block of code, when executed, will use the value of that parameter within the formatted print statement. The call on line 3 is where we pass the value into the function, known as an argument. In this example, we would get an output of "**Hello John**". We could can now call this function and pass in any string value we would like, and it will print it out. This function is now modular.

Passing a Single Parameter

Let's use the example from Figure 5-3 to create our first function that accepts a parameter:

```
# passing a single parameter into a function
def printName(full_name):
    print( "Your name is: { }".format(full_name) )
printName("John Smith")
printName("Amanda")
```

Go ahead and run the cell. We'll get two different outputs here that use the same function. Parameters allow us to pass different information for each call.

Multiple Parameters

The preceding example passes a string data type into a function, so let's check out how to pass numbers and create a nicely formatted print statement:

```
# passing multiple parameters into a function
def addNums(num1, num2):
        result = num1 + num2
        print( "{ } + { } = { }".format(num1, num2, result) )
addNums(5, 8)        # will output 13
addNums(3.5, 5.5)      # will output 9.0
```

Go ahead and run that cell. Our function definition is expecting two numbers to be passed into the parameters *num1* and *num2*. Within the function block, we reference these values passed in by their argument names.

Passing a List

Passing around a large amount of data is usually easiest when it is stored in a list. For that reason, functions are great at performing repetitive tasks on lists. Let's see an example:

```
# using a function to square all information
numbers1 = [ 2, 4, 5, 10 ]
numbers2 = [ 1, 3, 6 ]
def squares(nums):
        for num in nums:
                print(num**2)
squares(numbers1)
squares(numbers2)
```

Go ahead and run the cell. You can see that it will output all the numbers squared. This is much more efficient than writing the for loop twice for each list. This is the beauty of functions and passing in parameters.

Note   Remember that *nums* is an arbitrary name and is the variable that we reference within the function block.

Default Parameters

In many situations, a parameter can be associated with a default value. Take the value of *pi* for instance; it will always be 3.14, so we can set a parameter called *pi* to that exact value. This allows us to call the function with an already defined value for *pi*. If you wanted to have a more concise value for *pi* you could, but generally **3.14** is good enough:

```
# setting default parameter values
def calcArea(r, pi=3.14):
      area = pi * (r**2)
      print( "Area: { }".format(area) )
calcArea(2)      # assuming radius is the value of 2
```

Go ahead and run the cell. Now we can run the function without needing to pass a value for *pi*. Default parameters **MUST** always go after non-default parameters. In this example the radius must be declared first, then *pi*.

Making Parameters Optional

Sometimes you need to make functions that take optional arguments. The best example is always middle names; some people have them, and some don't. If we wanted to write a function that would print out properly for both situations, we would need to make the middle name an optional parameter. We do this by assigning an empty string value as the default:

```
# setting default parameter values
def printName(first, last, middle=""):
      if middle:
            print( "{ } { } { }".format(first, middle, last) )
      else:
            print( "{ } { }".format(first, last) )
printName("John", "Smith")
printName("John", "Smith", "Paul")      # will output with middle name
```

Go ahead and run the cell. Whether you pass in a middle name or not, the function will run efficiently either way. **Keep in mind the order of our parameters! Parameters must line up from left to right according to the function definition**. If *"Paul"* was placed as the second value after *"John"* in the second call, then our function would assign *"Paul"* into the parameter *"last."*

Named Parameter Assignment

During the function call, you can explicity assign values into parameter names. This is useful when you don't want to mix up the order of values being passed in, as they work from left to right by default. You can use parameter names to assign values for every parameter if you choose, but it's not necessary most of the time. Let's check out an example:

```
# explicity assigning values to parameters by referencing the name
def addNums(num1, num2):
        print(num2)
        print(num1)
addNums(5, num2 = 2.5)
```

Go ahead and run the cell. Here, we explicity assign the value of *num2* in the call using a keyword argument.

*args

The use of *args allows you to pass a variable number of arguments into a function. This allows you to make functions more modular. The magic isn't the *"args"* keyword here though; it's really the unary operator (*) that allows us to perform this feature. You could theoretically replace the word args with anyone, like "*data", and it would still work. However, args is the default and general standard throughout the industry. Let's see how we can use args in a function call:

```
# using args parameter to take in a tuple of arbitrary values
def outputData(name, *args):
    print( type(args) )
    for arg in args:
        print(arg)
outputData("John Smith", 5, True, "Jess")
```

Go ahead and run the cell. You'll notice that the args parameter takes in all values not assigned in the call as a tuple, as output with our first print statement. We then output each argument within that tuple. When you access the args parameter in the block, you do not need to include the unary operator. Notice that "**John Smith**" was not printed out. That's because we have two parameters in the function definition, *name* and *args*. The first argument in the function call is mapped to the name parameter, and the rest are inserted into the args tuple. This is a useful mechanism when you're not sure how many arguments to expect.

**kwargs

Like args, **kwargs** allows us to take in an arbitrary number of values in a function; however, it works as a dictionary with keyword arguments instead. **Keyword arguments** are values passed in with keys, which allow us to access them easily within the function block. Again, the magic here is in the two unary operators (**) not the keyword of kwargs. Let's check it out:

```
# using kwargs parameter to take in a dictionary of arbitrary values
def outputData(**kwargs):
    print( type(kwargs) )
    print( kwargs[ "name" ] )
    print( kwargs[ "num" ] )
outputData(name = "John Smith", num = 5, b = True)
```

Go ahead and run the cell. This time we can see that the type is a dictionary and we're able to output each key-value pair within the kwargs parameter like we would with any other dictionary. The keyword arguments within this cell are in the function call, where we specifically declare a key and value to be passed into the function.

```
┌─────────────────────────────────────────────────────────────────┐
│                      TUESDAY EXERCISES                            │
└─────────────────────────────────────────────────────────────────┘
```

1. **User Input**: Ask the user to input a word, and pass that word into a function that checks if the word starts with an uppercase. If it does output "**True**", otherwise "**False**".

2. **No Name**: Define a function that takes in two arguments, *first_name* and *last_name,* and makes both optional. If no values are passed into the parameters, it should output "**No name passed in**"; otherwise, it should print out the name.

Today was all about function parameters and how to use them. The use of parameters makes our functions modular within our program, so that we can successfully reduce the lines of code written.

Wednesday: Return Statement

Up to this point, we've been printing out the data that our functions alter, but what do you do if you need to access this information later? This is where the **return** statement is used. Functions can manipulate data and then send it back to where the function call occurred to save the information to be used for later. Today we'll learn how to do that and why it's useful.

To follow along with this lesson, let's continue from our notebook file "*Week_05*" and simply add a markdown cell at the bottom that says, "**Return Statement**."

How It Works

Figure 5-4 depicts how the two parameters passed into the function are calculated first and then returned to the original location of the call to be stored into a variable. This variable can now be used later in the program with that value.

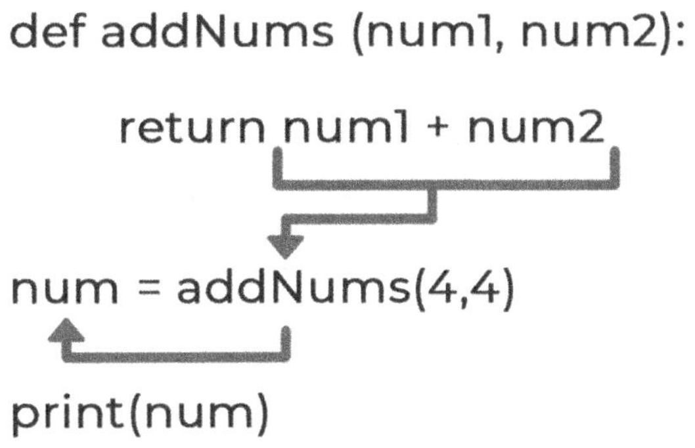

def addNums (num1, num2):

return num1 + num2

num = addNums(4,4)

print(num)

Figure 5-4. *Returning information and storing into a variable*

You can return any data type but may only return a single variable. When you need to return more than one piece of data, you would return a collection of data:

```
>>> def returnMultiple():
>>>            a = 5
>>>            b = 10
>>>            return [a, b]      # one data type holding multiple items
```

Using Return

The return statement is used to send information back to where the function call occurred. So far, we've used the print statement to output information, but this wouldn't work if we needed access to that value later in the program. Instead, we can return the value and save it into a variable that we can work with later. Let's check out a couple examples:

```
# using return keyword to return the sum of two numbers
def addNums(num1, num2):
      return num1 + num2
num = addNums(5.5, 4.5)      # saves returned value into num
print(num)
print( addNums(10, 10) )      # doesn't save returned value
```

Go ahead and run the cell. We'll get **10** and **20** for an output. When we call *addNums* the first time, it runs the function with **5.5** and **4.5** and returns the sum. It then stores that returned value within *num*. The second time we call the function, we simply print it in place. From here, we could reuse the value stored in num, but not the value returned by the second call.

Ternary Operator

A ternary operator is a shorthand Python branching statement. These operators can be used to assign values into a variable, or in this case, deciding what the return from a function:

```
# shorthand syntax using a ternary operator
def searchList(aList, el):
     return True if el in aList else False
result = searchList( [ "one", 2, "three" ], 2)    # result = True
print(result)
```

Go ahead and run the cell. The ternary operator returns True because the given condition is met. The same code written out normally would look like the following:

```
>>> if el in aList:
>>>          return True
>>> else:
>>>          return False
```

It's generally good practice to write less if you can, but it's not a necessity.

WEDNESDAY EXERCISES

---

1. **Full Name**: Create a function that takes in a first and last name and returns the two names joined together.

2. **User Input**: Within a function, ask for user input. Have this function return that input to be stored in a variable outside of the function. Then print out the input.

Today we learned how to retrieve information from a function. This will allow us to save the data it manipulates for later use.

Thursday: Scope

Today we're going to discuss an important concept called scope. This concept deals with accessibility of variables declared within a program. We'll go over the different types of scope and how to do handle them.

To follow along with this lesson, let's continue from our previous notebook file "*Week_05*" and simply add a markdown cell at the bottom that says, "**Scope.**"

Types of Scope

In Python, there are three types of scope: **global, function, and class**. We haven't gone over classes just yet, so we'll discuss class scope in a later chapter. Without knowing it, we've used the other two types of scope. **Global scope** is when you declare a variable to be accessible to an entire file or application. Most of the variables we've declared so far have been global; however, in most programs you write, you will want to avoid global variables. It's okay in Jupyter Notebook for now though. **Function scope** is in reference to variables being declared and accessible only within functions. A variable declared inside of a function cannot be accessed outside of the function, as once the function terminates, so do the variables declared within it.

Global Scope Access

When global attributes are defined, they're accessible to the rest of the file. However, we must keep in mind how function scope works. Even when you declare a variable accessible to the entire file, it will not be accessible within the function. Let's see an example:

```
# where global variables can be accessed
number = 5
def scopeTest( ):
      number += 1      # not accessible due to function level scope
scopeTest( )
```

Go ahead and run the cell. We'll end up receiving an error because the function is limited to variables declared within it or passed in.

Note   When passed in, it only passes the value, not the variable.

Handling Function Scope

When dealing with variables declared in a function, you generally won't need to access it outside of the function. However, in order to access that value, best practice is to return it:

```
# accessing variables defined in a function
def scopeTest( ):
    word = "function"
    return word
value = scopeTest( )
print(value)
```

Go ahead and run the cell. Now we have access to the word defined within the function, we simply assign the returned value to another variable to work with.

In-Place Algorithms

When passing variables into a function, you're simply passing the value of that variable and not the variable itself. Such that the following will not alter the variable *num*:

```
>>> num = 5
>>> def changeNum(n):
>>>        n += 5
>>>        print(num)
```

This is different when changing information via index though. Due to how index's work, via memory location and not by reference, changing an element in a list by the index location will alter the original variable. Let's check out an example:

```
# changing list item values by index
sports = [ "baseball", "football", "hockey", "basketball" ]
def change(aList):
    aList[ 0 ] = "soccer"
print("Before Altering: { }".format(sports) )
change(sports)
print( "After Altering: { }".format(sports) )
```

Go ahead and run the cell. Notice how the first item in the *sports* list changes when the function is called. This is due a change in value by the index itself when the list is passed in. These are known as **in-place algorithms** because no matter where you alter the information, it will change the values in the memory location directly.

THURSDAY EXERCISES

1. **Names**: Create a function that will change the list passed in with a parameter of name at a given index. Such that if I were to pass in *"Bill"* and index *1*, it would change *"Rich"* to *"Bill."* Use the list and function definition in the following:

   ```
   >>> names = ['Bob', 'Rich', 'Amanda']
   >>> def changeValue(aList, name, index):
   ```

Today was important in understanding how variable accessibility works. Knowing this information will keep our variables secure.

Friday: Creating a Shopping Cart

For today's project, we're going to build an application that stores products within a list. We'll be able to add, remove, clear, and show the products in the cart. All the concepts taught throughout the past few weeks will be used.

To follow along with this lesson, let's continue from our previous notebook file *"Week_05"* and add a markdown cell at the bottom that says, "**Friday Project: Creating a Shopping Cart.**"

Final Design

As we've introduced functions this week, the final design will be based around the logic of our program's actions. Functions perform a specific task, which is usually an action. For our shopping cart program, the actions that we need to consider are the tasks of adding, removing, clearing, and showing the items within the cart. The logical design will look like Figure 5-5.

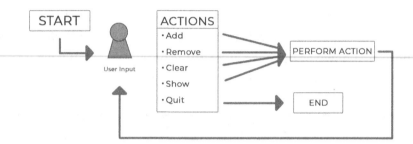

Figure 5-5. *Shopping cart program logic*

We'll be sure to have one main function that will contain the loop and handle user input.

Initial Setup

Like the project from last week, we'll be creating the program in a single cell, so make sure you familiarize yourself with the concepts we used in that project. To start, let's import the clearing function *from Jupyter Notebook* and declare a global variable to work with:

```
1| # import necessary functions
2| from IPython.display import clear_output
4| # global list variable
5| cart = [ ]
```

We wanted to declare a global variable of *cart* to work with throughout this program. We're going to use a list, as we'll need to store several items. Using a list will also allow us to edit the variable directly without having to pass it around because of how item assignments work.

Adding Items

As stated in the initial design, we'll want to create our functions first. We'll start with the function for adding items to our *cart* variable:

```
 7| # create function to add items to cart
 8| def addItem(item):
 9|         clear_output( )
10|         cart.append(item)
11|         print( "{ } has been added.".format(item) )
```

We won't call this function until later when we create the main loop. When called, this function will clear the output, append the *item* passed into the parameter, and output to the user.

Removing Items

Next, we'll create the function that will remove items from our *cart* variable:

```
13| # create function to remove items from cart
14| def removeItem(item):
15|         clear_output( )
16|         try:
17|         cart.remove(item)
18|         print( "{ } has been removed.".format(item) )
19|         except:
20|         print("Sorry we could not remove that item.")
```

We want to be sure to include a **try and except** clause around the remove statement because when removing an item that doesn't exist, the program would crash. This prevents that occurrence and will either remove the item properly or output to the user that it didn't work.

Showing the Cart

We want the user to be able to view the cart at any time, which uses a simple loop:

```
22| # create a function to show items in cart
23| def showCart( ):
24|          clear_output( )
25|           if cart:
26|          print("Here is your cart:")
27|          for item in cart:
28|                          print( "- { }".format(item) )
29|          else:
30|          print("Your cart is empty.")
```

Within the function, we clear the output first, then check to see if there are items within the cart. If it's empty, we let the user know; otherwise, we'll loop over the items and output one per line.

Clearing the Cart

One of the last functions we need is the ability to clear the cart:

```
32| # create function to clear items from cart
33| def clearCart( ):
34|          clear_output( )
35|          cart.clear( )
36|          print("Your cart is empty.")
```

Using the built-in clear method, we clear the cart of all items and let the user know.

Creating the Main Loop

So far, we've been creating the functions for handling the user's actions. Now we need to set up the program's main function which will contain the master loop and ending functionality:

```
38| # create main function that loops until the user quits
39| def main( ):
40|          done = False
42|          while not done:
43|          ans = input("quit/add/remove/show/clear: ").lower( )
45|          # base case
46|          if ans == "quit":
47|                       print("Thanks for using our program.")
48|                       showCart( )
49|                       done = True
51| main( )    # run the program
```

Go ahead and run the cell. You should now be able to type in **"quit"** and exit the program; otherwise, it will continue to run. We haven't set up what to do other than exiting; however, we've made sure that our base case is set up properly, as to not create an infinite loop. We also use the boolean variable *done* in order to keep track of whether the master loop is complete.

Handling User Input

The last step of this program is to add the functions we previously created to handle user input:

```
49|            done = True     □□□
50|     elif ans == "add":
51|                    item = input("What would you like to add? ").title( )
52|                    addItem(item)
53|     elif ans == "remove":
54|                  showCart( )
55|                  item = input("What item would you like to remove? ")
                          .title( )
56|                  removeItem(item)
57|     elif ans == "show":
58|                  showCart( )
59|     elif ans == "clear":
```

```
60|                          clearCart( )
61|      else:
62|                          print("Sorry that was not an option.")
64| main( )    # run the program
```

Go ahead and run the cell. We've included several *elif statements* to handle the user's input. Now, depending on what they choose, we'll be able to call the necessary function. On lines **51** and **55**, we accept a second input from the user to type in the item they would like to add or remove, but we make sure to change it to title case for case sensitivity purposes. If they don't choose a proper task to perform, we make sure that we let them know through the *else clause*.

Final Output

Congratulations on completing this project! Due to the size of the project, you may find the completed version of the code on *Github*. To find the specific code for this project, simply open or download the "**Week_05.ipynb**" file. If you ran into errors along the way, be sure to cross-reference your code with the code in this file and see where you may have gone wrong.

Today we were able to build out a full shopping cart program with the use of functions. We can see that our main loop is clean and easy to read. Even with this small program, we can see the power of functions.

Weekly Summary

This week was a big step forward into improving our programming skills. We learned that functions are useful in reducing the number of lines of code written. They help to make our program more efficient and easier to read. They can become modular using parameters or even return specific data using the *return* keyword. One of the last concepts we covered was how to deal with scope in a project and how it handles a variables accessibility. At the end of the week, we built the shopping cart program together to show the capabilities of using functions in a program. Next week we'll continue to build on our knowledge of advanced variables types called data collections.

Challenge Question Solution

The purpose of this challenge was to make you start thinking about possible errors in the steps laid out. Before you start programming the algorithm, you need to understand what could go wrong with the steps you've designed because computers are only as smart as you program them to be. There are several problems with this algorithm. Most notably between steps 2 and 3, where we try to replace the bulb. Did you check to see if the bulb was too hot to touch? In this case we did not, so anybody following this algorithm directly could get burned. As humans, basic instincts take over, and we would stop touching it, but computers will continue to perform the task they're told. Other glaring problems would include checking the replacement bulb being the correct type, and what to do with the bulb that we just replaced. The algorithm doesn't specify a step to dispose of it properly, so do we just leave it in our hand forever? These are steps we need to consider when replacing a bulb. When you begin to build your own algorithms, you need to not only make sure the algorithm works but that you've thought of how to handle error-prone situations.

Weekly Challenges

To test out your skills, try these challenges:

1. **Refactor Hangman**: This is a large task, so tread lightly, but try to refactor the Hangman project from last week to use functions. Think about what actions Hangman requires, and turn those tasks into functions.

2. **Removing by Index**: In the shopping cart program, set up the remove function so that you can remove via the index as well. Set the list up so that it prints out as a numbered list, and when asked to remove an item, the user can also type out a number next to the list item. For example, using the following you can type *"1"* to remove *"Grapes"*:

```
>>> 1) Grapes
>>> What would you like to remove? 1
```

CHAPTER 6

Data Collections and Files

There are several data stuctures in Python. We'll cover **dictionaries**, **sets**, **tuples**, and **frozensets** this week to add to our knowledge of collections. Each one has a specific purpose as we'll see the differences between each.

Knowing how to work with files in any language is important. In order to work with data, we'll need to know how to read and write from several types of files. We'll cover how to work with **text** files and **CSV** files.

Overview

- Understanding dictionaries

- Working with dictionaries

- Learning other important data collections

- Working with files

- Creating a sample database with files

CHALLENGE QUESTION

This week's challenge is to write a function that checks if a word is a palindrome. The function should take in a single parameter and return True or False. Try writing the function on paper first, then try programming it!

Monday: Dictionaries

Today, we'll be learning about a valuable data collection in dictionaries. They store information using keys and are much more efficient than Python lists.

129

© Connor P. Milliken 2020
C. P. Milliken, *Python Projects for Beginners*, https://doi.org/10.1007/978-1-4842-5355-7_6

To follow along with the content for today, let's open up Jupyter Notebook from our *"python_bootcamp"* folder. Once it's open, create a new file, and rename it to *"Week_06."* Next, make the first cell markdown that has a header saying: **"Dictionaries."** We'll begin working underneath that cell.

What Are Dictionaries?

A dictionary is a collection of **unordered** data, which is stored in **key-value** pairs. What is meant by *"unordered"* is the way it is stored in memory. It is not accessible through an index, rather it is accessed through a key. Lists are known as ordered data collections because each item is assigned a specific location. Dictionaries work like a real-life dictionary, where the key is the word and the values are the definition. Dictionaries are useful for working with large data, mapped data, CSV files, APIs, sending or receiving data, and much more.

Declaring a Dictionary

Like other variables, the name of the variable goes to the left of the equals operator, and on the right is the dictionary. All dictionaries are created by using open and closed curly brackets. In between the curly brackets, we define our key-value pairs. Keys can be declared with **ONLY** strings or numbers. There's a colon that separates the key and value. After the colon is the value, and this can be any data type including other data collections or even another dictionary:

```
# declaring a dictionary variable
empty = { }   # empty dictionary
person = { "name": "John Smith" }
    # dictionary with one key/value pair
customer = {
    "name": "Morty",
    "age": 26
}                    # dictionary with two key/value pairs
print(customer)
```

Go ahead and run the cell. Here we can see that we declare three different dictionaries, an empty one, one that has a single key-value pair, and another that has multiple key value pairs. All key-value pairs must be separated by a comma. We'll see how to access this data next.

Note   You could also use *dict( )* to declare an empty dictionary.

Accessing Dictionary Information

All data stored within a dictionary is accessed via the key associated with the value you're trying to access. We simply write the name of the dictionary followed by square brackets. Inside of the square brackets is the key. This will retrieve the value stored at that key:

```
# accessing dictionary information through keys
person = { "name": 'John' }
print( person[ "name" ] )        # access information through the key
```

Go ahead and run the cell. This will output "**John**" since that is what's stored at the "**name**" key.

Using the Get Method

Another way of retrieving information is to use the *get()* method. The major difference between using this method and the previous way of accessing a value is that the get method won't throw a key error. If the key doesn't exist, it will simply return *"None"*. You may also add in a second argument in the call, in order to have the program return a more specific data type. Let's try:

```
# using the get method to access dictionary information
person = { "name": 'John' }
print( person.get("name") )        # retrieves value of name key as before
print( person.get("age", "Age is not available.") )    # get is a secure
way to retrieve information
```

Go ahead and run the cell. On the second print statement, we'll receive the "**Age is not available**" message because the key "*age*" does not exist. This gives us a more secure way of retrieving information.

Dictionaries with Lists

Dictionaries become powerful when you start working with data collections as values:

```
# storing a list within a dictionary and accessing it
data = { "sports": [ "baseball", "football", "hockey", "soccer" ] }
print( data["sports"][0] )  # first access the key, then the index
```

Go ahead and run the cell. In order to access the list, we must first access the "*sports*" key. After that we can access items like any other list via the index. This will output "**baseball**". Keep in mind that we cannot create a dictionary that stores a list without first attaching a key:

```
# improperly storing a list within a dictionary
sports = [ "baseball", "football", "hockey", "soccer" ]
sports_dict = dict( sports )      # will produce error, no key
```

Go ahead and run the cell. This will produce an error because there is no key associated with the *sports* variable. To properly store this list, you would write the following:

```
>>> sports_dict = dict( { "sports" : sports } )
```

Lists with Dictionaries

The combination of lists within dictionaries and vice-versa can become confusing when trying to figure out how to access information. Always remember lists are indexed, and dictionaries use keys. Depending on the order of the data stored, you'll need to do one or the other first. When a list is storing a dictionary, you need to access that dictionary by the index first. After that you have access to the key-value pairs within the dictionary. Let's see an example:

```
# storing a dictionary within a list and accessing it
data = [ "John", "Dennis", { "name": "Kirsten" } ]
print( data[2] )   # the dictionary is in index 2
print( data[2]["name"] )   # first access the index, then access the key
```

Go ahead and run the cell. First, we access the item in the second index, which is our dictionary. Then we access the value stored at the *"name"* key, which is the output of **"Kirsten"**.

Note   Be very careful when using numbers for keys.

Dictionaries with Dictionaries

Dictionaries are very powerful and efficient due to how they're stored in memory. Often, you'll want to use dictionaries as the value for your key-value pairs. Let's see an example:

```
# storing a dictionary within a dictionary and accessing it
data = {
      "team": "Boston Red Sox",
      "wins": { "2018": 108, "2017": 93 }
}
print( data["wins"] )   # will output the dictionary within the wins key
print( data["wins"]["2018"] )   # first access the wins key, then the next key
```

Go ahead and run the cell. This will output **"108"** in the second statement. We're able to access this information by accessing the first key of *"wins"* followed by the second key of *"2018"*.

MONDAY EXERCISES

---

1. **User Input**: Ask the user for their name and age, and then create a dictionary with those key-value pairs. Output the dictionary once created.

2. **Accessing Ingredients**: Output all the ingredients from the following list within the *"ingredients"* key using a for loop:

```
>>> pizza = {
>>>     'ingredients': ['cheese', 'sausage', 'peppers']
>>> }
```

Data collections allow us to work with large data as they are stored in key-value pairs. Remember that data is accessed through keys.

Tuesday: Working with Dictionaries

Today's lesson will cover how to add data, manipulating data, removing key-value pairs, and iterating through dictionaries.

To follow along with this lesson, let's continue from our previous notebook file "*Week_06*" and simply add a markdown cell at the bottom that says, "**Working with Dictionaries.**"

Adding New Information

You'll often need to add new key-value pairs after declaring a dictionary. Let's see how:

```
# adding new key/value pairs to a dictionary
car = { "year": 2018 }
car["color"] = "Blue"
print( "Year: { } \t Color: { }".format( car["year"], car["color"] ) )
```

Go ahead and run the cell. To add new pairs, on the left side of the equals operator, you provide the dictionary name, followed by the new key within brackets. On the right side is whatever you want the value to be. This will output a nicely formatted string with our car information.

Note   As of Python, 3.7 dictionaries are ordered by default. In older versions of Python, key-value pairs didn't always keep their order. You would have needed to use an *OrderedDict( )*.

Changing Information

Altering key-value pairs is exactly like adding a new pair. If the key exists, it simply overwrites the previous value; however, if it doesn't exist, it will create a new key-value pair for you:

```
# updating a value for a key/value pair that already exists
car = { "year": 2018, "color": "Blue" }
car["color"] = "Red"
print( "Year: { } \t Color: { }".format( car["year"], car["color"] ) )
```

Go ahead and run the cell. Like how we declared a new key-value pair earlier, since the key "*color*" already exists in the dictionary, it simply overwrites the previous value.

Deleting Information

Sometimes you'll need to remove a certain pair. To do so, you'll need to use the *del* function:

```
# deleting a key/value pair from a dictionary
car = { "year": 2018 }
try:
    del car["year"]
    print(car)
except:
    print("That key does not exist")
```

Go ahead and run the cell. Be very careful when deleting key-value pairs. If the key you're trying to remove doesn't exist, it will crash the program. To avoid that problem, we use a try/except.

Looping a Dictionary

Dictionaries are iterable like lists. However, they have three different methods for doing so. You can iterate over both the keys and values together, only keys, or only values.

Looping Only Keys

To iterate through a dictionary while only accessing the keys, you'll use the *.keys()* method:

```
# looping over a dictionary via the keys
person = { "name": "John", "age": 26 }
for key in person.keys( ):
    print(key)
    print( person[key] )  # will output the value at the current key
```

Go ahead and run the cell. As we iterate over *person*, our temporary variable of *key* will be equal to each key name. This still gives us the ability to access each value by using our *key* variable.

Looping Only Values

When you don't need to access the keys, using the *.values( )* method is best:

```
# looping over a dictionary via the values
person = { "name": "John", "age": 26 }
for value in person.values( ):
    print(value)
```

Go ahead and run the cell. We won't have access to the key names, but for this method, we're only trying to get the values anyways. Our temporary variable *value* will store each value from the key-value pairs as we iterate over *person*.

Looping Key-Value Pairs

If you need the ability to access both the key and value, then you'll want to use the .items() method. This approach will assign two temporary variables instead of one:

```
# looping over a dictionary via the key/value pair
person = { "name": "John", "age": 26 }
for key, value in person.items( ):
    print( "{ }: { }".format(key, value) )
```

Go ahead and run the cell. As we iterate over *person*, the key-value pairs are assigned to their respective temporary variables of key and value. We now have access to both easily.

Note   The temporary variable names are usually called "*k*" and "*v.*"

---

1. **User Input**: Declare an empty dictionary. Ask the user for their name, address, and number. Add that information to the dictionary and iterate over it to show the user.

2. **Problem-Solving**: What is wrong with the following code:

```
>>> person = { 'name', 'John Smith' }
>>> print(person['name'])
```

Today was important in understanding how to work with dictionaries. Remember that adding and altering key-value pairs are the same syntax.

Wednesday: Tuples, Sets, Frozensets

Python includes several other data collections that all have their own features. Today, we'll look at another three that can be useful at times.

To follow along with this lesson, let's continue from our notebook file "*Week_06*" and simply add a markdown cell at the bottom that says, "**Tuples, Sets, Frozensets.**"

What Are Tuples?

A **tuple** is identical to a list, except it is **immutable**. When something is immutable, it means that it cannot be altered once declared. Tuples are useful for storing information that you don't want to change. They're ordered like lists, so you can iterate through them using an index.

Declaring a Tuple

To declare a **tuple**, you use a comma to separate two or more items. Lists are denoted by their square brackets on the outside, whereas tuples can be declared with optional parenthesis. It's more likely they're declared with parenthesis as it's easier to read. Let's see an example:

```
# declaring a tuple
t1 = ("hello", 2, "hello")    # with parens
t2 = True, 1                  # without parens
print( type(t1), type(t2) )    # both are tuples
t1[0] = 1    # will crash, tuples are immutable once declared
```

Go ahead and run the cell. You can see that we output the types of our variables, which both output "**tuple**". As stated, tuples are declared with and without parenthesis. The last line in this cell will create an error because a tuple's items cannot be altered once declared. The only way to overwrite the data within a tuple is to re-declare the entire tuple.

What Are Sets?

Sets share the same characteristics of *lists* and *dictionaries*. A *set* is a collection of information like a list; however, like a key in a dictionary, sets can only contain **unique values**. They are also an **unordered collection**. This means that they cannot be accessed by index but rather by the value itself like dictionary keys. They can be iterated through though, like how dictionary keys can be looped over. Sets are practical in situations of storing unique items.

Declaring a Set

There are two ways to declare a set. The first way is by using the keyword "**set**" followed by parenthesis and enclosing square brackets. The second way, which is more practical, looks like a dictionary being declared by using a set of curly brackets. Let's check it out:

```
# declaring a set
s1 = set( [1, 2, 3, 1] )      # uses the set keyword and square brackets
s2 = {4, 4, 5}                # uses curly brackets, like dictionary
print( type(s1), type(s2) )
s1.add(5)        # using the add method to add new items to a set
s1.remove(1)     # using the remove method to get rid of the value 1
print(s1)        # notice when printed it removed the second "1" at the end
```

Go ahead and run the cell. We'll see that it outputs the types for both variables as "**sets**". When we output the value of our *s1* variable, it ends up outputting "**1, 2, 3**" only. Remember that sets are unique items, so it drops the second **"1"** value. Sets have various methods that allow us to add, remove, and change information within them, as seen with the add/remove lines.

What Are Frozensets?

Frozensets are essentially the combination of a set and a tuple. They are **immutable**, **unordered**, and **unique**. These are perfect for sensitive information like bank account numbers, as you wouldn't want to alter those. They can be iterated over, but not indexed.

Declaring a Frozenset

To declare a frozenset, you use the keyword "**frozenset**" followed by parenthesis and enclosing square brackets. This is the only way you can declare a frozenset. Let's check out an example:

```
# declaring a frozenset
fset = frozenset( [1, 2, 3, 4] )
print( type(fset) )
```

Go ahead and run the cell. We won't use frozensets too often in this book, but all these data collections serve a specific purpose for use in the Python language.

Data Collection Differences

Table 6-1 shows a summary of the differences between each collection.

Table 6-1. *Collection similarities and differences*

Data Collection	Ordered	Iterable	Unique	Immutable	Mutable
List	Yes	Yes	No	No	Yes
Dictionary	No	Yes	Keys only	Keys only	Values only
Tuple	Yes	Yes	No	Yes	No
Set	No	Yes	Yes	No	Yes
Frozenset	No	Yes	Yes	Yes	No

WEDNESDAY EXERCISES

1. **User Input**: Ask the user to input as many bank account numbers as they'd like, and store them within a list initially. Once the user is done entering information, convert the list to a frozenset and print it out.

2. **Conversion**: Convert the following list into a set of unique values. Print it out after to check there are no duplicates:

   >>> nums = [3, 4, 3, 7, 10]

Today we were able to view three other data collections. Each one has a purpose, even though we mostly work with dictionaries and lists.

Thursday: Reading and Writing Files

Depending on the type of program you're writing, you'll need to save or access information. To do so, you'll need to understand how to work with files, whether it be **creating**, **writing**, or **reading**.

To follow along with this lesson, let's continue from our previous notebook file "*Week_06*" and simply add a markdown cell at the bottom that says, "**Reading & Writing Files.**"

Working with Text Files

By default, Python comes with an **open()** function that allows us to create or modify files. This function accepts two parameters, the *file name*, and the *mode*. If the file name exists, then it will simply open the file for modification; otherwise, it will create the file for you. The mode is in reference to how Python opens and works with the file. For instance, if you simply need to grab information from the file, you would open it up to read. This would allow you to work with the file while not accidentally changing it. Let's look at how to open, write, and read text files:

```
1| # opening/creating and writing to a text file
2| f = open("test.txt", "w+")   # open file in writing and reading mode
3| f.write("this is a test")
4| f.close( )
5| # reading from a text file
6| f = open("test.txt", "r")
7| data = f.read( )
8| f.close( )
9| print(data)
```

Go ahead and run the cell. Let's walk through this line by line. We open the file in writing and reading mode for full editing and assign the value into the variable *f*. On line **3** we use the **write()** method to write our sentence to the file. Then we close the file. **Anytime you open a file, you must always close it**. After we've created and written to our test file, we open it back up in read-only mode. On line **7** we use the **read()** method in order to read all the contents of the file into a single string, which is assigned to our *data* variable. Then we output the info.

Note   Mode "w" will overwrite the entire file. Use "a" for appending.

Writing to CSV Files

CSV files work with data by separating a comma between each cell. This is known as a tabular data structure. To get started working with them, Python has a default library called "csv." We'll need to import that in order to work with them. After importing this library, we'll use the second method of opening files using the **"with"** keyword. This concept works like a while loop, so that while the file is open, we can work with it, and once the block of code is done running, it closes the file automatically for us. Let's check out the example:

```
1| # opening/creating and writing to a csv file
2| import csv
3| with open("test.csv", mode="w", newline="") as f:
4|     writer = csv.writer(f, delimiter=",")
5|     writer.writerow( ["Name", "City"] )
6|     writer.writerow( ["Craig Lou", "Taiwan"] )
```

Go ahead and run the cell. Let's walk through this line by line. We import the *CSV* library on line **2**. Then we open the file in write mode as the variable *f*. We've also set the *newline* parameter to an empty string so that it doesn't create empty lines between rows. On line **4**, we create a *writer* variable that allows us to write to the CSV file. The last two lines write a couple lines of data to the CSV file. Once the block is complete, the file closes automatically, and we're done. Go ahead and check out the file; you'll see the new data output. Remember that write mode will always overwrite any data that was in the file previously.

Reading from CSV Files

In order to read the data from the CSV file we just created, we can simply set the mode to read:

```
1| # reading from csv files
2| with open("test.csv", mode="r") as f:
3|     reader = csv.reader(f, delimiter=",")
4|     for row in reader:
5|             print(row)
```

Go ahead and run the cell. You'll notice that it outputs each row as a list with two items inside. We opened the file in read mode as the variable *f*. We then create a *reader* object through the *CSV* library which reads the contents in the file for us. Then we loop over the *reader* variable and print out each piece of data.

Note   Objects will be covered in a later week.

File Modes in Python

Table 6-2 shows a few more file modes that you can use in Python.

Table 6-2. *File Modes*

Mode	Description
'r'	This is the default mode. It opens the file for reading only.
'w'	Opens file for writing. If file doesn't exist, it creates one.
'x'	Creates a new file. If file exists, the operation fails.
'a'	Open in append mode. If file doesn't exist, it creates one.
'b'	Open in binary mode.
'+'	Will open a file for reading and writing. Good for updating.

THURSDAY EXERCISES

---

1. **User Input**: Ask a user for their favorite number, and save it to a text file.

2. **Data Dumping**: Using the dictionary of following data, save the information to a csv file with the keys as the headers and the values as the rows of data:

```
>>> data = {
'name' : ['Dave', 'Dennis', 'Peter', 'Jess'],
'language': ['Python', 'C', 'Java', 'Python']
}
```

Today we learned how to work with text and CSV files. There are two methods for working with files, each has their own purpose, but generally the with statement is easier to work with.

Friday: Creating a User Database with CSV Files

For this week's project, we'll be building a replica of a user database with CSV files. We'll be able to take input and allow users to log in/log out/register.

To follow along with this lesson, let's continue from our previous notebook file "*Week_06*" and add a markdown cell at the bottom that says, "**Friday Project: Creating a User Database with CSV Files.**"

Final Design

This week's project is all about logic. We need to understand how to set up a step-by-step process for logging users in and out. There are three main parts to this program, registering a user, logging a user in, and the main loop that will run the program. Knowing that the first two are tasks, we can make functions out of them and call them when necessary in the main loop. Let's go ahead and lay out the logical process for this program:

1. Check to see if user is logged in.

    a. If logged in, ask if they would like to log out/quit.

        i. Either quit or log out user and restart.

    b. Else, ask if they would like to log in/register/quit.

        i. If log in, ask user for e-mail/password.

            1. If correct, log user in and restart.

            2. Else, display error and restart.

        ii. If register, ask for e-mail/password/password2.

            1. If passwords match, save user and restart.

            2. Else, display error and restart.

        iii. If quit, say thank you and exit program.

This is the program flowchart for our main loop. Now that you know exactly how the program should run, I urge you to try and build it yourself before continuing. By doing so, you'll be able to reference my code, see where you may have made mistakes, etc. The loop will continue to run until the user quits and allow them to register or log in. Once logged in, you'll only be able to log out or quit. It's simple but will provide some insight on how to handle menu systems.

Setting Up Necessary Imports

First, let's start by importing the necessary files and functions we need to run the program:

```
1| # import all necessary packages to be used
2| import csv
3| from IPython.display import clear_output
```

We'll be writing all the code in a single cell, so no need to run the cell right now. We've gone ahead and imported the CSV library to be able to work with CSV files, as well as the clear output function that allows us to clear our notebook statements from the cell.

Handling User Registration

Next, we'll design the function for registering users. Let's check out that functionality:

```
 5| # handle user registration and writing to csv
 6| def registerUser( ):
 7|   with open("users.csv", mode="a", newline="") as f:
 8|         writer = csv.writer(f, delimiter=",")
10|         print("To register, please enter your info:")
11|         email = input("E-mail: ")
12|         password = input("Password: ")
13|         password2 = input("Re-type password: ")
15|         clear_output( )
17|         if password == password2:
18|                 writer.writerow( [email, password] )
```

```
19|                    print("You are now registered!")
20|         else:
21|                    print("Something went wrong. Try again.")
```

We start by defining the function and opening a CSV file called *"user.csv"*. This will be the file where we store our data. We create a writer object with that file that will allow us to append additional data. After asking the user for their information, we check that both passwords entered are the same, and either add the user with the writer object we created, or we let the user know that something went wrong. Feel free to call this function and try it out. You should see the file be created after the first attempt.

Handling User Login

The second task that we need to design is the ability to log users in. Let's see how to do that:

```
23| # ask for user info and return true to login or false if incorrect info
24| def loginUser( ):
25|   print("To login, please enter your info:")
26|   email = input("E-mail: ")
27|   password = input("Password: ")
29|   clear_output( )
31|   with open("users.csv", mode="r") as f:
32|          reader = csv.reader(f, delimiter=",")
34|          for row in reader:
35|                  if row == [email, password]:
36|                          print("You are now logged in!")
37|                          return True
39|   print("Something went wrong, try again.")
40|   return False
```

In the user login function, we ask the user to enter their information. We then open the file where the user information is being stored as read-only mode. A reader object is created using the CSV library, and we loop through the data row by row on line 34. Each row we read is in the form of a list with two items. The first item is always the e-mail, and the second is the password. On line 35 we're checking the row information against a temporary list filled with the information that the user inputs. If the data matches, we log them in and return True; otherwise, we tell them something went wrong and return False. Try calling this function after registering.

Note   The file is stored in the same directory as the notebook file.

Creating the Main Loop

Here's where the magic happens. Thus far, we've created the two main functionalities of the program, registering and logging a user. This main loop will handle the menu system and what to show based on the user being logged in or not. Let's go ahead and complete this program;

```
42|  # variables for main loop
43|  active = True
44|  logged_in = False
46|  # main loop
47|  while active:
48|    if logged_in:
49|          print("1. Logout\n2. Quit")
50|    else:
51|          print("1. Login\n2. Register\n3. Quit")
53|    choice = input("What would you like to do? ").lower( )
55|    clear_output( )
57|    if choice == "register" and logged_in == False:
58|          registerUser( )
59|    elif choice == "login" and logged_in == False:
60|          logged_in = loginUser( )
61|    elif choice == "quit":
62|          active = False
63|          print("Thanks for using our software!")
64|    elif choice == "logout" and logged_in == True:
65|          logged_in = False
66|          print("You are now logged out.")
67|    else:
68|          print("Sorry, please try again!")
```

Go ahead and run the cell. Before the loop starts, we define a couple variables for the program. These variables will keep track of the user being logged in and whether the program should continue to run. Then we enter the main loop and display the proper menu, depending on the user being logged in. As the user is never logged in when the program starts, the second menu will be displayed. We then ask the user what they would like to do using the *input()* method. The next section is where the logic of our menu system occurs. Depending on the user's choice, we perform a specific action. We've made it so that the user can only log in or register if they are not already logged in. Likewise, they can only log out if they are logged in. If they choose to log in or register, we call the respective functions to perform their operations. For logging the user in, remember that the function returns **True** or **False**, which we then set the *logged_in* variable equal to. If the user decides to quit, we set our *active* variable to **False** and exit the program. Until then, the program will continually show the proper menu based on the user being logged in. If they choose anything but the options included, we display our error message.

Today we were able to understand the logic behind a user registration process with the use of CSV files. We'll use similar concepts later in this book for storing data.

Weekly Summary

Throughout this week we learned about one of the more important data collections, dictionaries. They are important when working with data as they allow us to assign key-value pairs and retrieve information at a high speed. We also covered some other data collections that serve a purpose in specific situations. After understanding collections, we were able to learn about working with files. Writing and reading from files give us the ability to add extra features to our programs, as we saw on the Friday project when we created a user registration app. We'll be able to apply this knowledge to programs that we create later in this book.

Challenge Question Solution

If you didn't know what a palindrome was, hopefully you looked it up. It's where a word is spelled the same forward and backward, like "racecar." There are a couple different ways you could've gotten the answer to this question. The following is an example of a simple and clean solution to the problem:

```
>>> def palindrome(word):
>>> return True if word == word[::-1] else False
```

Remember that we covered ternary operators in the previous chapter, which allow us to write a one-line conditional statement. If you wrote out the entire if else statement but were able to achieve the same result, then good job! Going forward you should start trying to understand how to condense your code further to be properly optimized.

Weekly Challenges

To test out your skills, try these challenges:

1. **Changing Passwords**: Add a function called "*changePassword*" to the project from Friday that will allow users to change their password when logged in.

2. **Favorite Food**: Write a new program that will ask users what their favorite food is. Save the answers to a CSV file called "*favorite_ food.csv*". After answering, display a table of tallied results. Example of table:

Favorite Food?	# of Votes
Turkey	5
Salad	3

CHAPTER 7

Object-Oriented Programming

Many languages are known as **object-oriented programming (OOP)** languages. Python, JavaScript, Java, and C++ are just a couple of names that use OOP. Throughout this week, we'll begin to understand what OOP is, why it's so useful, and how to implement it within a program.

In Python *(and most languages),* we create objects through **classes** that we build. You can think of a class as a blueprint for how an object is created. Take a first-person shooter video game, for instance. All players, vehicles, and weapons are objects. There could be five people each on two teams, but each one of those people are created from the same blueprint. They all have similar features like weight, height, hair color, etc. Rather than writing the same lines of code for ten different people, you write a single blueprint and create each person from that blueprint. This condenses code and makes programs easier to manage and maintain. At the end of the week, we'll build out a full game of Blackjack together and see the power of Python classes!

Overview

- Understanding the basics of object-oriented programming

- What and how to use attributes (variables within a class)

- What and how to use methods (functions within a class)

- Understanding the basics of inheritance (parent or base classes)

- Creating Blackjack with classes

© Connor P. Milliken 2020
C. P. Milliken, *Python Projects for Beginners*, https://doi.org/10.1007/978-1-4842-5355-7_7

CHALLENGE QUESTION

What is the result of the following code?

```
>>> values = { 4:4, 8:8, "Q":10, "ACE":11 }
>>> card = ("Q", "Hearts")
>>> print("{ }".format(values[ card[ 0 ] ] ) )
```

Monday: Creating and Instantiating a Class

All objects in Python are created from **classes**. The point of OOP is to reuse the same code while giving flexibility to create each object with their own features. Today, we'll learn the terms and stages of OOP, as well as how to write our first class.

To follow along with the content for today, let's open up Jupyter Notebook from our "*python_bootcamp*" folder. Once it's open, create a new file, and rename it to "*Week_07.*" Next, make the first cell markdown that has a header saying: "**Creating & Instantiating a Class.**" We'll begin working underneath that cell.

What Is an Object?

Look at your surroundings, what do you see? There may be a couch, chair, TV, book, etc., around you right now. In programming, all of these would be referenced as objects. Even people would be referenced as objects. This is because all objects come from a specific blueprint. In Python, those blueprints are known as classes. Let's take a car, for instance. All cars have similar features and can be built from a template. Each car will generally have wheels, color, make, model, year, VIN number, etc. What classes allow us to do is build out a blueprint that has all these features within it and create different cars from it. This will lessen the code we have to write and give us the ability to give any car we create personal characteristics specific to that object. Figure 7-1 illustrates this concept of creating multiple objects from the same class.

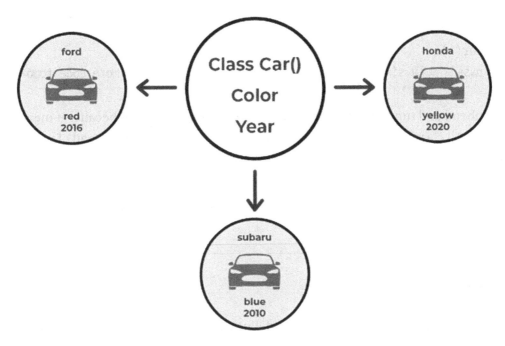

Figure 7-1. Creating three similar cars from the same class blueprint

OOP Stages

There are two stages when using classes. The first stage is the **class definition**. Like function definitions, this stage is where you write the blueprint to be used when called. The second stage is called **instantiation**. It is the process of creating an object from the class definition. After an object is instantiated, it is known as an **instance**. You may have multiple instances from a single class definition. Let's begin to look at how to define a class and make an instance!

Creating a Class

The first step in using classes is creating the class definition or "*blueprint.*" To create a new class, the syntax is like functions, but you use the *class* keyword instead of *def*. Within the indentation of this class block, we would write the blueprint for our class **attributes** and **methods**. Don't worry about those for now though; we'll go over those on Tuesday and Wednesday. For now, we'll just use the keyword *pass*. Let's check out an example:

```
# creating your first class
class Car( ):
      pass      # simply using as a placeholder until we add more code tomorrow
```

Go ahead and run the cell. Nothing will happen, but that's good because it means it worked! All classes will be created with the same structure, except instead of writing *pass*, we'll fill the block with code that gives objects features.

> **Note**   In Python, data types are also classes at their base. Printing out the type of an integer results in <class 'int'>.

Creating an Instance

Now that we know how to create the class definition, we can begin to understand how to create an instance of an object. Like storing a data type into a variable name, we use similar syntax, except after the name of the class, we use parenthesis. We'll go over what these parentheses are used for in tomorrow's lesson. Let's check it out:

```
# instantiating an object from a class
class Car( ):          # parens are optional here
      pass
ford = Car( )    # creates an instance of the Car class and stores into the
variable ford
print(ford)
```

Go ahead and run the cell. You'll get an output like "**<__main__.Car object at 0x0332DB>**". This is describing the class that the instance was built from "*Car*," and the location in memory that the class itself is stored "*0x0332DB*." We've successfully created an instance of the Car object and stored it into our "*ford*" variable.

Creating Multiple Instances

Remember that you can create as many instances as you want from each class; however, you store them in separate variables or data collections. Let's create two *instances* from our class:

154

```
# instantiating multiple objects from the same class
class Car( ):
      pass
ford = Car( )
subaru = Car( )    # creates another object from the car class
print( hash(ford) )
print( hash(subaru) )    # hash outputs a numerical representation of the
                          location in memory for the variable
```

Go ahead and run the cell. When we output the hash values for our variables, we get two different numbers. These numbers are a numerical representation of the variables' location in memory. Meaning that although the two variables are created from the same source, they are stored as separate entities within the program. This is the beauty of objects, as each instance can have personal characteristics.

MONDAY EXERCISES

1. **Animals**: Create a class called "Animals," and create two instances from it. Use two variables with names of "lion" and "tiger."

2. **Problem-Solving**: What's wrong with the following code?

   ```
   >>> class Bus:
   >>>     pass
   >>> school_bus = Bus( )
   ```

Today was the first step into the world of object-oriented programming. In order to build objects in Python, we must first create class definitions, also known as blueprints. From there, we can create single or multiple instances from that class. This process is known as instantiation. Tomorrow we'll see how we can give features to each instance.

Tuesday: Attributes

Yesterday we saw how to create a class definition. Today, we'll begin to understand how to give personalized features, known as **attributes**, to classes and their instances. Attributes are just variables defined within a class, nothing more than that. If you hear someone talking about attributes, you'll immediately know that they're speaking about classes. An attribute is how we store personal information for each object instance. Think of an attribute as a source of information for an object. For a car, an attribute could be the color, number of wheels, number of seats, the engine size, etc.

To follow along with this lesson, let's continue from our previous notebook file "*Week_07*" and simply add a markdown cell at the bottom that says, "**Attributes.**"

Declaring and Accessing Attributes

Like variables, we declare *attributes* with a name and value; however, they are declared inside of the class. We've talked about scope in a previous week; *attributes* are only available within classes they are defined, so in order to access an attribute, you must create an *instance*:

```
# how to define a class attribute
class Car( ):
        sound = "beep"      # all car objects will have this sound attribute
                              and its' value
        color = "red"          # all car objects will have this color
                                attribute and its' value
ford = Car( )
print(ford.color)      # known as 'dot syntax'
```

Go ahead and run the cell. The output will result in "**red**". When we instantiated the *ford* variable from the *Car* class, it was created with two attributes. These attributes were automatically set within the class definition, so every instance created from the *Car* class will be given the sound "**beep**" and the color "**red.**" We'll see how we can change this later. In order to access an object's attribute, you use *dot syntax*. You start by writing the name of the instance, followed by a dot and the attribute you want to access. All classes use this similar dot syntax in order to access attributes and methods (*more on methods tomorrow*).

Changing an Instance Attributes

Not all objects you create are going to have the same characteristics, so you need to have the ability to change an attributes value. To do this, you'll need to use dot syntax:

```
# changing the value of an attribute
class Car( ):
    sound = "beep"
    color = "red"
ford = Car( )
print(ford.sound)     # will output 'beep'
ford.sound = "honk"        # from now on the value of fords sound is honk,
                           this does not affect other instances
print(ford.sound)    # will output 'honk'
```

Go ahead and run the cell. You'll notice that we'll output the *sound* attribute of the *ford* instance before and after we change it. Using dot syntax, we're able to assign the *sound* attribute a new value. This is no different than changing a variables' value. The *ford* object's *sound* attribute will now be **"honk"** until we decide to change it.

Using the __init__() Method

So far, we've been creating classes in a very basic form. When you want to instantiate an object with specific properties, you need to use the **initialization** (*init*) method. Whenever an instance is created, the *init* method is called immediately. You can use this method to instantiate objects with different attribute values upon creation. This allows us to easily create class instances with personalized attributes. Now, we'll go over methods tomorrow, so don't worry too much about the syntax, but more so the understanding of how to use this method. The declaration for this method has two underscores before and after the word *init*. It also includes the **"self"** keyword (*more on this in the next section*) inside of the parenthesis as a mandatory parameter. For this example, we'll create an instance with a color defined at instantiation. Let's go ahead and try it out:

```
1| # using the init method to give instances personalized attributes upon
   creation
3| class Car( ):
4|    def __init__(self, color):
5|            self.color = color        # sets the attribute color to the
                                             value passed in
7| ford = Car("blue")      # instantiating a Car class with the color blue
9| print(ford.color)
```

Go ahead and run the cell. We'll get a resulting output of **"blue".** When we create the *ford* instance, it is initialized with the attribute *color* set to blue. All of this occurs on the 5th line. When we declare the *ford* variable to be instantiated, it passed the argument *"blue"* into the initialization method immediately. The self argument is ignored and *"blue"* is passed into the *color* parameter. Within the *init* method is where we set our *color* attribute to the argument that was just passed in. Hence the value *"blue."* Keep in mind that parameters for this method work the same as functions and need to be in the correct order.

The "self" Keyword

The **self** keyword is a reference to the current instance of the class and is used to access variables and methods associated with that instance. Think about a soccer team you've never seen play before. How do you distinguish each player from the next? You would probably use the numbers on the back of their jerseys. Even though each player is a person with different features, it's easy for you to pick out any of them based on their number. In Python, it's essentially how objects that are created from the same source are identified. In the previous cell, we printed out the attribute *color* from the *ford* instance. The reason Python knew where to access this value, specifically for *ford*, is because we used the *self* keyword. We didn't need it for basic classes because those attributes were globally accessible, which will be covered later today. For now, just know that when you want to instantiate an object with personalized attributes, you need to have the *init* method declared and use the *self* keyword to save each attributes value.

Instantiating Multiple Objects with __init__()

To truly understand how the *init* method works, let's instantiate a couple instances with two attributes of different values:

```
# defining different values for multiple instances
class Car( ):
     def __init__(self, color, year):
             self.color = color       # sets the attribute color to the
                                         value passed in

             self.year = year
ford = Car("blue", 2016)       # create a car object with the color blue
                                  and year 2016

subaru = Car("red", 2018)     # create a car object with the color red and
                                  year 2018

print(ford.color, ford.year)
print(subaru.color, subaru.year)
```

Go ahead and run the cell. The two print statements at the bottom will output each instance's attributes. When we instantiated the *ford* and *subaru* objects, we gave them different values for each of their respective attributes. This is the beauty of OOP. We're able to build two different objects from the same source using just two lines. Even if the class itself was thousands of lines long, to create ten different instances would only take ten lines of code.

Global Attributes vs. Instance Attributes

Without knowing it, you've been using both **globally accessible** attributes and **instance accessible** attributes. Global attributes can be referenced by the class directly and all its instances, whereas instance attributes (*which are defined within the init method*) can only be accessed by the class instances. If an attribute is declared inside of a class, but not within the *init* method, then it is known as a *global attribute*. Any attributes declared within the *init* method using the *self* keyword are *instance attributes*. Let's see an example:

```
1| # using and accessing global class attributes
3| class Car( ):
4|        sound = "beep"   # global attribute, accessible through the class itself
6|        def __init__(self, color):
7|                self.color = "blue"      # instance specific attribute, not
                                            accessible through the class itself
9| print(Car.sound)
11| # print(Car.color)   won't work, as color is only available to
                            instances of the Car class, not the class itself
13| ford = Car("blue")
15| print(ford.sound, ford.color)   # color will work as this is an instance
```

Go ahead and run the cell. On the 6th line we print out the sound **"beep"** by directly accessing it through the class blueprint with dot syntax. You do this by using the name of the class, instead of the name of an instance. We're able to do this because the *sound* attribute is set up as a globally accessible attribute. The entire 7th line is commented out because it would produce an error since the *color* attribute is declared within the *init* method and is only accessible to instances, not the class itself. Lastly, on the 9th line, after we instantiate the *ford* instance, we print out both the *sound* and the *color* attribute. All class instances have access to global and instance level attributes, which is why we're able to output the sound. What you must keep in mind, however, is that we weren't able to give the *ford* instance a personalized value for the *sound* attribute. Only when attributes are declared in the *init* method are we able to give instances personal values upon instantiation. Currently, in order to give *ford* a different value for the *sound* attribute, we would have to change it after its instantiation.

TUESDAY EXERCISES

1. **Dogs**: Create a *Dog* class that has one global attribute and two instance level attributes. The global attribute should be "*species*" with a value of "*Canine.*" The two instance attributes should be "*name*" and "*breed.*" Then instantiate two dog objects, a **Husky** named **Sammi** and a **Chocolate Lab** named **Casey**.

2. **User Input**: Create a *Person* class that has a single instance level attribute of "*name.*" Ask the user to input their name, and create an instance of the *Person* class with the name they typed in. Then print out their name.

Today we learned all about attributes and how we can give classes personalized variables. The use of the initialization method and self keyword allow us to declare attributes at the time of instantiation. Lastly, the difference between global and instance level attributes is key. Those attributes in the initialization method cannot be accessed directly through the class but rather through instances of the class.

Wednesday: Methods

When you think about objects, you associate certain features and actions with them. Take a car, for instance. They'll have attributes like color and wheels but also actions, such as stop, accelerate, turn, etc. In classes, these actions are known as **methods**. *Methods* are essentially functions that are within classes. If you hear someone talking about methods, you'll instantly know that they are talking about OOP. Today, we'll see how we can declare methods for our classes, how to call them, and why they are useful.

To follow along with this lesson, let's continue from our notebook file "*Week_07*" and simply add a markdown cell at the bottom that says, "**Methods.**"

Defining and Calling a Method

Defining a *method* is the same as defining a function; however, you simply put the code within the class indentation block. When declaring a *method* that you intend to access through instances, you must use the *self* parameter in the definition. Without the *self* keyword, the *method* can only be accessed by the class itself. In order to call a method, you use dot syntax. As methods are just functions, you must call them with parenthesis after the name of the instance:

```
# defining and calling our first class method
class Dog( ):
    def makeSound(self):
            print("bark")
sam = Dog( )
sam.makeSound( )
```

Go ahead and run the cell. We'll get "**bark**" as our output. When we created the class definition, it included the method *makeSound* within the blueprint. Once we created an instance of the *Dog* class, we were able to access the method by calling it using dot syntax. You may have as many methods as you'd like within a class.

Accessing Class Attributes in Methods

Within the methods you create, you'll often need access to attributes defined within the class. To do so, you need to use the *self* keyword in order to access the attribute. Remember that *self* is in reference to the instance accessing the class. When we create multiple instances, *self* is what allows the program to understand which sound attribute to return. This is true even for global attributes. Let's see an example:

```
# using the self keyword to access attributes within class methods
class Dog( ):
        sound = "bark"
        def makeSound(self):
                print(self.sound)      # self required to access attributes
                                       defined in the class
sam = Dog( )
sam.makeSound( )
```

Go ahead and run the cell. We'll get an output of "**bark**" again, except this time, it was because we accessed the *sound* attribute declared within the class. Anytime you need to reference an attribute using *self*, you must include *self* within the method parameters.

Method Scope

Like global attributes, you may have *methods* that are accessible through the class itself rather than an instance of the class. These may also be known as **static methods**. They are not accessible by instances of the class. Depending on the class your building, it may help to have a method that is only accessible through the class and not the instances. Let's see an example:

```
 1| # understanding which methods are accessible via the class itself and
       class instances
 3| class Dog( ):
 4|    sound = "bark"
 6|    def makeSound(self):
 7|            print(self.sound)
 9|    def printInfo( ):
10|            print("I am a dog.")
12| Dog.printInfo( )        # able to run printInfo method because it does
                               not include self parameter
14| # Dog.makeSound( )    would produce error, self is in reference to
                             instances only
16| sam = Dog( )
18| sam.makeSound( )     # able to access, self can reference the instance of sam
20| # sam.printInfo( )      will produce error, instances require the self
                              parameter to access methods
```

Go ahead and run the cell. We've defined two methods within our *Dog* class this time. One method has *self* within the parameter, while the other does not. The method without the *self* parameter can be accessed through the class itself, which is why line 8 outputs "**I am a dog.**". The 9th line is commented out because *makeSound* can only be accessed by instances of our *Dog* class, not the class itself. Lastly, we can see that the 12th line is also commented out because methods that are not defined with *self* as a parameter cannot be accessed by instances of the class. Otherwise, we would produce an error. This is the importance of the *self* keyword.

Passing Arguments into Methods

Methods work the same way as functions, where you can pass arguments into the method to be used. When these arguments are passed in, they do not need to be referenced with the self parameter, as they are not attributes, but rather temporary variables that the method can use:

```
# writing methods that accept parameters
class Dog( ):
     def showAge(self, age):
            print(age)     # does not need self, age is referencing the
                             parameter not an attribute
sam = Dog( )
sam.showAge( 6 )    # passing the integer 6 as an argument to the showAge method
```

Go ahead and run the cell. We'll get an output of **6**. After defining an instance of *Dog*, we called the method *showAge* and passed the argument of the integer **6** into the method. The method was then able to print out *age*. We did not need to say "**self.age**" because *self* is in reference to class attributes, not parameters.

Using Setters and Getters

In programming there is a concept called **setters** and **getters**. They are methods that you create to re-declare attribute values and return attribute values. We've seen how we can alter attribute values by directly accessing them; however, this can sometimes lead to problems or accidentally altering the value. Good practice is to create a method that will alter the attribute value for you and call that method when you need to set a new value. The same goes for when you want to access a given attributes value; instead of accessing it directly, you call a method that will return the value. This gives us a safer way to access an instances attributes. Let's see how we can:

```
1| # using methods to set or return attribute values, proper programming practice
3| class Dog( ):
4|   name = ' '      # would normally use init method to declare, this is
                      for testing purposes
6|   def setName(self, new_name):
7|          self.name = new_name      # declares the new value for the
                                       name attribute
9|   def getName(self):
10|         return self.name      # returns the value of the name attribute
11| sam = Dog( )
13| sam.setName("Sammi")
15| print( sam.getName( ) )      # prints the returned value of self.name
```

Go ahead and run the cell. We've created two methods, one *setter* and one *getter*. These methods will generally have their respective keywords "*set*" and "*get*" at the beginning of the method names. On line 4 we define a *setter* to take in a parameter of *new_name* and change the attribute name to the value passed in. This is better practice to alter attribute values. On the 6th line we create a *getter* method that simply returns the value of the *name* attribute. This is better practice to retrieve an attributes value. Lines 9 and 10 call both methods in order to alter and print out the returned value.

Incrementing Attributes with Methods

Like setters, when you want to alter an attributes value by incrementing or decrementing it rather than just changing it completely, the best way is to create a method to complete the task:

```
# incrementing/decrementing attribute values with methods, best
programming practice
class Dog( ):
      age = 5
      def happyBirthday(self):
             self.age += 1
sam = Dog( )
sam.happyBirthday( )    # calls method to increment value by one
print(sam.age)    # better practice use getters, this is for testing
purposes
```

Go ahead and run the cell. For this example, we created a method called *happyBirthday* that will increment the *age* of the dog by one each time it is called. This is simply better practice, but not a required method of altering class attribute values.

Methods Calling Methods

When calling a method from another method, you need to use the self parameter. Let's create a getter method and a method that prints out the information of the dog based on the value:

```
1| # calling a class method from another method
3| class Dog( ):
4|   age = 6
6|   def getAge(self):
7|           return self.age
9|   def printInfo(self):
10|          if self.getAge( ) < 10:      # need self to call other method
                                          for an instance
11|                  print("Puppy!")
13| sam = Dog( )
15| sam.printInfo( )
```

Go ahead and run the cell. We'll get an output of "**Puppy**" here. We can get the returned value from our *getter* because of how we referenced the getAge method within our printInfo method. It was using the self keyword and dot syntax. The condition proved true, as the returned value was **6**, so it proceeded to run the print statement within the block.

Magic Methods

While they have a funny name, **magic methods** are the underlying of classes in Python. Without knowing, you've already used one, the initialization method. All magic methods have two underscores before and after their name. When you print out anything, you're accessing a magic method called __str__. When you use operators (+, -, /, *, ==, etc.), you're accessing magic methods. They are essentially functions that decide what operators and other tasks in Python perform. Don't get too hooked on them, as we won't use them too much, but I wanted to introduce you to them. As mentioned, the __str__ magic method is called when using the print function; it stands for the string representation of a class. Let's alter what gets printed out when we print out a class that we defined ourselves:

166

```
# using magic methods
class Dog( ):
      def __str__(self):
            return "This is a dog class"
sam = Dog( )
print(sam)     # will print the return of the string magic method
```

Go ahead and run the cell. Previously when we printed out a class, it would output the name of the class blueprint and the memory location. Now, since we altered the _str_ magic method, we were able to output a completely different print statement. Keep in mind that the _str_ magic method was expecting a string to be returned, not printed. All magic methods require certain parameters and returned values. Feel free to look up a couple more and alter others to see how they work!

WEDNESDAY EXERCISES

1. **Animals**: Create a class definition of an animal that has a *species* attribute and both a setter and getter to change or access the attributes value. Create an instance called "**lion**," and call the setter method with an argument of "**feline.**" Then print out the *species* by calling the getter method.

2. **User Input**: Create a class *Person* that takes in a *name* when instantiated but sets an *age* to 0. Within the class definition setup, a setter and getter that will ask the user to input their age and set the *age* attribute to the value input. Then output the information in a formatted string as "**You are 64 years old.**" Assuming the user inputs 64 as their age.

Today, we were able to learn about methods and how they essentially function within classes. In order to access other methods, we need to use the self parameter. Methods give classes extra functionality and are used in almost every class we create. This will give all instances of a given class the same functionalities.

Thursday: Inheritance

Sometimes you'll create classes that will have similar attributes or methods. Take a Dog and Cat class, for example. Both will have nearly the same code, attributes, and methods. Rather than writing the same code twice, we use a concept called **inheritance**.

To follow along with this lesson, let's continue from our previous notebook file "*Week_07*" and simply add a markdown cell at the bottom that says, "**Inheritance.**"

What Is Inheritance?

Inheritance is one of the concepts that allow classes to have code reusability within programming. When you have two or more classes that use similar code, you generally want to set up what is called a "**superclass.**" The two classes that will inherit all the code within the superclass are known as "**subclasses.**" A great way to think of *inheritance* is parents and their children. Parents pass down genes to their children, which are inherited and help to define the traits the child will be born with. *Inheritance* works the same way, where the subclass inherits all the attributes and methods within the superclass. Rather than writing the same attributes and methods twice for two classes, we can inherit a class and only need to write the code once.

Inheriting a Class

To inherit a class, we need to put the name of the class we're inheriting between the parentheses after the name of our subclass. Let's try it:

```
 1| # inheriting a class and accessing the inherited method
 3| class Animal( ):
 4|   def makeSound(self):
 5|         print("roar")
 7| class Dog(Animal):          # inheriting Animal class
 8|   species = "Canine"
10| sam = Dog( )
12| sam.makeSound( )     # accessible through inheritance
14| lion = Animal( )
16| # lion.species      not accessible, inheritance does not work backwards
```

Go ahead and run the cell. On line 5, we inherit the *Animal* class into our *Dog* class. This gives *Dog* the ability to access the *makeSound* method, which is why on line 8, we're able to use dot syntax to access *makeSound*. Remember though, inheritance does not work backward, so *Animal* does not have access to attributes and methods defined within the *Dog* class. For this reason, the 10th line is commented out because the *species* attribute does not exist in *Animal* and trying to access it would produce an error.

Using the super( ) Method

The **super** method is used to create forward compatibility when using inheritance. When declaring attributes that are required within the superclass, *super* is used to initialize its values. The syntax for *super* is the keyword super, parenthesis, a dot, the initialization method, and any attributes within the parenthesis of the *init* call. Let's see an example:

```
1| # using the super( ) method to declare inherited attributes
3| class Animal( ):
4|   def __init__(self, species):
5|          self.species = species
7| class Dog(Animal):
8|   def __init__(self, species, name):
9|          self.name = name
10|         super( ).__init__(species)    # using super to declare the species
                                           attribute defined in Animal
12| sam = Dog("Canine", "Sammi")
14| print(sam.species)
```

Go ahead and run the cell. On line 6 we declare the *name* attribute to equal the argument being passed in because this attribute is only defined within the *Dog* class. Line 7 is where the super method is called to initialize the *species* attribute because it is declared inside of the superclass *Animal*. The use of super here helps to reduce lines of code, which is more apparent when the superclass requires several attributes. Once the super method is called, our *species* attributes value is set to the argument passed in, and we can now access it through our *Dog* instance, which is why we're able to output the species on the 9th line.

Method Overriding

Sometimes when using inheritance, you want the subclass to be able to perform a different action when the same method is called. Take our *makeSound* method from the previously created *Animal* class. It prints out "**roar**", but that's not the sound you want dogs making when you create your *Dog* class. Instead, we use the concept of **method overriding** to change what the method does. Within the subclass, we redefine the method (*with the same name*) to perform the task differently. Python will always use the method defined within the subclass first, and if one doesn't exist, then it will check the superclass. Let's use method overriding to alter the *makeSound* method and print the proper statement for our *Dog* class:

```
1| # overriding methods defined in the superclass
3| class Animal( ):
4|   def makeSound(self):
5|           print("roar")
7| class Dog(Animal):
8|   def makeSound(self):
9|           print("bark")
11| sam, lion = Dog( ), Animal( )    # declaring multiple variables on a
                                            single line
13| sam.makeSound( )     # overriding will call the makeSound method in Dog
15| lion.makeSound( )    # no overriding occurs as Animal does not inherit
                             anything
```

Go ahead and run the cell. On the 8th line, we declare two instances *sam* and *lion*. The next line is where we call the *makeSound* method from our dog instance of *sam*. The output results in "**bark**" because of method overriding. As the method was inherited, but then redefined within the *Dog* class, it prints bark instead. On the 10th line, we call the same method with our *Animal* instance *lion*. This output is "**roar**" because *lion* is an instance of the *Animal* class. Remember that inheritance does not work backward. Subclasses cannot give superclasses any features.

Inheriting Multiple Classes

Thus far, we've seen how we can inherit from a single superclass. Now we're going to try inheriting from multiple classes. The main difference is how you super the attributes. Rather than using the super method, you call the class name directly and pass in the self parameter with the attributes. Let's see how:

```
 1| # how to inherit multiple classes
 3| class Physics( ):
 4|   gravity = 9.8
 6| class Automobile( ):
 7|   def __init__(self, make, model, year):
 8|          self.make, self.model, self.year = make, model, year
            # declaring all attributes on one line
10| class Ford(Physics, Automobile):      # able to access Physics and
                                           Automobile attributes and methods
11|   def __init__(self, model, year):
12|          Automobile.__init__(self, "Ford", model, year)    # super does
                                                                 not work
                                                                 with multiple
14| truck = Ford("F-150", 2018)
16| print(truck.gravity, truck.make)   # output both attributes
```

Go ahead and run the cell. We'll get an output of **9.8** and "**Ford**". On line 7 you'll notice that we inherit two classes within the parenthesis for the *Ford* class. The 9th line is where the magic occurs this time though. Instead of using super, we initialize the variables by calling the name of the inherited class directly. Using the *init* method, we pass the *self* parameter along with all the attributes that *Automobile* requires. Python knows which superclass to use because of the name at the beginning of the line. On the last line, we're able to see that we have access to both attributes declared within *Physics* and *Automobile*, where we are inheriting from.

```
THURSDAY EXERCISES
```

1. **Good Guys/Bad Guys**: Create three classes, a superclass called "*Characters*" that will be defined with the following attributes and methods:

    a. *Attributes: name, team, height, weight*

    b. *Methods: sayHello*

    The *sayHello* method should output the statement "*Hello, my name is Max* and *I'm on the good guys*". The team attribute should be declared to a string of either "**good**" or "**bad.**" The other two classes, which will be subclasses, will be "*GoodPlayers*" and "*BadPlayers*." Both classes will inherit "*Characters*" and super all the attributes that the superclass requires. The subclasses do not need any other methods or attributes. Instantiate one player on each team, and call the *sayHello* method for each. The output should result in the following:

    ```
    >>> "Hello, my name is Max and I'm on the good guys"
    >>> "Hello, my name is Tony and I'm on the bad guys"
    ```

Today was all about inheritance in OOP. Using inheritance, we can cut down on the repetitive lines that we write between similar classes. Inherited classes are known as superclasses, while those that perform the inheritance are known as subclasses. Also, the ability to override inherited methods is called method overriding and provides class customization for subclasses.

Friday: Creating Blackjack

Throughout this week, we've learned all about how to use classes in Python to improve our programs. Today, we'll put all that knowledge together and build the popular game Blackjack together. We'll use classes throughout the program, and you'll be able to see how we are able to structure a full-fledged object-oriented game in Python. It is assumed that you know how to play Blackjack. If not, feel free to look up the rules and steps on how to play.

To follow along with this lesson, let's continue from our previous notebook file "*Week_07*" and add a markdown cell at the bottom that says, "**Friday Project: Creating Blackjack.**"

Final Design

As with all previous Friday projects, we need to create a final design that we can follow. This week is a little different, as we need to design our classes first as well. This will help us figure out what attributes and methods our classes need to have before we even begin programming. Sticking to this blueprint will improve the programming process. First, let's think about what classes we need. In Blackjack, you have specific game rules, game actions, and the deck itself. Then we also need to consider that there is a player and a dealer playing the game. It seems that we need to create two classes, one for the game itself and one for the two players. You could argue that you need a separate class for the dealer and player; however, we are keeping this game design a bit simpler. Let's think about what the *Game* class needs first:

- **Game Attributes**
  deck – holds all 52 cards to be used within the game
  suites – used to create deck, tuple of all four suits
  values – used to create deck, tuple of all card values

- **Game Methods**
  makeDeck – creates new 52-card deck when called
  pullCard – pops random card from deck and returns it

The *Game* class is mainly going to keep track of the deck that we're playing with. We could certainly put all methods associated with the game inside of this class as well; however, I'd like to keep the classes simple for you to understand. If you'd like to refactor the game afterward, feel free to do so. Methods like *checkWinner, checkBust, handleTurn,* etc., could all be part of the *Game* class. For this lesson, we're not going to worry about adding these methods to *Game*. Knowing what the *Game* class is going to handle is going to help us understand what our *Player* class needs. Let's go ahead and plan out the attributes and methods for this class now:

- **Player Attributes**
  hand – stores cards within player's hand
  name – string variable that stores name of the player or dealer

- **Player Methods**

  calcHand – returns the calculated total of points in hand

  showHand – prints out player's hand in a nicely formatted statement

  addCard – takes in a card and adds it to the player's hand

As we can see, the *Player* class will be keeping track of each player's hand and any methods associated with altering the hand. Generally, you always want to put methods that alter an attribute within the same class that the attribute is stored. Now that we have a good idea of the attributes and methods needed for each class, we'll follow this guideline to program the game.

Setting Up Imports

Let's start writing this program by importing the necessary functions we'll be using:

```
1| # importing necessary functions
2| from random import randint          # allows us to get a random number
3| from IPython.display import clear_output
```

Feel free to test out the *randint* function. It takes in two arguments, a *min* and *max*, and will return a random number between those arguments. The other import we need is the ability to clear the output from the notebook cell.

Creating the Game Class

Next, we'll begin to write our main game class, which we'll call *Blackjack*. Looking at our design we created before, we'll need to initialize the class with the attributes *deck*, *suits*, and *values*:

```
 5| # create the blackjack class, which will hold all game methods and attributes
 6| class Blackjack( ):
 7|   def __init__(self):
 8|         self.deck = [ ]      # set to an empty list
 9|         self.suits = ("Spades", "Hearts", "Diamonds", "Clubs")
10|         self.values = (2, 3, 4, 5, 6, 7, 8, 9, 10, "J", "Q", "K", "A")
```

We set the *deck* attribute to an empty list because we're going to create a method that creates the deck for us. The other two attributes are created as tuples so that we can iterate over them without changing the items. We'll use them in order to make the cards for our deck.

Generating the Deck

Using *suits* and *values* defined within the *Blackjack* class, we're going to build our deck:

```
12|     # create a method that creates a deck of 52 cards, each card
        should be a tuple with a value and suit
13|     def makeDeck(self):
14|         for suit in self.suits:
15|             for value in self.values:
16|                 self.deck.append( (value, suit) )      # ex: (7,
                                                           "Hearts")

18| game = Blackjack( )
19| game.makeDeck( )
20| print(game.deck)        # remove this line after it prints out correctly
```

Go ahead and run the cell. Our *makeDeck* method has generated a full deck of 52 tuples, each with a value in the 0 index and a suit in the 1 index. We're storing each card as a tuple because we don't want to alter the value accidentally. In the last three lines, we create an instance of the game, call the *makeDeck* method, and output the value of the *deck* attribute. Be sure to remove the last line when you're done, as the print statement is only being used for debugging purposes.

Pulling a Card from the Deck

Now that we have the deck created, we can create a method to pull a card from the deck. We'll use the pop method so that we can get an item and remove it from the deck at the same time:

```
16|                          self.deck.append( (value, suit) )
                              #   ex: (7, "Hearts")  □□□
18|   # method to pop a card from deck using a random index value
19|   def pullCard(self):
20|             return self.deck.pop( randint(0, len(self.deck) - 1) )
22| game = Blackjack( )
23| game.makeDeck( )
25| print( game.pullCard( ), len(game.deck) )     # remove this line after
                                                  it prints out correctly
```

Go ahead and run the cell. You should get an output like "**(7, 'Hearts') 51**". The tuple is our card that we printed out, while the **51** is proving to us that it's removing a card from the deck. We set up the *pullCard* method so that it would pop a random card from the deck. It chooses randomly because of the arguments we passed into *randint*. The max number we want to allow is always one less than the size of the deck because indexing starts at zero. If the deck has 45 cards left in it, we want the random integer to be from 0 to 44. It then pops the item in that random index, removes it from the deck, and returns it back to where the method was called. Currently, we're just printing it out, but later we'll add it to a player's hand. Be sure to remove the last line when you're done, as the print statement is only being used for debugging purposes.

Creating a Player Class

With the game class working properly, we turn our focus to the player class. Let's begin by creating the class definition to accept a name and set the hand to an empty list:

```
20|             return self.deck.pop( randint(0, len(self.deck) - 1) )  □□□
22| # create a class for the dealer and player objects
23| class Player( ):
24|   def __init__(self, name):
25|           self.name = name
26|           self.hand = [ ]
28| game = Blackjack( )
29| game.makeDeck( )
31| name = input("What is your name?")
```

```
32| player = Player(name)
33| dealer = Player("Dealer")
34| print(player.name, dealer.name)    # remove after working correctly
```

Go ahead and run the cell. We'll get a printed statement of the name that was input, as well as "**Dealer**". We define the player class to be initialized with the *name* and *hand* attribute. The *name* attribute is taken in as an argument, while *hand* is set directly inside of the class. After we instantiate the *game* object, we ask the user for their name and create an instance of the *Player* class with their input. The *dealer* object will always be known as "*Dealer*", which is why we create the instance with that value being passed in during the instantiation.

Adding Cards to the Player's Hand

Once we have the player objects being instantiated properly, we can begin to work on the methods needed for the *Player* class. When looking at which method to program first, you always need to think about what methods rely on other methods. For this class, the *calcHand* and *showHand* methods rely on having cards in the hand. For this reason, we'll work on the *addCard* method and then focus on the other two:

```
26|        self.hand = [ ]  □□□
28|   # take in a tuple and append it to the hand
29|   def addCard(self, card):
30|        self.hand.append(card)
32| game = Blackjack( )   □□□
37| dealer = Player("Dealer")   □□□
39| # add two cards to the dealer and player hand
40| for i in range(2):
41| player.addCard( game.pullCard( ) )
42| dealer.addCard( game.pullCard( ) )
44| print( "Player Hand: { } \nDealer Hand: { }".format(player.hand,
    dealer.hand) )   # remove after
```

Go ahead and run the cell. We'll get an output of two random cards within each of the player's hands. The *addCard* method simply takes in a tuple that represents a card and appends it to the player's hand. On the 40th line, we begin a *for loop* that will add two cards to each hand. It does this by pulling a card using the *game* instance method *pullCard*. That method returns a tuple, and that tuple is then passed into the *addCard* method, which is then appended to the respective player's *hand*. This loop will suffice as the start of the game in which all players begin with two cards in their hand. Be sure to remove the last line, as it's used for debugging.

Showing a Player's Hand

In the previous section, we were printing out the full hand of each player. However, in actual Blackjack, you only show the second card dealt to the dealer. It's also bad practice to reference the attribute directly, so we'll need to create the *showHand* method to take care of both these problems. We'll use nicely formatted print statements to show the hands, but more importantly, we'll make sure that if it is still the player's turn, then you can only see one of the dealer's cards:

```
30|          self.hand.append(card)    □□□
32|    # if not dealer's turn then only show one of his cards, otherwise show all
33|    def showHand(self, dealer_start = True):
34|          print( "\n{ }".format(self.name) )
35|          print("===========")
37|          for i in range( len(self.hand) ):
38|                if self.name == "Dealer" and i == 0 and dealer_start:
39|                      print("- of -")  # hide first card
40|                else:
41|                      card = self.hand[ i ]
42|                      print( "{ } of { }".format( card[0], card[1] ) )
44| game = Blackjack( )    □□□
54|    dealer.addCard( game.pullCard( ) )    □□□
56| # show both hands using method
57| player.showHand( )
58| dealer.showHand( )
```

Go ahead and run the cell. The output results in the player's hand showing both cards, while the dealer only shows one. Let's walk through this step by step. On line 33 we declare the *showHand* method with the *dealer_start* parameter. This parameter will be a boolean value which tracks whether we hide the first card the dealer is dealt. We set the default value to **True** so that the only time we need to pass an argument of **False** into the method is at the end when we want to show the dealer's cards. The for loop on line 37 allows us to print out each card in the player object's hand. Line 38 is where we check two things:

1. The instance that called this method was the *dealer.*

2. It's not the dealer's turn yet *(dealer_start == True)*.

If both are true, then we hide the first card; otherwise, we'll show all the cards for both the *player* and the *dealer*. The *card* variable is declared for ease of use when reading the code, as we set it to one of the items within our hand, which represents a card. We then print a formatted statement with the tuple's values. This is done by accessing the **0** and **1** index of the tuples that represent each card. At the bottom of the cell, we call these methods for each player object.

Calculating the Hand Total

Now that we're able to call a method to show each of the player's hands correctly, we need to calculate the total of the cards within the hand. This method becomes a bit tricky, however, as we need to keep a few checks in mind:

1. Aces can be worth 11 or 1 point. They are worth 1 point if the total is over 21.

2. If the dealer is only showing one card, the value of his hand should only represent the value of that one card even though he has two cards in his hand.

3. All face cards (J, Q, K) are worth 10 points.

There are several ways to handle this method. What we'll program together is just one of those many ways. When thinking about how to calculate aces, we need to check for their value after we've calculated the total of all other cards. We'll keep track of how many aces we have first and then total them up afterward. To make sure we return the dealer's total properly, we'll keep track of whether it's his turn or not like we did in the *showHand* method. Lastly, to calculate the face card values, we'll create a dictionary of values to pull from:

```
42|                    print( "{ } of { }".format( card[0], card[1] ) )   □□□
43|                print( "Total = { }".format( self.calcHand(dealer_start) ) )
45|     # if not dealer's turn then only give back total of second card
46|     def calcHand(self, dealer_start = True):
47|         total = 0
48|         aces = 0     # calculate aces afterwards
49|         card_values = {1:1, 2:2, 3:3, 4:4, 5:5, 6:6, 7:7, 8:8, 9:9,
                10:10, "J":10, "Q":10, "K":10, "A":11}
51|         if self.name == "Dealer" and dealer_start:
52|                 card = self.hand[ 1 ]
53|                 return card_values[ card[ 0 ] ]
55|         for card in self.hand:
56|                 if card[ 0 ] == "A":
57|                         aces += 1
58|                 else:
59|                         total += card_values[ card[ 0 ] ]
61|         for i in range(aces):
62|                 if total + 11 > 21:
63|                         total += 1
64|                 else:
65|                         total += 11
67|         return total
69| game = Blackjack( )    □□□
```

Go ahead and run the cell. Starting at line 46, we declare our *calcHand* method with the parameter *dealer_start*. We'll set this parameter to a default of **True**, so that it defaults to only showing the total of one card for the dealer. Line 47 is where we declare our variable to keep track of the *total*. Line 48 is where we declare our variable to keep track of how many *aces* we have in our hand. On line 49, we declare a dictionary of key-value pairs that represent the card's value. Our conditional statement on line 51 checks to see if the *dealer* instance is the object calling this method, as well as if the *dealer_start* parameter is **True**. If they are both true, then we'll simply return the value of the second card in the dealer's hand. It's the second card because we set the *card* variable to equal the second item within the hand, which is the second card. Then we reference the *card_values* dictionary with the card variables' item in index **0**. This item is going to be one of the keys, and the dictionary will then return the value of that key-value pair. If the item at index **0** is "**J**", the dictionary will return a value of 10. The for loop starting on line 55 will loop over each card in the respective player's hand, reference the dictionary for a card value, and add that card value to the current total. If the card is an ace, it will simply add one to our *aces* variable and not add anything to the *total*. The next for loop on line 61 will loop as many times as there are aces in the player's hand. For each ace, we'll either add 1 point or 11 points depending on the *total*. If adding 11 points to the hand makes the *total* greater than 21, we simply add one point instead. At the end of the method, we return the *total*. Lastly, line 43 is where we call *calcHand* within the *showHand* method. We pass the *dealer_start* variable in case we're trying to show the hand during the dealer's turn. Later, during the dealer's turn, we'll pass the argument of **False**, which will then calculate the total of all the dealer's cards rather than just one.

Handling the Player's Turn

The class definitions are now complete. We can begin to focus on the main game flow. First, we'll tackle the player's turn. They should have the ability to **hit** or **stay**. If they stay, their turn is over. If they hit, then we need to pull a card from the deck and add it to their hand. After the card is added, we'll have to check if the player went over 21. If they do, they lose, and we'll need to keep track of that to determine an output later:

```
83|  dealer.showHand( )    □□□
85|  player_bust = False     # variable to keep track of player going over 21
87|  while input("Would you like to stay or hit?").lower( ) != "stay":
88|    clear_output( )
90|    # pull card and put into player's hand
91|    player.addCard( game.pullCard( ) )
93|    # show both hands using method
94|    player.showHand( )
95|    dealer.showHand( )
97|    # check if over 21
98|    if player.calcHand( ) > 21:
99|          player_bust = True       # player busted, keep track for later
100|          print("You lose!")        # remove after running correctly
101|          break   # break out of the player's loop
```

Go ahead and run the cell. For now, try hitting until you go over 21. This will cause an output of "**You lose!**". Nothing happens if you don't go over 21, as we haven't handled that yet, but we'll get there. On line 85, we declare a variable to keep track of the player going over 21. We then begin our while loop by asking the user if they'd like to hit or stay. If they choose anything but stay, then the loop will run. Within the loop, we'll clear the output, add a card to the player's hand, show the hand, and then check if they busted. There are two ways for the loop to end, they bust, or they choose to stay.

Handling the Dealer's Turn

The dealer's turn will be very similar to that of the player's, but we won't need to ask if the dealer would like to hit. The dealer automatically hits while under 17. We'll need to track if the dealer busts as well though:

```
100|          break   # break out of the player's loop    □□□
102| # handling the dealer's turn, only run if player didn't bust
103| dealer_bust = False
105| if not player_bust:
106|     while dealer.calcHand(False) < 17:          # pass False to
                                                       calculate all cards
107|         # pull card and put into player's hand
108|         dealer.addCard( game.pullCard( ) )
110|         # check if over 21
111|         if dealer.calcHand(False) > 21:         # pass False to
                                                       calculate all cards
112|             dealer_bust = True
113|             print("You win!")    # remove after running correctly
114|             break      # break out of the dealer's loop
```

Go ahead and run the cell. Try running the cell until you get the dealer to go over 21, resulting in the print statement running. We begin by declaring a variable on line 103 to track the dealer going bust. On line 105, we check to see if the player already busted, as the round would already be over and the dealer doesn't need to draw any cards. Line 106 is where our loop begins, which will add a card to the dealer's hand and check if he busted. The loop will continue until the dealer has more than 16 points, or he goes over 21.

When we call the *calcHand* method for the dealer this time, we pass the argument of
False. This is so that the method will calculate the complete total of the hand and not
just the second card, as we've been doing previously.

Calculating a Winner

The final piece of this game is to calculate who the winner is. Thus far, we've put a couple
checks in place to see if either the player has already lost by going over 21. We'll first check
to see if the player busted, then the dealer. If neither player busts, then we'll need to see
who has the higher point total. If they tie, then it's known as a push, and no one wins:

```
113|                      break       # break out of the dealer's loop    ☐☐☐
115| clear_output( )
117| # show both hands using method
118| player.showHand( )
119| dealer.showHand(False)     # pass False to calculate and show all
                                 cards, even when there are 2
121| # calculate a winner
122| if player_bust:
123|     print("You busted, better luck next time!")
124| elif dealer_bust:
125|     print("The dealer busted, you win!")
126| elif dealer.calcHand(False) > player.calcHand( ):
127|     print("Dealer has higher cards, you lose!")
128| elif dealer.calcHand(False) < player.calcHand( ):
129|     print("You beat the dealer! Congrats!")
130| else:
131|     print("You pushed, no one wins!")
```

Go ahead and run the cell. We now have a fully functioning game of Blackjack! To
start, we clear the output and show both player's hands. The main difference, though, is
on line 119. We pass the argument **False** into the *showHand* method for the dealer. This
is so that all the dealer's cards show, along with the complete total. Remember that we
were calling the *calcHand* method within *showHand* and passing the value of *dealer_
start*, which we set to **False** with this method call. After that we set up a few conditions
which will output the proper result based on the given condition.

Final Output

Congratulations on completing this project! Due to the size of the project, you may find the completed version of the code on *Github*. To find the specific code for this project, simply open or download the "**Week_07.ipynb**" file. If you ran into errors along the way, be sure to cross-reference your code with the code in this file and see where you may have gone wrong.

Even though today's project was long, we were able to see some great examples of object-oriented programming. Using classes gives us the ability to reuse several lines of code like we did for the player and dealer objects. This program could certainly be refactored to have more methods within the Blackjack class; however, I wanted you to be able to read the code a little easier. For this reason, I kept the classes shorter and the main game functionality separate. Be sure to test the game and add your own features to it if you'd like.

Weekly Summary

Throughout this week, we covered the concepts of object-oriented programming and why they are important in the programming world. In Python, we know them as classes. They allow us to reuse code and create multiple instances from one object. When storing variables or creating functions inside of classes, they're known as attributes and methods. We're able to reference these using dot syntax and the self parameter. Without classes, we would need to hard-code every line for all objects within our programs. This becomes especially apparent within larger-scale programs. To increase the reusability of the code, we're able to use inheritance. This allows subclasses to inherit attributes and methods from superclasses, much like that of a parent and their child. At the end of this week, we were able to create an object-oriented game of Blackjack. This showcased the capabilities of OOP, as we were able to create multiple instances of the player object. Going forward, be sure to think of the world around you as objects. It will help you adjust to the world of OOP and understanding what an objects' attributes and methods are.

Challenge Question Solution

The solution of the challenge question is **10**. The reasoning behind this output is due to how dictionaries work. Remember that when accessing information from dictionaries, you can access *key-value* pairs. When accessing a key from a dictionary, you get back the value of that *key-value* pair. The following line is accessing the value of the first item within the card variable:

```
>>> card[0]
```

This will result in **"Q"**, as it is the first item within the tuple assigned into card. When we access the dictionary, we're accessing the value of the **"Q"** key. The last line would look like this:

```
>>> print("{ }".format(values["Q"]))
```

This would then output the value of the **"Q:10"** key-value pair, which is **10**.

Weekly Challenges

To test out your skills, try these challenges:

1. **Game Loop**: Using the code from our Friday project, create a game loop so that you can continually play a new hand until the player decides to quit. The cell should only stop running if the player types in "**quit**"; otherwise, you should continue to play new hands.

2. **Adding Currency**: Using the code from our Friday project, add the ability to wager currency in the game. Be sure to track the currency within the *Player* class, as the attribute should belong to that object. Before each hand, ask the user how much they would like to wager; if they win, add that amount to their *currency*; if they lose, subtract that amount from what they currently have; and if they tie, nothing should happen.

## CHAPTER 8

Advanced Topics I: Efficiency

Now that we have a solid base to work from, we can begin to dive into more advanced topics. Over the next two weeks, we'll be covering concepts that help to reduce the amount of code you need to write. Many of these concepts will help prepare us for data analysis in Week 10.

Throughout this week, we'll be covering one-liners using **list comprehension** and **anonymous functions**. This will help to reduce the lines of code by condensing the same functionality within a single line. We'll then cover a few of the built-in Python functions that make working with data easier. The last concept we cover is when functions call themselves, known as a **recursive function**. Often, these types of functions lack efficiency, so we'll cover how to use a caching concept called **memoization**. As this week is all about advanced topics, we'll dive into one of the more important algorithms in programming... **Binary Search**! We'll see how to program this algorithm line by line and understand how searching algorithms are able to work efficiently.

Overview

- Building lists in one line using comprehensions
- Understanding one-line anonymous functions
- Using Python's built-in functions for list alteration
- Understanding recursive functions and how to improve them
- Writing the algorithm for Binary Search

© Connor P. Milliken 2020
C. P. Milliken, *Python Projects for Beginners*, https://doi.org/10.1007/978-1-4842-5355-7_8

CHALLENGE QUESTION

For this week's challenge, I'd like you to create a program that asks a user to input a number and tells that user if the number they entered is a prime number or not. Remember that prime numbers are only divisible by one and itself and must be above the number 2. Create a function called "*isPrime*" that you pass the input into, and return a **True** or **False** value. Be sure to keep efficiency in mind when programming the function.

Monday: List Comprehension

List comprehension allows us to create a list filled with data in a single line. Rather than creating an empty list, iterating over some data, and appending it to the list all on separate lines, we can use comprehension to perform all these steps at once. It doesn't improve performance, but it's cleaner and helps reduce the lines of code within our program. With comprehension we can reduce two or more lines into one. Plus, it's generally quicker to write.

To follow along with the content for today, let's open up Jupyter Notebook from our "*python_bootcamp*" folder. Once it's open, create a new file, and rename it to "*Week_08*." Next, make the first cell markdown that has a header saying: "**List Comprehension.**" We'll begin working underneath that cell.

List Comprehension Syntax

The syntax when using list comprehension depends on what you're trying to write. The general syntax structure for list comprehensions looks like the following:

```
>>> *result* = [   *transform*    *iteration*    *filter*   ]
```

For example, when you want to populate a list, the syntax would have the following structure:

```
>>> name_of_list = [ item_to_append for item in list ]
```

However, when you want to include an if statement, the comprehension would look like the following:

```
>>> name_of_list = [ item_to_append for item in list if condition ]
```

The item will only be appended to the new list if the condition is met; otherwise, it won't include it. Lastly, if you would like to include an else condition, it would look like the following:

```
>>> name_of_list = [ item_to_append if condition else item_to_append for item in list ]
```

When using the else conditional within list comprehension, the first item will be appended to the list only when the if statement proves True. If it is False, then the item that comes after the else statement will be appended to the list.

Generating a List of Numbers

Let's try generating a list of numbers from 0 all the way up to 100 using list comprehension:

```
# create a list of ten numbers using list comprehension
nums = [ x for x in range(100) ]        # generates a list from 0 up to 100
print(nums)
```

Go ahead and run the cell. You'll notice that we output a list that includes 100 numbers. List comprehension has allowed us to build out this list within a single line rather than writing out the for loop and append statement on separate lines. The comprehension from the preceding cell is an exact representation of the following code:

```
>>> nums = [ ]
>>> for x in range(100):
>>>         nums.append(x)
```

As you can see, we've reduced three lines down to one using comprehension. This doesn't improve performance but does reduce the number of lines within our code. It becomes more apparent in larger programs, and I highly recommend that you try to use comprehension when possible. Going forward we'll begin to use list comprehension when building out lists.

If Statements

Earlier, we went over how the syntax changes when including an if statement in your comprehension. Let's try an example by making a list of only even numbers:

```python
# using if statements within list comprehesion
nums = [ x for x in range(10) if x % 2 == 0 ]       # generates a list of
                                                    # even numbers up to 10

print(nums)
```

Go ahead and run the cell. For this comprehension, the variable *x* only gets appended to the list when the condition proves **True**. In our case, the condition is True when the current value of *x* is divisible by two. In the following, you'll find the same code that is needed without using comprehension:

```python
>>> nums = [ ]
>>> for x in range(10):
>>>         if x % 2 == 0:
>>>                 nums.append(x)
```

This time we were able to reduce four lines of code down to one. This can often improve readability of your code.

If-Else Statements

Let's take it one step further now and add in an else statement. This time we'll append the string "**Even**" when the number is divisible by two; otherwise, we'll append the string "**Odd**":

```python
# using if/else statements within list comprehension
nums = [ "Even" if x % 2 == 0 else "Odd" for x in range(10) ]    # generates
                                                                 # a list of
                                                                 # even/odd
                                                                 # strings

print(nums)
```

Go ahead and run the cell. This will output a list of strings that represent the numbers odd or even value. Here we append the string "**Even**" when the if conditional is True; otherwise, the else statement will be hit and append the string "**Odd**". The same representation of code without comprehensions can be found in the following:

```
>>> nums = [ ]
>>> for x in range(10):
>>>        if x % 2 == 0:
>>>               nums.append("Even")
>>>         else:
>>>               nums.append("Odd")
```

We've reduced the lines of code from six down to one. Comprehensions are great for quick generation of data; however, it becomes more difficult when the conditions are larger. Comprehensions don't allow for the use of elif statements, only if/else statements.

List Comprehension with Variables

Comprehension is great for generating data from other lists as well. Let's take a list of numbers and generate a separate list of those numbers squared, using comprehension:

```
# creating a list of squared numbers from another list of numbers using
list comprehension
nums = [2, 4, 6, 8]
squared_nums = [ num**2 for num in nums ]        # creates a new list of squared
                                                   numbers based on nums
print(nums)
```

Go ahead and run the cell. We'll get an output of **[4, 16, 36, 64]**. For this example, we were able to generate the squared numbers by appending the expression "*num**2*". The same representation of code without comprehension would look like the following:

```
>>> squared_nums = [ ]
>>> for num in nums:
>>>      squared_nums.append(num**2)
```

In this example, we were able to reduce the lines needed from three to one.

Dictionary Comprehension

Not only can you use comprehension on lists but also Python dictionaries as well. The syntax structure is the exact same, except you need to include a key-value pair instead of a single number to insert into the dictionary. Let's create a dictionary of even numbers as keys, where the value is the key squared:

```python
# creating a dictionary of even numbers and square values using comprehension
numbers = [ x for x in range(10) ]
squares = { num : num**2 for num in numbers if num % 2 == 0 }
print(squares)
```

Go ahead and run the cell. We'll get the following: "{0: 0, 2: 4, 4: 16, 6: 36, 8: 64}". We were able to add each key-value pair using comprehension while checking to see if they were an even number with the conditional statement.

MONDAY EXERCISES

1. **Degree Conversion**: Using list comprehension, convert the following list to Fahrenheit. Currently, the degrees are in Celsius temperatures. The conversion formula is "(9/5) * C + 32". Your output should be **[53.6, 69.8, 59, 89.6]**.

   ```
   >>> degrees = [ 12, 21, 15, 32 ]
   ```

2. **User Input**: Ask the user to input a single integer up to and including 100. Generate a list of numbers that are exactly divisible by that number up to and including 100 using list comprehension. For example, if the number 25 was input, then the output should be **[25, 50, 75, 100]**.

Today's focus was all about generating lists using a concept called list comprehension. Depending on the expression needed, you'll use a certain syntax structure. Comprehension doesn't improve performance; instead it reduces the lines needed in our code to perform the same task. It can also improve readability.

Tuesday: Lambda Functions

Lambda functions, otherwise known as **anonymous functions**, are one-line functions within Python. Like list comprehension, lambda functions allow us to reduce the lines of code we need to write within our program. It doesn't work for complicated functions but helps to improve readability of smaller functions.

To follow along with this lesson, let's continue from our previous notebook file "*Week_08*" and simply add a markdown cell at the bottom that says, "**Lambda Functions.**"

Lambda Function Syntax

The syntax for lambda functions will generally remain the same, unlike list comprehensions when you begin to add the conditional statements. To start, let's look at the basic structure:

```
>>> lambda arguments : expression
```

Lambdas will always begin with the keyword lambda. Following that you'll find any arguments that are being passed in. On the right side of the colon, we'll see the expression to be performed and returned. Lambdas return the expression by default, so we don't need to use the keyword:

```
>>> lambda arguments : value_to_return if condition else value_to_return
```

Like list comprehension, the conditional statement goes at the end. This is as complex as lambda functions get. Anything more than this would require writing the function out completely.

Note   Lambdas basically use ternary operators on the right side of the colon.

Using a Lambda

When using lambdas without storing them into a variable, you need to wrap parenthesis around the function, as well as any arguments being passed in. Let's start small by writing a lambda function that will return the result of the argument squared:

```
# using a lambda to square a number
( lambda x : x**2 )( 4 )      # takes in 4 and returns the number squared
```

Go ahead and run the cell. We'll get an output of **16**. The first set of parenthesis holds the lambda function. The second set holds the argument being passed in. In this case, the integer **4** is passed into *x,* and the expression *x**2* is performed and the result returned. They are known as anonymous functions because they don't have a name. In the following, you'll find the code written for a normal function that would perform the same execution:

```
>>> def square(x):
>>>        return x**2
>>> square(4)
```

We've taken three lines and turned them into one. Once you get used to reading lambda syntax, programs become easier to read and write with these functions.

Passing Multiple Arguments

Lambdas can take in any number of arguments, like functions. Let's try passing in two arguments this time and multiplying them by each other:

```
# passing multiple arguments into a lambda
( lambda x, y : x * y )( 10, 5 )       # x = 10, y = 5 and returns the
result of 5 * 10
```

Go ahead and run the cell. We'll get an output of 50. This time the lambda function accepted two arguments of x and y on the left side of the colon. On the right side of the colon, it was able to perform the expression of multiplying those two arguments together and returning the result. In the following, you'll find the same code, as if we wrote a normal function:

```
>>> def multiply(x, y):
>>>        return x * y
>>> multiply(10, 5)
```

Same as before, we were able to save a couple lines of code to get the same result.

Saving Lambda Functions

Lambdas get there name anonymous function because they don't have a name to reference or call upon. Once a lambda function is used, it can't be used again unless it is saved into a variable. Let's use the same lambda function as before, except this time save it into a variable called "*square*" that can be referenced even after the lambda function is read:

```
# saving a lambda function into a variable
square = lambda x, y : x * y
print(square)
result = square(10, 5)      # calls the lambda function stored in the
square variable and returns 5 * 10
print(result)
```

Go ahead and run the cell. We'll get the same output as before, except this time we got it by calling *square* as a function. When functions are stored inside of variables, the variable name acts as the function call. When we stored a lambda inside of the *square* variable, we were able to call the lambda function by calling *square* and passing in the arguments.

Note   Even functions that are defined normally can be saved into variables and referenced by the variable name.

Conditional Statements

Once you begin adding conditional statements into a lambda function, they act the same way that ternary operators do. The only difference is that you must provide both the if and else statements. You can't use just an if statement; it will render a syntax error, as it always needs an expression to return . Let's create a lambda that will return the greater number between two arguments passed in:

```
# using if/else statements within a lambda to return the greater number
greater = lambda x, y : x if x > y else y
result = greater(5, 10)
print(result)
```

Go ahead and run the cell. We'll get an output of **10** as it is the higher value. Lambdas are extremely useful when you need a function that can perform a simple conditional such as this. The same code written as a normal function can be seen in the following:

```
>>> def greater(x, y):
>>>        if x > y:
>>>                return x
>>>        else:
>>>                return y
>>> result = greater(5, 10)
```

When conditional statements are used, it's easy to see the power of lambda functions. In this case we were able to turn five lines of code into one.

Returning a Lambda

Where lambda functions shine is in their ability to make other functions more modular. Let's say we have a function that takes in an argument and we want that argument to be multiplied with an unknown number later in the program. We can simply create a variable that stores a returned lambda function while passing an argument. Let's try a couple examples:

```
# returning a lambda function from another function
def my_func(n):
      return lambda x : x * n
doubler = my_func(2)          # returns equivalent of lambda x : x * 2
print( doubler(5) )   # will output 10
tripler = my_func(3)          # returns equivalent of lambda x : x * 3
print( tripler(5) )     # will output 15
```

Go ahead and run the cell. We'll get an output of **10** and **15**. What occurs when we define our *doubler* variable is that we call *my_func* while passing in the integer value **2**. That value is used within the lambda function, and the lambda is then returned. However, the lambda isn't returned as "*lambda x : x * n*"; it is now returned with the integer **2** in place of *n*. Whenever *doubler* is called, it's really the lambda function being called. Which is why we get an output of **10** when we pass the value **5** into *doubler*. The same applies to our variable *tripler*. We're able to modify the result of *my_func* because of the returned lambda function.

TUESDAY EXERCISES

1. **Fill in the Blanks**: Fill in the blanks for the following code so that it takes in a parameter of "x" and returns "True" if it is greater than 50; otherwise, it should return "False":

   ```
   >>> ____ x _ True if x _ 50 ____ False
   ```

2. **Degree Conversion**: Write a lambda function that takes in a degree value in Celsius and returns the degree converted into Fahrenheit.

Today we were able to understand the differences between normal functions and anonymous functions, otherwise known as lambda functions. They're useful for readability and being able to condense your code. One of their most powerful features is being able to give functions more capabilities by being returned from them.

Wednesday: Map, Filter, and Reduce

When working with data, you'll generally need to be able to modify, filter, or calculate an expression from the data. That's where these important built-in functions come in to play. The **map** function is used to iterate over a data collection and modify it. The **filter** function is used to iterate over a data collection, and you guessed it... filter out data that doesn't meet a condition. Lastly, the **reduce** function takes a data collection and condenses it down to a single result, like the sum function for lists.

To follow along with this lesson, let's continue from our notebook file "*Week_08*" and simply add a markdown cell at the bottom that says, "**Map, Reduce, and Filter.**"

Map Without Lambdas

The **map** function is used when you need to alter all items within an iterable data collection. It takes in two arguments, the function to be applied on each element and the iterable data. When using map, it returns a **map object**, which is an **iterator**. Don't worry about what these are for now; just know that we can type convert them into a data type that we can work with, like a list. Let's try taking in a list of Celsius temperatures and convert all of them to Fahrenheit:

```
1| # using the map function without lambdas
2| def convertDeg(C):
3|     return (9/5) * C + 32
4| temps = [ 12.5, 13.6, 15, 9.2 ]
5| converted_temps = map(convertDeg, temps)        # returns map object
6| print(converted_temps)
7| converted_temps = list(converted_temps)        # type convert map object
   into list of converted temps
8| print(converted_temps)
```

Go ahead and run the cell. The first print statement will output "**<map object at 0x00DC3D3>**" or something similar. This is because the map function returns a map object, not a converted data collection. On line 7, we're able to convert the map object into a list, which results in the output of "**[54.5, 56.48, 59, 48.56]**". When *map* is called, the function begins to iterate over the the *temps* list passed in. As it iterates, it passed a single item into the *convertDeg* function until it passes all items in. The equivalent of the process is the following:

```
>>> for item in temps:
>>>        convertDeg(item)
```

Following the conversion, it appends the data to the map object. It isn't until we convert the map object that we're able to see the converted temperatures.

Map with Lambdas

Now that we've seen how to use *map* with a normally defined function, let's try it with a lambda function this time. As *map* requires a function as the first parameter, we can simply program a lambda in place of the name of a defined function. We can also type convert it on the same line:

```
# using a map function with lambdas
temps = [ 12.5, 13.6, 15, 9.2 ]
converted_temps = list( map( lambda C : (9/5) * C + 32,
temps) )    # type convert the map object right away
print(converted_temps)
```

Go ahead and run the cell. We'll get the same output as we did before but in far less lines of code. This is the beauty of combining these two concepts. The lambda function takes in each item as the *map* function iterates over the *temps* list and returns the converted value. The same process that we're performing can be found in the lines of code in the following:

```
>>> def convertDeg(degrees):
>>>        converted = [ ]
>>>        for degree in degrees:
>>>                result = (9/5) * degree + 32
>>>                converted.append(result)
>>>        return converted
>>> temps = [ 12.5, 13.6, 15, 9.2 ]
>>> converted_temps = convertDeg(temps)
>>> print(converted_temps)
```

As you can see, the use of lambda functions and map help to reduce the lines of code used when we need to alter our data.

Filter Without Lambdas

The **filter** function is useful for taking a collection of data and removing any information that you don't need. Like the *map* function, it takes in a function and an iterable data type and returns a filter object. This object can be converted into a working list like we did with our map object. Let's use the same data and filter out any degrees that aren't above 55 degrees Fahrenheit:

```
# using the filter function without lambda functions, filter out temps below 55F
def filterTemps(C):
    converted = (9/5) * C + 32
    return True if converted > 55 else False        # use ternary operator
temps = [ 12.5, 13.6, 15, 9.2 ]
filtered_temps = filter(filterTemps, temps)      # returns filter object
print(filtered_temps)
filtered_temps = list(filtered_temps)      # convert filter object to list
                                    of filtered data
print(filtered_temps)
```

Go ahead and run the cell. The first output results in "**<filter object at 0x00DC3D3>**", like our map object output. The second statement results in the output of "**[56.48, 59]**". When we used *filter* and passed in *temps*, it looped over the list one item at a time. It would then pass each item into the *filterTemps* function, and whether the return was **True** or **False,** it would add the item to the filter object. It's not until we type convert the object into a list that we're able to output the data. Using a lambda function can reduce the lines of code needed even further.

Filter with Lambdas

Let's perform the same steps as earlier, except this time we'll use a lambda function:

```
# using the filter function with lambda functions, filter out temps below 55F
temps = [ 12.5, 13.6, 15, 9.2 ]
filtered_temps = list( filter( lambda C : True if (9/5) * C + 32 > 55 else
False, temps) )  # type convert the filter
print(filtered_temps)
```

Go ahead and run the cell. We'll get the same output as we did earlier, except this time we were able to reduce the number of lines used with our lambda function. The same process that we're performing can be found in the lines of code in the following:

```
>>> def convertDeg(degrees):
>>>        filtered = [ ]
>>>        for degree in degrees:
>>>              result = (9/5) * degree + 32
>>>              if result > 55:
>>>                    filtered.append(degree)
>>>        return filtered
>>> temps = [ 12.5, 13.6, 15, 9.2 ]
>>> filtered_temps = convertDeg(temps)
>>> print(filtered_temps)
```

Like the map function using lambdas, coupling the filter function with a lambda cuts our code down greatly.

The Problem with Reduce

Although I'm going to show you how to use the *reduce* function, you should understand that there's a better method than using the actual function. Per the creator of Python himself:

> *So now reduce( ). This is actually the one I've always hated most, because, apart from a few examples involving + or *, almost every time I see a reduce( ) call with a non-trivial function argument, I need to grab pen and paper to diagram what's actually being fed into that function before I understand what the reduce( ) is supposed to do. So in my mind, the applicability of reduce( ) is pretty much limited to associative operators, and in all other cases it's better to write out the accumulation loop explicitly.*[1]

In his own words, he's saying that *reduce* only serves a couple purposes, but other than that, it's useless, so it makes more sense to use a simple *for loop*. Let's look at both examples.

Note   Reduce was a built-in function in Python 2, since then it has been moved into the functools library.

Using Reduce

The reduce function accepts two arguments, the function to perform the execution and the data collection to iterate over. Unlike filter and map, however, reduce iterates two items at a time instead of one. The result of reduce is to always return a single result. In the following example, we want to multiply all the numbers with each other. Let's use reduce to execute this example:

```
# for informational purposes this is how you use the reduce function
from functools import reduce
nums = [ 1, 2, 3, 4 ]
result = reduce( lambda a, b : a * b, nums )    # result is 24
print(result)
```

---

[1]www.artima.com/weblogs/viewpost.jsp?thread=98196

Go ahead and run the cell. The output will be 24. As the reduce function takes in two arguments, it condenses the nums list down to a single returned value. In the following, you'll see the suggested way of executing the same procedure:

```
>>> total = 0
>>> for n in nums:
>>>        total = total * n
```

For the most part, it's easy to see why Rossum was so adamant on suggesting *for loops* instead, as *reduce* can become tough to understand when you try more complex data collections like lists within lists.

WEDNESDAY EXERCISES

1. **Mapping Names**: Use a lambda and map function to map over the list of names in the following to produce the following result "**["Ryan", "Paul", "Kevin Connors"]**".

    ```
    >>> names = [ "    ryan", "PAUL", "kevin connors      " ]
    ```

2. **Filter Names**: Using a lambda and filter function, filter out all the names that start with the letter "A." Make it case insensitive, so it filters out the name whether it's uppercase or not. The output of the following list should be **["Frank", "Ripal"]**.

    ```
    >>> names = [ "Amanda", "Frank", "abby", "Ripal", "Adam" ]
    ```

Today we learned about a few important built-in functions that we can use when working with data in Python. Coupling *map* and *filter* with lambdas helps to improve our code readability and shorten the lines of code needed. Lastly, *reduce* can be helpful in a few situations; however, a for loop will generally be more readable.

Thursday: Recursive Functions and Memoization

Recursion is a concept in programming where a function calls itself one or more times within its block. These types of functions can often run into issues with speed, however, due to the function constantly calling itself. **Memoization** helps this process by storing values that were already calculated to be used later. Let's first understand more about recursive functions.

To follow along with this lesson, let's continue from our previous notebook file *"Week_08"* and simply add a markdown cell at the bottom that says, "**Recursive Functions and Memoization.**"

Understanding Recursive Functions

All **recursive functions** have what is known as a "**base case**," or a stopping point. Like loops, you need a way to break out of a recursive call. Without one you create an infinite loop that will eventually crash. For example, let's imagine we set a base case of **1** for the following questions:

1. Can you calculate the sum of 5?

2. Can you calculate the sum of $5 * 4$?

3. Can you calculate the sum of $5 * 4 * 3$?

4. Can you calculate the sum of $5 * 4 * 3 * 2$?

5. Can you calculate the sum of $5 * 4 * 3 * 2 * 1$?

6. Yes, we reached our base case; the result is 120.

In this example, we started our recursive call at 5 and wanted to reach our base case before we calculated the total. On each new call, we add a number to the expression, which was the previous number minus one. This was an example of a factorial function performing a recursive call. Depending on the task, functions could perform two recursive calls at once. The most obvious example of this is the **Fibonacci sequence**. We'll program both together.

You may be asking yourself, how are these useful? In general, you can program a loop to perform the same task that a recursive call can. So why use them? In certain instances, recursive functions are easier to understand rather than programming a loop. They're used often in searching and sorting algorithms because of the repetitive tasks that occur.

Imagine you needed to search through a 4-dimensional array, otherwise known as a list within a list within a list within a list. Rather than writing a bunch of for loops to iterate through each list, you could write a recursive function that calls itself every time a new dimension is found. The code would produce far less lines and be easier to read. Let's check out some examples!

Writing a Factorial Function

Factorials are one of the easier examples of recursion because they are the result of a given number multiplied by all previous numbers until zero is reached. Let's try programming it:

```
# writing a factorial using recursive functions
def factorial(n):
        # set your base case!
        if n <= 1:
                return 1
        else:
                return factorial( n - 1 ) * n
print( factorial(5) )       # the result of 5 * 4 * 3 * 2 * 1
```

Go ahead and run the cell. As we know from the example previously, we'll get an output of **120**. The recursive call occurs within the else block. The return statement calls the factorial function within itself because in order to get the result of *factorial(5)*, it must calculate "**factorial(4)** ∗ **5**". Then it must calculate "**factorial(3)** ∗ **4**" in order to get the result of *factorial(4)* as shown in the following:

1. factorial(5) = factorial(4) ∗ 5

2. factorial(4) = factorial(3) ∗ 4

3. factorial(3) = factorial(2) ∗ 3

4. factorial(2) = factorial(1) ∗ 2

5. factorial(1) = 1

This occurs until the base case is reached at *factorial(1)*, which does not have a recursive call and returns the value **1**. As soon as the base case is reached, it can begin to return all the calculated values back to the original call, as shown in the following:

1. factorial(1) = 1

2. factorial(2) = 1 ∗ 2 = 2

3. factorial(3) = 3 ∗ 3 = 6

4. factorial(4) = 9 ∗ 4 = 24

5. factorial(5) = 24 ∗ 5 = 120

Recursive functions work their way down until the base case is reached. Once a single value is returned, it can then work its way back to the previous calls and return a result.

The Fibonacci Sequence

The Fibonacci sequence is one of the most famous formulas in mathematics. It's also one of the most well-known recursive functions in programming. Each number in the sequence is the sum of the previous two numbers, such that *fib(5) = fib(4) + fib(3)*. The base case for the Fibonacci sequence is **0** and **1** because the result of *fib(2)* is "*fib(2) = fib(1) + fib(0)*". In order to create the recursive sequence, we'll need to return the respective value once below the value of two:

```
# writing the recursive fibonacci sequence
def fib(n):
    if n <= 1:
        return n
    else:
        return fib( n - 1 ) + fib( n - 2 )
print( fib(5) )    # results in 5
```

Go ahead and run the cell. We get **5** as the output. Remember that it's not the result of 3 + 4 but rather the result of *fib(3) + fib(4)*. The Fibonacci sequence utilizes two recursive calls in a single return, which makes it much more complex than our factorial function. In order to calculate *fib(5)*, *fib(1)* must be calculated five times. This is because of the two-part recursive call. When these recursive calls occur, they essentially break out into a pyramid-like structure. Let's look at Figure 8-1, for instance.

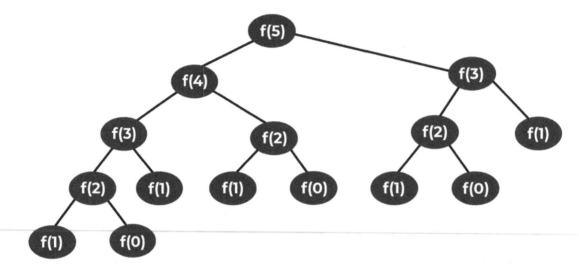

Figure 8-1. *Fibonacci sequence recursive sequence tree*

This figure represents all the recursive calls that need to occur in order to calculate the result of *fib(5)*. As the number passed in grows, so to does the structure and number of recursive calls. It's exponential, which can slow down the program dramatically. Even trying to execute *fib(40)* can take a couple minutes, and *fib(100)* will generally break because of maximum recursion depth issues. Which leads us to our next topic on how to solve this issue… *memoization.*

Understanding Memoization

When you go to a web page for the first time, your browser takes a little while to load the images and files required by the page. The second time you go to the exact same page, it usually loads much faster. This is because your browser is using a technique known as "**caching.**" When you loaded the page the first time, it saved the images and files locally. The second time you accessed the web page, instead of re-downloading all the images and files, it simply loaded them from the cache. This improves our experiences on the Web.

In computing, **memoization** is an optimization technique used primarily to speed up computer programs by storing the results of previously called functions and returning the saved result when trying to calculate the same sequence. This is simply known as "*caching,*" and the preceding paragraph is a real-life example of how memoization can improve performance. Let's look at some examples of how memoization can improve our recursive functions.

Using Memoization

In order to apply *memoization* to the Fibonacci sequence, we must understand what the best method of caching values would be. In Python, dictionaries give us the ability to store values based on a given key. They are also based on constant time in terms of *Big O Notation*. We'll get to this topic in the next week. For now, just understand that dictionaries are much faster at returning information than most other data collections. Due to the speed and unique key structure of dictionaries, we can use them to store the value of each Fibonacci sequence. This way, once a single sequence like *fib(3)* has been calculated, it does not need to be calculated again. It is simply stored into the cache and retrieved when needed. Let's try it out:

```
 1| # using memoization with the fibonacci sequence
 3| cache = { }          # used to cache values to be used later
 5| def fib(n):
 6|     if n in cache:
 7|         return cache[ n ]       # return value stored in dictionary
 9|     result = 0
11|     # base case
12|     if n < = 1:
13|         result = n
14|     else:
15|         result = fib( n - 1 ) + fib( n -2 )
17|     cache[ n ] = result     # save result into dictionary with n as
                                        the key
19|     return result
21| print( fib(50) )    # calculates almost instantly
```

Go ahead and run the cell. Notice this time it was able to calculate *fib(50)* almost instantly. If we ran this without caching values, it could have taken hours or days to execute the same calculation. This is the beauty of memoization at work. The process begins by passing the argument into *fib*. The program then checks to see if the argument appears as a key within the *cache*. If it does, it simply returns the value. If not, however, it needs to calculate the proper result by using recursion until the base case is reached. Once the base is reached, the values begin to save as key-value pairs within the cache.

As the recursive calls begin to work their way back up the structure, they simply pull the values from the dictionary. Rather than having to calculate *fib(2)* thousands of times, it only calculated it once thanks to memoization.

Note   Memoization is not perfect; there is a limit to how much you can store in a single cache.

Using @lru_cache

Now that we know how to create a caching system ourselves, let's use Python's built-in method for memoization. It's known as "**lru_cache**" or **Least Recently Used Cache**. It performs the same way our memoization technique did earlier; however, it'll do it in less lines of code because we apply it as a decorator. Let's check it out:

```
# using @lru_cache, Python's default moization/caching technique
from functools import lru_cache
@lru_cache( )        # python's built-in memoization/caching system
def fib(n):
    if n <= 1:
            return n
    else:
            return fib( n - 1 ) + fib( n - 2 )
fib(50)        # calculates almost instantly
```

Go ahead and run the cell. We'll get the same output as we did in the preceding cell but this time with less lines. It's performing the exact same technique, except it's applied as a decorator rather than directly within the function. There's no better way, as far as performance goes, but using *lru_cache* is much easier on the eyes.

THURSDAY EXERCISES

---

1. **Factorial Caching**: Apply either the lru_cache built-in decorator to the factorial function that we created previously, or set up your own caching system.

2. **Searching Data**: Create a function that takes in two arguments, a list of data and an item to search for. Search through the list of data passed in and return True if the item to search for appears, otherwise, return False. If one of the items is another list, create a recursive call so that you don't need to create another loop. Use the example call in the following as a reference on what data to expect:

```
>>> searchList( [ 2, 3, [ 18, 22 ], 6 ], 22 )
```

Today, we learned all about recursive functions and how to improve them with the concept of memoization. We were able to use a simple caching technique in order to store previously computed values. Recursive functions can be useful when it makes sense to use them, but in most cases a simple for loop would suffice, since recursive functions can become slow over time.

Friday: Writing a Binary Search

This week's project is all about understanding one of the more efficient algorithms in programming... **Binary Search**. When you need to search a list full of data, you need to do it efficiently. It may not make sense to create an algorithm for a list of ten items but imagine if it was one million items. You don't want to search through the list item by item to try and find what you're looking for. Instead, we use algorithms like Binary Search to perform these tasks.

To follow along with this lesson, let's continue from our previous notebook file "*Week_08*" and add a markdown cell at the bottom that says, "**Friday Project: Writing a Binary Search.**"

Final Design

Although the program itself will be relatively small, we must understand how the algorithm for Binary Search works. For our design concept this week, we're going to lay out the steps that we need to follow. Remember that algorithms are nothing more than a set of steps. Binary Search is no different. Each step for this algorithm is as follows:

1. Sort the list.

2. Find the middle index.

3. Check the value at the middle index; if it's the value we're looking for, return True.

4. Check the value at the middle index; if it's greater than the value we're looking for, cut off the right half of the list.

5. Check the value at the middle index; if it's less than the value we're looking for, cut off the left half of the list.

6. Repeat steps 2 through 6 until the list is empty.

7. If the while loop ends, it means there's no items left, so return False.

Let's walk through an example together with the following arguments: [14, 0, 6, 32, 8], and we'll be looking for the number **14**. See Table 8-1 for a step-by-step walk-through.

Table 8-1. *Binary Search example description*

Step	Value of Variable	Description	Code
1	list: [0, 6, 8, 14, 32]	Sort the list immediately	*list.sort( )*
2	mid: 2	Find the middle, 5 / 2, round down	*len(list) // 2*
3	value: 8	Don't return True, 8 is not 14	*list[2]*
4	condition: False	8 is less than 14 don't run block	*if list[2] > 14*
5	list: [14, 32]	Run block, cut off first half of list	*list = list[mid + 1 :]*
2	mid: 1	Middle index is 1 because 2 / 2	*len(list) // 2*
3	value: 32	Don't return True, 32 is not 14	*list[1]*
4	list: [14]	Run block, cut off second half of list	*list = list[: mid - 1]*
2	mid: 0	Find the middle, 1 / 2, round down	*len(list) // 2*
3	return True	Value at mid index is 14 return True	*return True*

A linear search would require us to search the list item by item to see if the number we're looking for was in the list. When thinking about efficiency and how long a search may take to complete the task, it would be based on the length of the list. As the length of the list grows, so does the time it takes to find the number we're looking for. With a Binary Search, however, the time it takes to find a number within a list only takes a minimal number of steps even when the list is a million numbers. For example, when you search a list of one million numbers, a linear search could take one million tries to find the number, but a Binary Search would be able to find it within 20 guesses. As it searches, it cuts the list in half. Within 10 guesses you're already working with a list of under 2,000 items. This is the beauty of an efficient algorithm. Let's walk through each step together to understand how the algorithm is programmed.

Program Setup

Before we begin to write our algorithm, we need to set up a way to generate a random list of numbers. Let's import the random module and use list comprehension to generate some data:

```
1| # setting up imports and generating a list of random numbers to work with
2| import random
4| nums = [ random.randint(0, 20) for i in range(10) ]     # create a list
                                                           of ten numbers
                                                           between 0 and 20

6| print( sorted(nums) )       # for debugging purposes
```

Go ahead and run the cell. We import the random module in order to generate a list of 20 random numbers with our list comprehension. For debugging purposes, we output a sorted version of *nums* on line 6 in order to see the data that we'll be working with.

Step 1: Sort the List

The first step in the algorithm is to sort the list. Generally, you sort the list before passing it in, but we want to take all precautions that this algorithm works even with unsorted lists. Let's begin by defining the function definition, as well as sorting the list passed in:

```
 4| nums = [ random.randint(0, 20) for i in range(10) ]    # create a ...   □□□
 6| def binarySearch(aList, num):
 7|   # step 1: sort the list
 8|   aList.sort( )
10| print( sorted(nums) )        # for debugging purposes
12| print( binarySearch(nums, 3) )
```

We've added the function call at the bottom and will be printing the returned value, but for now nothing will happen when you run the cell. Let's move on to step 2.

Step 2: Find the Middle Index

In this step, we need to find the middle index. I'm not talking about the value of the item in the middle of the list but rather the actual index number. If we're searching a list of one million items, the middle index would be 500,000. The value at that index could be any number, but again, that's not what this step is for. Let's write out the second step:

```
 8|   aList.sort( )      □□□
10|   # step 2: find the middle index
11|   mid = len(aList) // 2         # two slashes means floor division - round
                                      down to the nearest whole num
13|   print(mid)      # remove once working
15| print( sorted(nums) )      # for debugging purposes      □□□
```

Go ahead and run the cell. In order to find the middle index, we need to divide the length of the list by two and then round down to the nearest whole number. We need to use whole numbers because an index is only ever a whole number. You could never access index *1.5*. Also, we round down because rounding up would cause index out of range errors. For example, if there is one item within the list, then *1 / 2 = 0.5* and rounding up to one would cause an error, as the single item within the list is at index zero. The output will result in **5**, as we're working with a list of ten numbers. Go ahead and remove the print statement at line 13 when you're done.

Step 3: Check the Value at the Middle Index

Now that we have the middle index, we want to see if the value at that given index is the number that we're looking for. If it is, then we want to return *True*:

```
11|  mid = len(aList) // 2      # two slashes ...    □□□
13|  # step 3: check the value at middle index, if it is equal to num
     return True
14|  if aList[mid] == num:
15|          return True
17| print( sorted(nums) )      # for debugging purposes    □□□
```

Go ahead and run the cell. You'll get an output of either **True** or **None**, depending on the list that was randomly generated for you. If the number 3 appears at index 5, then your output will be **True** as our condition on line 14 is True and will run the return statement.

Step 4: Check if Value Is Greater

If the number that we're looking for isn't at the middle index, then we need to figure out which half of the list to remove. Let's first check if the value at the middle index is greater than the number we're searching for. If it is, we need cut off the right half of the list:

```
15|          return True    □□□
17|  # step 4: check if value is greater, if so, cut off right half of list
       using slicing
18|  elif aList[mid] > num:
19|          aList = aList[ : mid ]
21|          print(aList)    # remove after working properly
23| print( sorted(nums) )      # for debugging purposes    □□□
```

Go ahead and run the cell. On line 18 we check to see if the value at the middle index of the list is greater than the argument that we passed in during the function call. Line 19 is where the magic of Binary Search occurs though. Using slicing, we're able to re-declare the value of *aList* to the beginning half of the list.

Note   Remember that slicing allows you to input the start, stop, and step. If you don't input a number like earlier, it implies that you are using default values. Default values are start = 0, stop = len(list), and step = 1.

We imply that we want to keep the all items from index zero up to the middle index. Remove line 21 after you're done, as it will simply output the result of our new *aList*.

Step 5: Check if Value Is Less

This step is the exact same as step 4 but with the opposite condition. If the value at the middle index is less than the number we're looking for, we want to remove the left half:

```
19|          aList = aList[ : mid ]      □□□
21|   # step 5: check if value is less, if so, cut off left half of list
      using slicing
21|   elif aList[mid] < num:
22|          aList = aList[ mid + 1 : ]
23|   print(aList)     # remove after working properly
25|   print( sorted(nums) )      # for debugging purposes      □□□
```

Go ahead and run the cell. On line 22 we perform the opposite slice from step 4. This time we declare "*mid + 1*" because we don't want to include the middle index, as it's already been checked. The logic has now been implemented for our Binary Search. All that's left is to set up a loop to repeat steps 2 through 5 and return *False* if we don't find what we're looking for.

Step 6: Set Up a Loop to Repeat Steps

We'll need to loop until the argument is found, or until the list is empty. This sounds like a great case for a *while* loop. After creating the *while* statement, we need to make sure we execute the code for steps 2 through 5 within the loop:

```
 8|   aList.sort( )      □□□
10|   # step 6: setup a loop to repeat steps 2 through 6 until list is empty
11|   while aList:
12|           mid = len(aList) // 2
14|           if aList[mid] == num:
15|                   return True
16|           elif aList[mid] > num:
17|                   aList = aList[ : mid ]
18|           elif aList[mid] < num:
19|                   aList = aList[ mid + 1 : ]
21|           print(aList)    # remove after working properly
21| print( sorted(nums) )      # for debugging purposes      □□□
```

Go ahead and run the cell. Our Binary Search is now performing all the necessary steps to either return *True* when the argument is found or create an empty list, in which case the loop will end. Remember that our preceding *while* statement is the same as "*while len(aList) > 0:*". All that's left is to return *False* if the loop ends, as that means that the list does not contain our number.

Step 7: Return False Otherwise

To complete our Binary Search, we simply need to return *False* after the *while* loop ends:

```
19|                   aList = aList[ mid + 1 : ]      □□□
21|   # step 7: return False, if it makes it to this line it means the list
       was empty and num wasn't found
22|   return False
24| print( sorted(nums) )      # for debugging purposes      □□□
```

Go ahead and run the cell. We've now completed the Binary Search algorithm! Now when you run the cell, you'll get an output of either **True** or **False**. Feel free to print out the list within the while loop, so you can see how the list is being truncated on each step.

Final Output

You can find all the code for this week, as well as this project in the *Github* repository. The final output in the following won't include any of the comments we added in previous blocks so that you may see the complete version unobstructed:

```
1| # full output of binary search without comments
2| import random
4| nums = [ random.randint(0, 20) for i in range(10) ]
6| def binarySearch(aList, num):
7|   aList.sort( )
9|   while aList:
10|           mid = len(aList) // 2
12|           if aList[mid] == num:
13|                   return True
14|           elif aList[mid] > num:
15|                   aList = aList[ : mid ]
16|           elif aList[mid] < num:
17|                   aList = aList[ mid + 1 : ]
19|   return False
21| print( sorted(nums) )
22| print( binarySearch(nums, 3) )
```

Go ahead and run the cell. If you ran into any problems, be sure to reference this code. Try increasing the number of items within the list you pass in and see how quickly it can find your number. Even on large lists, this algorithm will execute with extreme speed.

Today was important in understanding not only how Binary Search works, but how we can program an algorithm from a set of step-by-step instructions. Algorithms can be simple to understand, yet difficult to translate into code. Using this algorithm, we can begin to understand how searches can be efficient, even when there are large amounts of data to sift through.

Weekly Summary

Throughout this week, we were able to go over some of the more advanced topics within Python. As you begin to build your programming experience, you should always be thinking about efficiency. First and foremost, we need to make sure that our programs are correct in their execution, but then we need to be aware of their speed. If an algorithm or program could give you the price of a stock to the cent, but it took ten years to execute, it would be worthless. That's the importance of a great algorithm. Along with efficiency, we want to keep in mind the readability of our code. Although sing list comprehension, lambdas, and recursive functions don't improve the speed of our program, it helps to improve our ability to read what's happening. During the lessons next week, we'll be covering algorithmic complexity and the importance of performance when using certain data types.

Challenge Question Solution

In the following, you can find the solution to the challenge question this week:

```
 1|  # ask user for input, return whether it is prime or not
 3|  def isPrime(num):
 4|    for i in range( 2, int(num**0.5) + 1 ):
 5|          if num % i == 0:
 6|                    return False
 7|    else:
 8|          return True
10|  n = int( input("Type a number: ") )
12|  if isPrime(n):
13|    print("That is a prime number.")
14|  else:
15|    print("That is not a prime number")
```

The most important part of this program is on line 4. Although you may have gotten it correct, we wanted to create this program so that it was efficient. The statement on line 4 could have also looked like the following:

```
>>> for i in range(2, num):
```

The problem with this line, however, is that it's not efficient. When you are trying to calculate whether a number is prime or not, the square root of the number is as high as you need to go. If a number isn't divisible between two and the square root of itself, then it means it's a prime number. If we didn't take the square root of the number passed in to calculate prime, then we would've had to loop all the way to the prime number itself. Let's take the number 97, for instance, which is a prime number. Using the second for loop statement, we would've looped for a total of 96 iterations. With the statement written in the code block, however, we would only loop for a total of nine iterations. As the number you're passing in gets larger, so too does the iteration count. Therefore, it's always important to keep efficiency in mind when programming.

Weekly Challenges

To test out your skills, try these challenges:

1. **Recursive Binary Search**: Turn the Binary Search algorithm that we created together into a recursive function. Rather than using a while loop, it should call itself in order to cut the list down and eventually return **True** or **False**.

2. **Efficient Algorithms**: Looking at the Binary Search we wrote, how could you possibly make it even more efficient?

3. **Case-Sensitive Search**: Rewrite the Binary Search so that it works with a list that holds both numbers and letters. It should be case sensitive. Use the following function call to understand the parameters being passed in. **Hint**: *"22" < 'a' will return True.*

   ```
   >>> binarySearch( [ 'a', 22, '3', 'hello', 1022, 4, 'e' ] ,
   'hello')  # returns True
   ```

CHAPTER 9

Advanced Topics II: Complexity

This week is the continuation of advanced python concepts and will cover more topics that a developer has to understand on the job.

To begin the week, we'll cover a concept that you've been using this whole time, **generators and iterators**. Over the following couple of days, we'll cover **decorators** and **modules**, which will help us in building larger-scale applications. These concepts will help to understand how frameworks are used, like *Flask* and *Django*.

Although I don't like talking about theory within this book, it's important to understand how time complexity works with algorithms. On Thursday, we'll dive into **Big O Notation** and understanding algorithms further. All the lessons within the book have led you to the point of being able to further your education into becoming a Python developer. This all leads us into our Friday project, which is **interview prep**. As this book is set up as a tool for improving or changing your career, an important piece of that is the interview process. There will be information about the process, what to expect, and how to handle some interview questions that you may be asked.

Overview

- Understanding generator and iterator objects

- Using and applying decorators

- Creating and importing modules

- What is time complexity and Big O Notation?

- Knowing how to handle interviews, questions, and more

219

© Connor P. Milliken 2020
C. P. Milliken, *Python Projects for Beginners*, https://doi.org/10.1007/978-1-4842-5355-7_9

CHALLENGE QUESTION

As a programmer you must think about the time it takes to execute a program. Even a program that will give you 100% accurate answers can be useless if it doesn't give the answer to you in time. Without looking it up, do you think lists or dictionaries are more efficient when needing to retrieve and store information?

Monday: Generators and Iterators

In previous sections of this book, you may have seen the words **generators** or **iterators** mentioned. Without knowing, you've been using them the entire time. Today, we'll dive into what each of these concepts are and how to use them.

To follow along with the content for today, let's open up Jupyter Notebook from our *"python_bootcamp"* folder. Once it's open, create a new file, and rename it to *"Week_09."* Next, make the first cell markdown that has a header saying: **"Generators and Iterators."** We'll begin working underneath that cell.

Iterators vs. Iterables

An **iterator** is an object that contains items which can be iterated upon, meaning you can traverse through all values. An **iterable** is a collection like lists, dictionaries, tuples, and sets. The major difference is that iterables are not iterators; rather they are containers for data. In Python, iterator objects implement the magic methods *iter* and *next* that allow you to traverse through its values.

Creating a Basic Iterator

We can create iterators easily from iterables. You can simply use the *iter()* function to do so:

```
1| # creating a basic iterator from an iterable
3| sports = [ "baseball", "soccer", "football", "hockey", "basketball" ]
5| my_iter = iter(sports)
7| print( next(my_iter) )     # outputs first item
```

```
 8| print( next(my_iter) )        # outputs second item
10| for item in my_iter:
11|    print(item)
13| print( next(my_iter) )        # will produce error
```

Go ahead and run the cell. Iterators will always remember the last item that they returned, which is why we get an error on line 13. Using the *next()* method, we're able to output the next item within the iterator. Once all the items within the iterator have been used, however, we can no longer traverse through the iterator, as there are no more items left. Iterators are great for looping as well, and like lists and dictionaries, we can simply use the in keyword *(see line 10)*. You can still loop over the list like we normally do, and it will always begin from index 0, but once our iterator is out of items, we can no longer use it.

Creating Our Own Iterator

Now that we've seen how to create an iterator from a Python iterable, let's create our own iterator class that will output each letter in the alphabet. To create an iterator, we'll need to implement the magic methods *__iter__()* and *__next__()*:

```
 1| # creating our own iterator
 3| class Alphabet( ):
 4|   def __iter__(self):
 5|         self.letters = "abcdefghijklmnopqrstuvwxyz"
 6|         self.index = 0
 7|         return self
 9|   def __next__(self):
10|         if self.index <= 25:
11|               char = self.letters[ self.index ]
12|               self.index += 1
13|               return char
14|         else:
15|               raise StopIteration
17| for char in Alphabet( ):
18|    print(char)
```

Go ahead and run the cell. The output results in the entire alphabet being printed one letter at a time. We begin by creating an iterator with the name "*Alphabet.*" We then use the *iter* method to declare the attributes associated with this iterator. Think of the *iter* method as the initialization method for iterators. At the end of the *iter* method, you must always return *self.* The *next* method is declared so that when called upon, the iterator can return the next character in the string of letters. We stored an attribute called *index* in order to track which item was supposed to be returned next. Lastly, we added a condition on line 14 so that it raises a *StopIteration* error if it has already output all the letters. Iterators are useful when you're in need of traversing through Python collections in a specific way.

What Are Generators?

Generators are functions that yield back information to produce a sequence of results rather than a single value. They're a way to simplify the creation of an iterator. Normally, when a function has completed its task and returned information, the variables declared inside of the function will be deleted. With generators, however, they use the "**yield**" keyword to send information back to the location it was called without terminating the function. Generators don't always have to yield back integers though you can yield any information you'd like. Let's look at a couple examples with both numbers and single characters.

Note   Generators are simplified iterators.

Creating a Range Generator

Although the *range* function is not a generator, we can make our own version that's created from a generator using the *yield* keyword. Let's try it out:

```
1| # creating our own range generator with start, stop, and step parameters
3| def myRange(stop, start=0, step=1):
4|   while start < stop:
5|         print( "Generator Start Value: { }".format(start) )
6|         yield start
```

```
 7|            start += step        # increment start, otherwise infinite loop
 9| for x in myRange(5):
10|   print( "For Loop X Value: { }".format(x) )
```

Go ahead and run the cell. The two print statements are used to show you when the generator *myRange* is accessed, compared to when the *for loop* outputs the result. We're able to call *myRange* like we would a normal range function because of the way that generators operate. On line 3 we declare the function like we would any other, accepting the same arguments as *range* would. We begin a while loop within the function on line 4 that will *yield* back the *start* value. Once the information is yielded back to the for loop, it's able to use that value for the current iteration. Once the for loop completes its code block, it returns to the generator as the while loop condition has not been met. Normally, once a function has returned information, it is not called upon again; however, generators continue to return and store information until their condition is met. If we didn't increment the *start* value with *step*, we would create an infinite loop. Generators, like iterators, can be useful when you need a specific sequence for iterating. Generators are useful when you need to be memory aware. Although they are not as efficient when it comes to performance, they are memory efficient when storing information. They're useful in situations when you need to create a data pipeline, which is when you need to perform a set of executions on pieces of data.

MONDAY EXERCISES

1. **Reverse Iteration**: Create an iterator that takes in a list, and when iterated over, it returns the information in a reverse order. **Hint**: When accepting arguments into an iterator, you need to use the *init* method, as well as *iter* and *next*. The following call should result in "**5, 4, 3, 2, 1**".

   >>> *for i in RevIter([1, 2, 3, 4, 5]):*

2. **Squares**: Create a generator that acts like the range function, except it yields a squared number every time. The result of the following call should be "**0, 1, 4, 16**".

   >>> *for i in range(4):*

Today we were able to understand how to build our own *range* function, as well as how data collections can be iterated over. Generators are simplified version of iterators but use the *yield* keyword to return information. Iterators must always be created by using the *iter* and next *methods* and are useful for creating our own sequence for iterating.

Tuesday: Decorators

If you want to learn about frameworks, or understand how to improve functions within Python, then you need to understand what a **decorator** is and how it works. It will help to simplify our code as well as reduce the lines necessary to improve our programs.

To follow along with this lesson, let's continue from our previous notebook file "*Week_09*" and simply add a markdown cell at the bottom that says "**Decorators.**"

What Are Decorators?

Decorators, also known as *wrappers*, are functions that give other functions extra capabilities without explicitly modifying them. They are denoted by the "**@**" symbol in front of the function name, which is written above a function declaration like the following:

```
>>> @decorator
>>> def normalFunc( ):
```

Decorators are useful when you want to perform some functionality before or after a function executes. For example, let's imagine you wanted to restrict access to a function based on a user being logged in. Rather than writing the same conditional statement for every function you create, you could put the code into a decorator and apply the decorator onto all functions. Now, whenever a function is called, the conditional statement will still run, but you were able to save yourself several lines. This is a real-life example for the Flask framework, which restricts access to certain pages based on user authentication using decorators. We'll see a minimal example of this later today.

Higher-Order Functions

A *higher-order function* is a function that operates on other functions, either by taking a function as its argument or by returning a function. We saw this done in last week's lesson with *lambdas, map, filter, and reduce*. Decorators are higher-order functions because they take in a function and return a function.

Creating and Applying a Decorator

We'll need to declare a function that takes in another function as an argument in order to create a decorator. Inside of this decorator, we can then define another function to be returned that will run the function that was passed in as an argument. Let's see how this is written:

```
1| # creating and applying our own decorator using the @ symbol
3| def decorator(func):
4|   def wrap( ):
5|         print("======")
6|         func( )
7|         print("======")
8|   return wrap
10| @decorator
11| def printName( ):
12|   print("John!")
14| printName( )
```

Go ahead and run the cell. We'll get an output of "**John!**" with equal signs above and below the name that act as a border. On line 10 we attached our decorator to the *printName* function. Whenever the *printName* function is called, the decorator will run, and *printName* will be passed in as the argument of "*func*". Within *decorator* we declare a function called *wrap*. This *wrap* function will print a border, then call the func argument, and then print another border. Remember that decorators must return a function in order to run. Our decorator that we declared can be attached to any function that we write. All functions with this decorator will simply run with a border above and below them.

Decorators with Parameters

Although decorators simply add extra capabilities to functions, they can also have arguments like any other function. Let's take the following example where we want to run a function *x* times:

```
1| # creating a decorator that takes in parameters
3| def run_times(num):
4|   def wrap(func):
5|           for i in range(num):
6|                       func( )
7|   return wrap
9| @run_times(4)
10| def sayHello( ):
11|   print("Hello!")
```

Go ahead and run the cell. This cell will output "**Hello!**" four times. The syntax changes when the decorator accepts an argument. Our decorator this time accepted an argument of *num*, and the *wrap* function accepted the function as the argument this time. Within our *wrap* function, we created a for loop that would run the function attached to our decorator as many times as the argument declared on the decorator on line 9.

Note   When passing an argument into a decorator, the function is automatically run, so we do not need to call sayHello in this instance.

Functions with Decorators and Parameters

When you need a function to accept arguments, while also having a decorator attached to it, the *wrap* function must take in the same exact arguments as the original function. Let's try it:

```
1| # creating a decorator for a function that accepts parameters
3| def birthday(func):
```

```
 4|  def wrap(name, age):
 5|           func(name, age + 1)
 6|   return wrap
 8| @birthday
 9| def celebrate(name, age):
10|   print( "Happy birthday { }, you are now { }.".format(name, age) )
12| celebrate("Paul", 43)
```

Go ahead and run the cell. This will output a nicely formatted string with the information passed in on line 12. When we call *celebrate*, the decorator takes in *celebrate* as the argument of *func*, and the two arguments "**Paul**" and "**43**" get passed into *wrap*. When we call our function within *wrap*, we pass the same arguments into the function call; however, we increment the *age* parameter by one.

Restricting Function Access

You're probably wondering how decorators can serve a purpose, since the last few cells seem meaningless. For each one of them, we could have simply added those lines within the original function. That was just for syntax understanding though. Decorators are used a lot with frameworks and help to add functionality to many functions that you'll write within them. One example is being able to restrict access of a page or function based on user login credentials. Let's create a decorator that will help to restrict access if the password doesn't match:

```
 1| # real world sim, restricting function access
 3| def login_required(func):
 4| def wrap(user):
 5|         password = input("What is the password?")
 6|         if password == user["password"]:
 7|                 func(user)
 8|         else:
 9|                 print("Access Denied")
10|    return wrap
12| @login_required
13| def restrictedFunc(user):
```

```
14|   print( "Access granted, welcome { }".format(user[ "name" ]) )
16| user = { "name" : "Jess", "password" : "ilywpf" }
18| restrictedFunc(user)
```

Go ahead and run the cell. On line 13 we declared a normal function that would take in a user and output a statement with their name and accessibility. Our decorator was attached on line 12 so that when we call *restrictedFunc* and pass in our created user, it would run through the decorator. Within the *wrap* function, we ask the user for a password and check whether the password is correct or not on line 6. If they type in the correct password, then we allow them to access the function and print out "**Access Granted**". However, if the password is incorrect, then we output "**Access Denied**" and never run *restrictedFunc*. This is a simple example of how *Flask* handles user restrictions for pages, but it proves the importance of decorators. We can now attach *login_required* to any of the functions that we feel should be accessed only by users.

TUESDAY EXERCISES

1. **User Input**: Create a decorator that will ask the user for a number, and run the function it is attached to only if the number is less than 100. The function should simply output "**Less than 100**". Use the function declaration in the following:

   ```
   >>> @decorator
   >>> def numbers( ):
   >>>          print("Less than 100")
   ```

2. **Creating a Route**: Create a decorator that takes in a string as an argument with a wrap function that takes in *func*. Have the wrap function print out the string, and run the function passed in. The function passed in doesn't need to do anything. In Flask, you can create a page by using decorators that accept a URL string. Use the function declaration in the following to start:

   ```
   >>> @route("/index")
   >>> def index( ):
   >>>          print("This is how web pages are made in Flask")
   ```

Today was an important lesson in preparation for other technologies that use Python, such as frameworks. Decorators help to improve function execution and can be attached to any function necessary. This helps to reduce code and give improved functionality.

Wednesday: Modules

Most programs tend to include so many lines of code that you wouldn't store it all within a single file. Instead you separate the code into several files, which helps to keep the project organized. Each one of these files is known as **modules**. Within these modules are variables, functions, classes, etc., that you can import into a project. Luckily, Python has a large following of developers that create modules for us to use in order to enhance our own projects. Today, we'll look at some modules that are included with Python, how to import them, how to use them, and how to write our own modules to be used within Jupyter Notebook.

To follow along with this lesson, let's continue from our notebook file "*Week_09*" and simply add a markdown cell at the bottom that says, "**Modules.**"

Importing a Module

For the next few examples, we'll be working with the *math* module, which is one of Python's built-in modules. This specific module has functions and variables to help us with any problem related to math, whether it's rounding, calculating pi, or many other math-related tasks. For this first cell, we're going to import the entire *math* module and its contents:

```
# import the entire math module
import math
print( math.floor(2.5) )     # rounds down
print( math.ceil(2.5) )      # rounds up
print(math.pi)
```

Go ahead and run the cell. We'll get an output of "**2**", "**3**", and "**3.14**". When we imported *math*, we were able to access all of *math*'s functions, variables, and classes. In this example, we call two functions and one variable that are stored within the *math* module. In order to import the entire module and its contents, you simply put the keyword import before the name of the module. Whenever you'd like to access any of its contents, you need to use dot syntax. Now we can use any of math's code.

Importing Only Variables and Functions

When you know that you won't need to use the entire module, but rather a couple functions or variables, you can import them directly. You should always make sure you import only what you need. In the previous cell, we imported the entire *math* module; however, we didn't really need to, as we only used two functions and a variable from it. To import something specifically, you'll need to include the *from* keyword and the name of what you'd like to import:

```
# importing only variables and functions rather than an entire module,
  better efficiency
from math import floor, pi
print( floor(2.5) )
# print( ceil(2.5) )      will cause error because we only imported floor
                          and pi, not ceil and not all of math
print(pi)
```

Go ahead and run the cell. We'll get an output of "**2**" and "**3.14**". The import statement changes slightly when importing specific parts of the module. To separate multiple imports from a single module, you use a comma. We comment out the print statement for *ceil* because it won't work. We only imported *floor* and *pi* directly, but not the *ceil* function. Notice that we don't need to reference the *math* module with dot syntax before the names either. This is because we imported the *floor* function and *pi* variable directly, so we can now reference them without using dot syntax. Remember to only import what you need.

Note   You can import classes from modules the same way as earlier; simply use the name of the class.

Using an Alias

Often, the name of what you'd like to import can be lengthy. Rather than having to write out an entire name each time you'd like to use it, you can give an "**alias**" or nickname when importing:

```
# using the 'as' keyword to create an alias for imports
from math import floor as f
print( f(2.5) )
```

Go ahead and run the cell. We'll get the same output as we do in the previous two cells, except this time we were able to reference the *floor* function as just the letter "*f*". This is because of how we wrote our import statement using the "*as*" keyword. You can rename anything that is imported, although it's generally best to only do so on larger names.

Creating Our Own Module

Now that we know how to import and call a module, let's create our own. Go ahead and open any text editor you have on your computer like *Notepad* or *TextEdit*. Write the following code in the file, and save it within the same folder that your "*Week_09*" file is located, with the name "*test.py*". If the two files aren't in the same directory, it produces an error:

```
# creating our own module in a text editor
# variables to import later
length = 5
width = 10
# functions to import later
def printInfo(name, age):
    print( "{ } is { } years old.".format(name, age) )
```

See Figure 9-1 for an example of what the code will look like within a text editor.

```
test.py
 1    # create our own module in a text editor
 2
 3    # variables to import later
 4    length = 5
 5    width = 10
 6
 7    # functions to import later
 8  def printInfo(name, age):
 9      print("{} is {} years old.".format(name, age))
10
11
```

Figure 9-1. *test.py module with code in text editor (notepad++)*

You've just written your first module! Remember that modules are nothing more than code written in other files that we can import in any of our projects. Now let's see how to use them.

Using Our Module in Jupyter Notebook

In any other circumstance, you'd import the variables and function we wrote in *test.py* with the *import* and *from* keywords. Jupyter Notebook, however, works a little differently when using modules that you've created. We'll use the "**run**" command in order to load in the entire module that we've created. After we run the file, we can use the variables and functions that we wrote within the module. Let's check out how to do so:

```
# using the run command with Jupyter Notebook to access our own modules
%run test.py
print(length, width)
printInfo("John Smith", 37)        # able to call from the module because
                                   we ran the file in Jupyter above
```

Go ahead and run the cell. You'll notice that we're able to output the variables and function print statement that we declared within our *test.py* module. Keep in mind that the run command runs the file as if it were a single cell. Any function calls or print statements within our module would run immediately. To test this out, try putting a print statement at the bottom of the module. When you work in a development environment (*IDE*), you'll write the import as you would normally, like the following:

```
>>> from test import length, width, printInfo
```

This is just how Jupyter Notebook works with files that we create.

> **Note**   You can place any modules you create within the Python folder on your hard drive. Once the files are there, they can be accessed normally rather than using the run command.

WEDNESDAY EXERCISES

1. **Time Module**: Import the *time* module and call the *sleep* function. Make the cell sleep for 5 seconds, and then print "**Time module imported**". Although we haven't covered this module, this exercise will provide good practice for you to try and work with a module on your own. Feel free to use Google, Quora, etc.

2. **Calculating Area**: Create a module named "*calculation.py*" that has a single function within it. That function should take in two parameters and return the product of them. We can imagine that we're trying to calculate the area of a rectangle and it needs to take in the length and width properties. Run the module within Jupyter Notebook, and use the following function call within the cell:

```
>>> calcArea(15, 30)
```

Today's focus was all about modules, how to import them, how to use them, how to create our own, and how to call our own modules within Jupyter Notebook. Understanding how modules work will give you the ability to work with frameworks in Python. Flask, for example, uses a lot of different modules, as each module serves a specific purpose. When you need to keep your project organized, modules are the answer.

Thursday: Understanding Algorithmic Complexity

Throughout this book, we've been learning by doing. At the beginning, I spoke about how we wouldn't go much into theory, but rather we would learn by building projects together and coding along. Today's focus is primarily on the theory of programming and algorithms. If there is a theory in programming that you should understand, it should be **Big O Notation**.

To follow along with this lesson, let's continue from our previous notebook file "*Week_09*" and simply add a markdown cell at the bottom that says, "**Understanding Algorithmic Complexity.**"

What Is Big O Notation?

As a software engineer, you'll often need to estimate the amount of time a program may take to execute. In order to give a proper estimate, you must know the time complexity of the program. This is where algorithmic complexity comes in to play, otherwise known as **Big O Notation**. It is the concept to describe how long an algorithm or program takes to execute. Take a list, for example. As the number of items within the list grows, so does the amount of time it takes to iterate over the list. This is known as $O(n)$, where n represents the number of operations. It's called Big O Notation because you put a "*Big O*" in front of the number of operations.

Big O establishes a worst-case scenario runtime. Even if you search through a list of 100 items and find what you're looking for on the first try, this would still be considered $O(100)$ because it could possibly take up to 100 operations.

The most efficient Big O Notation is $O(1)$, also known as constant time. It means that no matter how many items or steps are required, it will always take the same amount of time and generally occurs instantly. If we took the same list of 100 items and accessed an index directly, this would be known as $O(1)$. We would retrieve the value in that index immediately without needing to iterate over the list.

One of the least efficient time complexities is $O(n**2)$. This is a representation of a double loop. Our Bubble Sort algorithm that we wrote uses a double for loop and is known as one of the less efficient sorting algorithms in programming; however, it is simple to understand, so it makes for a good introduction into algorithms. We'll see later today how Bubble Sort compares to another algorithm that is designed to be much more efficient.

When you compare a simple search that iterates through each element of a list to an efficient algorithm like Binary Search, you begin to see that they don't grow at the same rate over time. Take Table 9-1 that illustrates the amount of time to search for a given item.

Table 9-1. *Big O Notation growth rate comparison[1]*

Number of Elements	Simple Search	Binary Search
The runtime in Big O Notation	*O(n)*	*O(log n)*
10	10 ms	3 ms
100	100 ms	7 ms
10,000	10 sec	14 ms
1,000,000,000	11 days	32 ms

We can clearly see that efficient algorithms can help to improve our programs speed. Therefore, it's important to keep efficiency and time complexity in mind when writing your code. The picture in Figure 9-2 depicts the complexity of the number of operations over the number of elements.

---

[1]https://guide.freecodecamp.org/computer-science/notation/big-o-notation/

Big-O Complexity Chart

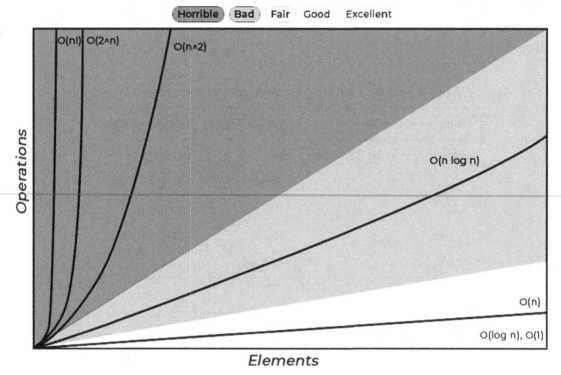

Figure 9-2. Big O Notation complexity over time chart

Not all of Big O Notation is covered here, so be sure to do some further research if you'd like to understand these concepts further. This is simply an introduction into what Big O is and why it is important when writing our programs.

Hash Tables

When we originally covered dictionaries, we went over **hashing** very briefly. Now that we've covered Big O Notation, understanding **hash tables** and why they're important is much easier. Dictionaries can be accessed in *O(1)* complexity because of how they are stored in memory. They use hash tables to store the key-value pairs. Before we cover hash tables though, let's have a quick refresher on the hash function and how to use it:

```
>>> a, c = 'bo', "bob"
>>> b = a
>>> print(hash(a), hash(b), hash(c))
```

From the preceding code, we would get the same values for *a* and *b* and a separate value for the hash of *c*. Hash functions are used to create an integer representation of a given value. In this case the integer for the string "**bo**" and the variables *a* and *b* are the same; however, "**bob**" and the *c* variable are completely different because they have a different value.

When dictionaries store key-value pairs into memory, they use this concept. A hash table is used to store a hash, a key, and a value. The hash stored is used for when you need to retrieve a given value by the key. Take Table 9-2, for instance. There are three key-value pairs in place, all with different hash values. When you want to acces the value for *name*, you would write:

```
>>> person[ "name" ]
```

What happens is Python hashes the string "**name**" and looks for the hash value rather than the key itself. You can think of this like retrieving an item within a list by its index. This is much more efficient as you can retrieve values based on hashes almost instantly at *O(1)* time.

Table 9-2. *Logical representation of Python hash table*

Hash	Key	Value
2839702572	Name	John Smith
8267348712	Age	32
-2398350273	Language	Python

Dictionaries are helpful data collections for not only keeping information connected but also improving efficiency. Keep this in mind when you're trying to answer programming questions or making a program faster. Like the information on Big O Notation, this is simply an introduction into hash tables. If you'd like to learn more, be sure to look it up using Google, Quora, etc.

Dictionaries vs. Lists

To understand the true power of a hash table and Python dictionaries, let's compare it against a list. We'll write a conditional statement to have Python check for a given item within a dictionary and list, and we'll time how long each one takes. We're going to separate the code into two cells. The first cell will generate the dictionary and list with 10 million items:

```
# creating data collections to test for time complexity
import time
d = { }          # generate fake dictionary
for i in range(10000000):
      d[ i ] = "value"
big_list = [ x for x in range(10000000) ]        # generate fake list
```

Go ahead and run the cell. Nothing will happen yet. We've simply made the variables within this cell so that we don't have to re-create them, as it takes a couple seconds depending on your computer. In the following cell, we're going to keep a timer on how long each data collection takes to find the last element. We'll use the *time* module in order to track the start and end time:

```
 1| # retrieving information and tracking time to see which is faster
 3| start_time = time.time( )      # tracking time for dictionary
 5| if 9999999 in d:
 6|   print("Found in dictionary")
 8| end_time = time.time( ) - start_time
10| print( "Elapsed time for dictionary: { }".format(end_time) )
12| start_time = time.time( )        # tracking time for list
14| if 9999999 in big_list:
15|    print("Found in list")
17| end_time = time.time( ) - start_time
19| print( "Elapsed time for list: { }".format(end_time) )
```

Go ahead and run the cell. On lines 3 and 12, we access the current time in UTC format. After checking our conditions, we get the current time in UTC format again; however, we subtract the start time from it to get the number of seconds the entire execution took. You'll notice there's a large difference between the two times. The list will usually take between **1** and **1.5** seconds, whereas the dictionary is almost instant every time. Now this doesn't seem like that big of a difference, but what if you needed to search for 1000 items. Using a list now becomes a problem, as a dictionary would continue to do it instantly, but the list would take much longer.

Note   The time module gets time in UTC (*universal time*) unless otherwise stated. UTC began on January 1, 1970. The number you see when you output time.time() is the number of seconds since that day at 12:00 AM.

Battle of the Algorithms

One of the most obvious ways to test time complexity is to run two algorithms against each other. This will allow us to really see the power behind an efficient algorithm. We're going to test **Bubble Sort** against another sorting algorithm called **Insertion Sort**. Although Insertion Sort isn't the most efficient algorithm when sorting, we'll find out that it's still much more powerful than Bubble Sort. Let's go ahead and write out the two sorting algorithms within the first cell:

```
1| # testing bubble sort vs. insertion sort
3| def bubbleSort(aList):
4|  for i in range( len(aList) ):
5|          switched = False
6|          for j in range( len(aList) - 1 ):
7|                  if aList[ j ] > aList[ j + 1 ]:
8|                          aList[ j ], aList[ j + 1 ] = aList[ j + 1 ],
                            aList[ j ]
9|                          switched = True
10|         if switched == False:
11|                 break
12|     return aList
14| def insertionSort(aList):
15|  for i in range( 1, len(aList) ):
16|          if aList[ i ] < aList[ i - 1 ]:
17|                  for j in range( i, 0, -1 ):
```

```
18|                              if aList[ j ] < aList[ j - 1 ]:
19|                                  aList[ j ], aList[ j + 1 ] = aList
                                     [ j + 1 ], aList[ j ]
20|                      else:
21|                          break
22|    return aList
```

Go ahead and run the cell. Now that we've defined the two functions we need to call, let's set up some random data to be sorted and set up a timer like we did in the previous section:

```
1| # calling bubble sort and insertino sort to test time complexity
2| from random import randint
4| nums = [ randint(0, 100) for x in range(5000) ]
6| start_time = time.time( )     # tracking time bubble sort
7| bubbleSort(nums)
8| end_time = time.time( ) - start_time
9| print( "Elapsed time for Bubble Sort: { }".format(end_time) )
11| start_time = time.time( )     # tracking time insertion sort
12| insertionSort(nums)
13| end_time = time.time( ) - start_time
14| print( "Elapsed time for Insertion Sort: { }".format(end_time) )
```

Go ahead and run the cell. It's not even a contest. Insertion Sort is a more efficient algorithm than its counterpart. Although both use the concept of a double for loop, Bubble Sort's steps are much more inefficient because it starts at the front of the list each time. It's always important to keep time complexity in mind when designing your program and algorithms. If you're ever unsure what's best to use, try testing it like we have here.

THURSDAY EXERCISES

1. **Merge Sort**: Do some research, and try to find out the "Big O" representation for a Merge Sort algorithm.

2. **Binary Search**: What is the max number of guesses it would take for a Binary Search to find a number within a list of 10 million numbers?

Although today was more about theory than any other part of this book, it's one of the most important aspects of programming. Big O Notation helps us to understand the efficiency of our programs and algorithms. It's always important to understand why we use certain data collections like dictionaries or lists. When efficiency is important, dictionaries can be implemented to improve a program. This is another reason why we use dictionaries for caching.

Friday: Interview Prep

If you're looking for a new career or job as a Python developer, then all these lessons would be for naught if you can't pass the interview process. For this Friday, we're going to cover the process of a general software development interview. We'll cover each stage, what to do before and after the interview, whiteboarding, answering general and technical questions, and how to contour your resumes and profiles. This lesson is meant to be helpful for those either struggling on the interview process or those of you who have never had a formal software development interview. If you have no interest in this section, and wish to continue, use today as a break from this book's schedule.

Developer Interview Process

The interview process for a developer role can be broken down into many different stages. In the following, you'll find the main stages that many companies in the industry practice. Keep in mind that this is a general interview process and not every company will follow these to a tee. Use this section as more of a guide on what to possibly expect:

- **Stage 1**
    - Basic questions about yourself along with past work experience. The first step will usually be a phone call with a 3rd party recruiter, internal recruiter, HR, or talent acquisition of the company. During the first step of the interview process, the interviewer is trying to gauge if you are the correct fit for the role. They are looking for you to mention the "*Buzzwords*" along with providing

241

information on why you are a good fit for the position. You want to relate yourself to the position. Be sure to talk about your experience using the languages and technologies they're looking for. The interviewer is looking for you to meet half of the requirements to make yourself a good match. No one will ever know everything, but it is good to show them what you know and your willingness to learn.

Note   Buzzwords are keywords that the position is looking for. For example, a back-end position using Python would expect to hear words like *API, JSON, Python, Flask, Django, Jinja, Relational Databases, PostgreSQL*, etc.

- **Stage 2**
    - If you've made it past the phone screen, you'll usually be asked to come in for an in-person interview. This stage is generally where you meet other developers that currently work at the company. Although they'll ask you interview questions, this stage is generally for the employees to see if they would like to work with you and get to know you on a more personal level. Generally, you'll interview with small groups of employees at a time. You'll have about two to five of these sessions that will last around 10–15 minutes each. Before hiring an individual, these groups will generally get together to discuss potential candidates for the next stage. During this stage, be sure to properly introduce yourself and shake each person's hand. Get to know each employee, and try to relate with them on a personal level.

- **Stage 3**
    - This is the technical round. In this stage, questions will be asked to assess the developer's skills and abilities. Generally, there will be a whiteboarding question, a couple technical questions on paper, and a brain teaser. This stage is generally conducted with the hiring manager, or team manager that you'll be working with. When asked a question, make sure you understand it clearly. You are more than welcome to ask as many questions as you need to

clearly understand the problem before answering the question. If you do not know the answer to the question, let the interviewer know that you have not worked with that concept or do not see the problem. The interviewer during this stage will know if you have no idea what you're talking about so don't try and make something up. They'll be more impressed with your honesty and try to guide you through the problem. During this stage, they don't care if you're right or wrong. They're more interested in how you think and how well you can problem-solve.

- **Stage 4**

  - At this point, you're generally sitting with the hiring manager or an HR personnel. In this stage, you can ask questions about the company, as well as the job role. If you've made it this far, the company has seen value in you as a potential employee. Usually, this is where contract negotiations and salary conversations occur. At the end of the interview, always have questions ready to ask and lots of them. If you have no questions, it's generally a sign of not being prepared or laziness.

What to Do Before the Interview

In almost everything that you do in life, you can never be too prepared. The same goes for interviewing. The following are tips for what you should do before your interview:

- **Research**

  - Be sure to research the company you're interviewing for. Don't just understand what products they create, or services they offer, but know what charities they support, the companies they partner with, etc. It shows that you're involved and care about the companies' well-being. A little goes a long way.

- **Be Prepared**

  - Put together a folder or portfolio of that includes your resume, a pad of paper for taking notes during the interview, examples of work, etc.

- **Resume**

  - Always print on resume on higher quality paper.

  - Contour your resume to the job you're interviewing for. For example, for back-end roles, mention Python, SQL, database-related technologies, etc.

  - Keep your resume to a single page.

  - Don't add any fluff.

  - Keep it organized with sections like experience, skills, and education.

  - Think of your resume as a 30-second elevator pitch.

  - Often, it helps to have a designer overlook your resume. Some sites will do this for a small fee but help to make your resume look more professional and organized.

- **Portfolio Web Site**

  - Not all developers have personal web sites, but it certainly looks bad when you don't. Imagine going to a dentist that has no teeth. View yourself as the product that you're trying to sell to companies, you should have a web site that shows your skills and allows others to contact you.

- **Github**

  - Almost every hiring agency and company will look to your Github to see the projects you've worked on.

  - It's best to have complete projects on your portfolio as well. One major project will always stand out better than 10 minor projects.

  - Include your Github account in your resume, portfolio web site, and e-mails.

- **LinkedIn**

  - Most recruiters and companies are on LinkedIn for one reason, and that's to look for potential candidates for a job posting.

- Make sure your profile is up to date with all relative information and projects that you've worked on.

- Your profile picture should be professional. You don't need to be in a suit and tie, but it's best not to have a picture of you on a beach.

- Look at this web site as your professional networking service.

- Post often with information from the field you want to work in. The more you post, the more apt a recruiter is to recognize you.

- **Social Media**

  - Make it private or keep it clean. You better believe companies will look at your posts for a way to understand who you are, and if they don't like what they see, you won't be getting a call back.

- **Apply Directly**

  - It always looks more professional to send in an application directly to the company. Often, you'll find a job you like on Indeed or ZipRecruiter; however, these companies get flooded with applications every day on these sites, and they generally have algorithms to eliminate most candidates. Sending a direct e-mail shows that you put time and effort into directly contacting the company.

General Questions

The following is a list of general nontechnical questions, followed by an example of a good answer. These questions were selected because they are usually asked and answered improperly:

- **What salary are you looking for?**

  - "I don't have an exact number right now. I'd like to do some more research on what other companies are offering for a similar position. What do you pay your employees on average for this position?"

  - Never state a number when they ask, this provides leverage for them during any negotiation process.

- Counter their question with another question.

- If they continue to ask you for a number, simply state the same response.

- **Where do you see yourself in five years?**

  - "I'm more so focused on my skills over the next five years. I know that focusing on continuing my education and improvement of myself will lead me to where I need to be."

  - Focusing on improving your skills shows compassion.

- **Why did you want to be a software developer?**

  - "I've always been intrigued by being able to build something out of nothing, and I've always enjoyed a challenge. When you're able to solve problems and build applications, it's a wonderful feeling."

  - Show the passion that you have as a developer; it will always come off as a strength.

  - Never mention it's about money, even if it is.

- **Why are you changing careers?**

  - "It felt like I wasn't being challenged enough in my previous career and I've always been interested in programming and the thrill that comes with building applications that improve people's lives."

  - Like the previous question, show the passion and drive that you have for this career.

  - Explaining that you like to be challenged shows your not lazy.

  - Never mention it's about money, even if it is.

- **Why do you want to work here?**

  - "The applications that you build here help so many users around the world, and I'd love to be a part of that."

  - Talk about the applications or charities that the company works with. It shows that you have passion, work well in teams, and that your driven.

– Mentioning the culture of the company would be a great answer as well.

– Do not mention salary, benefits, or even worse... have no answer.

- **Tell me about a tough software problem and how you solved it.**

    – "I was working on a project where I was assigned to implement the Steam API into the application. Unfortunately, the API wouldn't connect properly. Using the debugger, I set break points at the import and function call locations. After realizing that they weren't being hit at all, I figured it must be an issue with connecting. Having tried several import variations, and reading through the documentation, I decided to set up the application to close when the function was hit. When I ran the program the next time, it closed instantly. Realizing that the function is being called, but the application isn't running properly, I figured it had to be an import issue. It wasn't until I tested the API in a more up-to-date application that the problem was due to the code being written in version 2.2, when the API required version 3.6. In order to connect the API, I had to manually import the library through a mapper function that could translate the code between versions. After realizing that the mapper worked, I was able to implement the libraries that the Steam API included in its SDK."

    – Go as in depth as you can with the problem. They want to know every little detail that caused the issue, how you fixed the problem, and all the ideas you had in trying to solve the problem. Although the preceding answer may not have made much sense to you right now, it shows the problem, what I did to try and find the issue, as well as how I came up with a solution once I found the problem.

Whiteboarding and Technical Questions

This section is a list of tips that you should consider using during the third stage of the interview process for both whiteboarding and technical questions:

- **Take Your Time**

    - There's absolutely no rush to solve a problem. Think through a proper solution first before answering the question. Often, you'll think of two or three different solutions given time.

- **Speak Out Loud**

    - Always talk through your thought process. It makes the interviewer feel more comfortable so that you're both not sitting in a quiet room while you think.

    - It shows the interviewer your ability to problem-solve.

    - Even if you don't give the correct answer, they can at least understand where you went wrong and offer some guidance.

- **Steps > Syntax**

    - When whiteboarding, you'll need to write out a function or some lines of code on the board in front of the interviewer. The most important thing to remember is that your thought process is more important than your actual code.

    - You can have syntactical bugs on a whiteboard and still pass the interview; however, having an incorrect algorithm or set of steps will cause you to fail.

- **Ask Questions**

    - If you're unsure, ask questions. It's perfectly fine to ask questions when trying to solve a problem.

    - Keep in mind the questions you ask matter though. There's a big difference in asking what a sort method does, compared to what type of sort method would you like me to use.

- **Algorithmic Complexity**

  - Always keep in mind the complexity of an algorithm. You'll generally be asked after you write your code if there is a way to improve the performance of it even further.

  - Know the Big O Notation category of the algorithm you just wrote.

  - Think about what data types or collections would work best for your scenario.

- **Be Honest**

  - If you don't know an answer, absolutely do not try and talk your way through it. The interviewer during this stage is a professional developer and can pick apart anything that doesn't make sense.

  - Being honest and saying you're not sure but are willing to learn the material will always prove to be a better method of answering questions you don't know how to solve.

End of Interview Questions

You never want to be empty handed at the end of an interview when they ask if you have any questions. It's usually good practice to take notes during an interview and write down questions as you think of them. In the following, you'll find a list of questions that you should consider asking:

- *How is the commute?*

- *Is parking free?*

- *Do you hold social events?*

- *If I wanted to further my career skills, do you guys offer any services or tuition reimbursement?*

- *What kind of benefits do you offer?*

- *What is the company culture like?*

- *How many people will be working on the team with me?*

- *Will there be mentoring involved?*

- *Can you tell me more about the day-to-day responsibilities of this role?*

- *What do you like best about working for this company?*

- *What is the typical career path within this company for someone in this role?*

- *What are the next steps in the interview process?*

- *What might I expect in a typical day?*

- *What charities does this company support?*

- *Are there any company activities, like sports teams?*

What to Do After the Interview

Even if you pass the first three stages, you can still fail miserably if you don't execute the proper steps following the interview. In the following, you'll find examples of what you should do once the interview process is complete:

- **Follow Up**

  - **Always, always, always** send an e-mail to the interviewer immediately, thanking them for their time. It shows respect and is a courteous gesture.

- **Critique Yourself**

  - Understand your own mistakes. Don't take it personal; the only way you can get better is by understanding and self-reflecting.

- **Continue Building**

  - Always be working on projects and trying to improve your portfolio.

  - Stay up to date with the latest libraries, languages, and technologies.

  - Update your resume and portfolio often.

- **Adventure Out**

  - Go out to local networking events in your area. This is where you'll meet most of your connections. It's always easier to land a job when you know someone who works in the company.

–   Events like code alongs, or hackathons, are a great way to meet other developers looking to work together.

- **Rejection**

    –   It happens, you won't always get the job. If it does occur, be sure to ask the interviewer in a courteous manner as to why you didn't get the job. Don't take it personally; instead use this information to become a better developer and improve.

Today was all about understanding the interview process and how you can improve your interviewing skills. Even the greatest programmers can be terrible interviewers. It takes a lot of hard work and focus to land the proper job, and even then, it may not work out. The best advice is to just continue to improve your skills and network with other software developers.

Weekly Summary

This week was the second portion of the more advanced Python concepts. Much of the lessons taught this week were important for not only interviewing but for improving the performance of your projects. Iterators and generators are a type of object that can be used to create better looping structures and algorithms. Being able to use decorators will help to improve function capabilities and are widely used within frameworks like Flask or Django. Modules allow us to use other developer's code by importing the functions or entire files into our program. Being able to write our own modules allows us to reduce the amount of code in each file. You generally want to stay as organized as possible because it makes the project easier to read, maintain, and fix. If there's one topic you need to understand from this week, however, it would be Big O Notation. Understanding how Big O works can help in job interviews and knowing how to improve the speed of an application. There are more advanced topics to cover on Python and programming in general, but these last two weeks will give you enough to start building your own projects and even move on to learning about frameworks and larger-scale applications using databases.

Challenge Question Solution

We were able to review the exact answer to this question during the lesson from Thursday. It was easy to see that dictionaries are clearly the more efficient way to store and retrieve data. It's always important to keep in mind the proper data structures to use when working with large sets of data. You can be sure that similar questions will be asked in an interview process.

Weekly Challenges

To test out your skills, try these challenges:

1. **Understanding the Market**: Go on to a job application web site like Indeed or Monster, and look up potential jobs that you're interested in. Make notes of the qualifications and technologies they're looking for. After looking at several job descriptions, what are the top three technologies? These should be your focus going forward.

2. **Shopping Cart Module**: Take the code from our Shopping Cart program that we wrote a few weeks back, and put it into a module. In Jupyter Notebook, run the module, and get the program to work properly.

3. **Enhanced Shopping Cart**: Add a new feature into the program that allows the user to save the cart. Upon running the program, the saved cart should load. The method should be written within the module. **Hint**: Use a CSV or text file.

4. **Code Wars**: Make an account on `www.codewars.com` and try to solve some problems. Code Wars has been used for interview practice problems, improving your algorithm and problem-solving skills, and much more. It will help to increase the skills taught in this book. Try to solve a problem a day, and you'll notice your Python programming skills will improve.

CHAPTER 10

Introduction to Data Analysis

Up to this point, we've covered enough Python basics and programming concepts to move on toward bigger and better things. This week will encompass a full introduction into the data analysis libraries that Python has to offer. We won't go in depth like other books that focus on this subject; instead we'll cover enough to get you well on your way to analyzing and parsing information.

We'll learn about the **Pandas** library and how to work with tabular data structures, web scraping with **BeautifulSoup** and understanding how to parse data, as well as data visualization libraries like **matplotlib**. At the end of the week, we'll use all these libraries together to create a small project that scrapes and analyzes web sites.

Overview

- Working with Anaconda environments and sending requests

- Learning how to analyze tabular data structures with Pandas

- Understanding how to present data using matplotlib

- Using the BeautifulSoup library to scrape the Web for data

- Creating a web site analysis tool

© Connor P. Milliken 2020
C. P. Milliken, *Python Projects for Beginners*, https://doi.org/10.1007/978-1-4842-5355-7_10

CHALLENGE QUESTION

Imagine you're a data analyst and you've just been handed a set of data that shows the number of accidents for all drivers, their ages, and the size of their engines. You need to figure out a way to display this information so that it tells a story. Normally you would create a graph with x, y, z coordinates; however, that can become complicated, and you don't have time for that. How would you render the information so that it's still considered 3-dimensional, but you can only use the x and y axis?

Monday: Virtual Environments and Requests Module

Today we'll be learning all about **virtual environments**, why we need them and how to use them. They're necessary for what we need to do this week, which is downloading and importing a few libraries to work with. We'll also get into the **requests** module and cover **APIs** briefly.

For today's lesson, we won't be starting out in Jupyter Notebook; instead open the terminal and cd into the "python_bootcamp" folder if you haven't already. If you have the terminal running Jupyter Notebook, be sure to stop it, as we need to write some commands in the terminal.

What Are Virtual Environments?

Python virtual environments are essentially a tool that allows you to keep project dependencies in a separate space from other projects. Most projects in Python need to use modules that are not included by default with Python. Now, you could simply download the modules (or libraries) into your Python folder to use; however, that could cause some issues down the road. Let's say you're working on two separate projects, where the first one uses Python version 2.7 and the second project uses Python version 3.5. If you try and use the same syntax for both, you'll run into several issues. Instead, you would create two separate virtual environments, one for each project. This way both projects can run properly using the correct dependencies because of the personalized virtual environment.

Note   When creating a virtual environment, a folder called "*venv*" will appear. This is where all the libraries that you download are saved. Simply put, a virtual environment is not much more than a folder that stores other files.

As an analogy to understand virtual environments, first picture our own planet. Now think of it as an environment filled with grass, sun, clouds, air, etc. In the case of programming, Python would be like the planet, and the grass, sun, clouds, and air would be like libraries that you need to include in the environment. As Python does not come included with them, we would create a virtual environment to store these libraries so that we may import them into our project when needed. If you think of Mars, that would be another project, with a separate virtual environment specifically made for that program.

Virtual environments can often be a tough concept to grasp for anyone seeing it for the first time, so here's another analogy. Imagine you've planned two vacations, one to the beach and the other to go skiing. Rather than using the same suitcase filled with mixed clothes, you've decided to pack two separate suitcases. The one for the beach will include a bathing suit, sunglasses, and flip-flops. The other suitcase will include a jacket, skiis, and boots. In the following, you can find the relationships within this analogy:

- Vacations ➤ Projects

- Suitcases ➤ Virtual Environments

- Clothes and Accessories ➤ Project Dependencies/Files

Note   Remember from the first chapter, when working in terminal, you'll see the $ next to the commands that we enter. For the next few sections, we'll be working inside of terminal.

What Is Pip?

Pip is the standard package manager for Python. Anytime you need to download, uninstall, or manage a library or module to use within your project, you use *pip*. It has been included in all installations of Python since *v3.4*. To check your version of *pip*, write the following in terminal:

```
$ pip --version
```

Feel free to visit the **Python Package Index** (*PyPI*) to view all the possible libraries that you're able to download. You can use any of them in your future projects. For today, we'll learn how to install and use the *requests* module, but first, let's create and activate a virtual environment.

Creating a Virtual Environment

One of the big reasons Anaconda is such a wonderful tool is because of its ability to organize virtual environments for us. We're going to use it to create our first virtual environment. While in terminal, type in the following command:

```
$ conda create --name data_analysis python=3.7
```

Go ahead and run the command. It'll then ask you if you'd like to proceed by typing in "**y**" or "**n**", simply type "**y**" for yes and hit enter. A folder will be created within the Anaconda directory in our program files. The folder will be given the name of "*data_analysis.*" We've just created our own virtual environment using Python version *3.7*. In order to use it, we must activate it. If you wanted to use Python's default virtual environment system, you can use the keyword "virtualvenv." Be sure to look that up if you're interested. We will use Conda's environments for the ease of use throughout this chapter.

Note   You can create a conda environment from anywhere; you do not need to be *cd'ed* into a specific folder.

Activating the Virtual Environment

The second step in using a virtual environment is activating it. Activating an environment allows the computer to execute our scripts from a separate executable. By default, we use the Python executable file stored in our program's directory. We can see the PATH of the executable by entering the following commands into the terminal:

We need to activate the Python shell first:

```
$ python
```

Now we can view the PATH by typing in the following lines:

```
>>> import os
>>> import sys
>>> os.path.dirname(sys.executable)
```

You'll notice that the PATH is your default folder where Python was originally installed. Go ahead and exit the Python shell once you're done. We'll come back to these same commands at the end of this section to see how the PATH has changed once the environment is activated.

Once you create the environment, you don't need to create it again; you can simply activate it anytime you need to use it. Before you're able to download libraries into the environment, you must first activate it. Depending on your operating system, write the following command in terminal:

For Windows:

```
$ activate data_analysis
```

After activating the environment, you'll see the name appear within parenthesis on the left side of the terminal. It will be shown like the following:

```
>>> (data_analysis) C:\Users...
```

For Mac/Linux:

```
$ source activate data_analysis
```

Like Windows, after activating the environment, you'll see the name to the left of your directory:

```
>>> (data_analysis)
```

If you can see the name on the side, you've successfully activated the environment. Before we move on, let's see where our executable is now by running the same commands in the Python shell from the beginning of this section, to view the PATH of the executable:

```
>>> import os
>>> import sys
>>> os.path.dirname(sys.executable)
```

After running those same lines, you'll notice that a different PATH has been output. This is the executable of our Conda environment that will be running our scripts. Now we can begin to install any libraries or packages we may need to work with.

Installing Packages

To install packages into the virtual environment, we'll use *pip*. The syntax is always the same to install any package. It's the keywords *pip install*, followed by the package name. In our case, we'll be working with the requests package today. Let's write the following command:

```
$ pip install requests
```

Go ahead and run the command. We've just installed the requests module into our environment to work with. To be sure that it installed properly, write the following command:

```
$ conda list
```

This command lists out all the packages that are installed within this environment. You'll be able to see the requests package that we just downloaded as well as the other packages that were downloaded initially when we created the environment.

APIs and the Requests Module

The *requests* module allows us to make HTTP requests using Python. It is the standard library for making *API* calls and requesting information from outside resources.

Note   If you're unfamiliar with HTTP requests, I suggest checking out the *w3schools*[1] resource for more information, as this book is not designed to cover networking.

An **application programming interface** (*API*) is a set of functions and procedures that allow applications to access the features or data of an operating system, application, or other service. In a simpler description, *APIs* allow us to interact with web pages and software designed by other developers. Imagine you need some data on housing prices. Rather than collecting all that information yourself, you could use the resources that major companies like *Zillow* and *Trulia* have put together. In order to access that information, you need to call their *API*, which will return the data that you need. *APIs* make a developer's life easier because we can use data or tools created by other companies within our projects.

Using the Requests Module

Now that we've created and activated our environment and installed the package that we'll be working with for the rest of the day, we can open Jupyter Notebook.

Note   If you do not have the environment activated or the *requests* module installed, then you will receive errors. Be sure to activate the environment, and check that the *requests* module is installed.

To follow along with the content for the rest of the lesson, open up Jupyter Notebook from our "*python_bootcamp*" folder in terminal. Once it's open, create a new file, and rename it to "*Week_10.*" Next, make the first cell markdown that has a header saying: "**Virtual Environments and Requests Module**." We'll begin working underneath that cell.

---

[1]www.w3schools.com/tags/ref_httpmethods.asp

Sending a Request

For this lesson, we'll be requesting information from an *API* created by *Github*. Generally, *APIs* require a key in order to use their service; however, we'll be using one that doesn't require an *API key*. To begin, we must send a request to a specific URL, which will send a response back to us. That response will include data that we'll be able to parse through. Write the following:

```
1| # sending a request and logging the response code
3| import requests
5| r = requests.get("https://api.github.com/users/Connor-SM")
7| print( r )
8| print( type( r ))
```

Go ahead and run the cell. In order to use *requests,* you must import it, which is what we do on line 3. Next, we use the **get()** method within the *requests* object in order to request information from the given URL that we pass in. The data we expect to get back will be the profile information for my *Github* account. Feel free to replace "*Connor-SM*" in the URL with your own profile username. The first print statement will output a response code. You should get back "**<Response [200]>**"; if you don't, be sure to check your Internet connection. This output is letting us know that we were successful in requesting information from the *Github* URL. For a list of response codes and what they mean, be sure to visit *w3schools*[2] resource. The second print statement will output the type of our variable, which is a request object. All request objects come preloaded with default methods and attributes that we can access. This will allow us to work with the data that we received.

Accessing the Response Content

In order to access the data that we get back in the response, we need to access the **content** attribute within our requests object:

```
# accessing the content that we requested from the URL
data = r.content
print(data)
```

---

[2]www.w3schools.com/tags/ref_httpmessages.asp

Go ahead and run the cell. We'll get a byte string output with lots of brackets and information in a way that's difficult to read. Responses from *APIs* are generally sent in string format, as strings are much lighter data types than objects. The actual response that we get back is in *JSON* formatting. JavaScript Object Notation (*JSON*) format is the equivalent of a Python dictionary and is the default format to send data via a request. The next step is to convert the data from a *JSON* formatted string into a dictionary that we can parse.

Converting the Response

Luckily for us, the requests object comes with a built-in JSON conversion method called **json()**. After we convert the response to a dictionary, let's output all the key-value pairs:

```
# converting data from JSON into a Python dictionary and outputting all
key-value pairs
data = r.json( )        # converting the data from a string to a dictionary
for k, v in data.items( ):
      print("Key: { } \t Value: { }".format(k, v))
print(data["name"])      # accessing data directly
```

Go ahead and run the cell. All the information is now easy to read and access, as seen through the for loop implementation and the simple print statement.

Passing Parameters

Most *API* calls that you perform will require extra information like parameters or headers. This information is taken in by the *API* and used to perform a specific task. Let's perform a call this time while passing parameters in the URL to search for Python-specific repositories on *Github*:

```
# outputting specific key-value pairs from data
r = requests. get("https://api.github.com/search/repositories?q=language:
python")
data = r.json( )
print(data["total_count"])     # output the total number of repositories
                               that use python
```

Go ahead and run the cell. There are a couple different ways that we can send parameters through the request. In this case, we've written them directly into the URL string itself. You may also define them within the *get* method like the following:

```
>>> requests.get("https://api.github.com/search/repositories",
>>>              params = { 'q' = 'language:python' } )
```

When sending parameters through the URL, you separate the URL and the parameters with a question mark. To the right of the question mark are a set of key-value pairs that represent the parameters being passed. For our example, the parameter being passed has a key of "**q**" and a value of "**requests+language:python**". The *API* on *Github* will take this information and give us back the data on repositories that use Python, because that's what we asked for in our parameters. Not all *APIs* require parameters, however, like our first call previously in this lesson. To figure out what is required when calling an *API*, always read the documentation. Good documentation for *APIs* is everything and can make your life as a developer much easier.

Note   To stop running the virtual environment, simply write into the terminal "*deactivate.*" You will be asked to activate the environment before each lesson this week.

MONDAY EXERCISES

1. **Test Environment**: Create a new virtual environment called "*test.*" When creating it, install Python version *2.7* instead of the current version. After it's completed, make sure it installed the proper version of Python by checking the list.

2. **JavaScript Repositories**: Using the *requests* module and the *Github API* link in our last lesson, figure out how many repositories on *Github* use JavaScript.

Today was an important introduction into data analysis. Not only did we cover how to use virtual environments and why, but we also went over the *requests* module with a brief introduction into APIs. When using any library for the rest of the week, we'll need to activate our *data_analysis* virtual environment. At the end of the week, we'll cover web scraping, which requires us to use the *requests* module.

Tuesday: Pandas

When you need to work with data, **Pandas** is the ultimate tool. It's essentially Excel on steroids. If you're familiar with the SQL language, this will come easier to you, as Pandas is a mix of Python and SQL. By the end of the day, you'll be able to analyze and work with tabular data in a more efficient way than other traditional methods.

Like how yesterday's lesson began, we need to install the Pandas library into our virtual environment. To follow along with today's lesson, cd into the "*python_bootcamp*" folder, and activate the environment. We'll begin today within the terminal.

Note If you can't remember how to activate the environment, go back to yesterday's lesson.

What Is Pandas?

Pandas is a flexible data analysis library built within the C language, which is excellent for working with tabular data. It is currently the de facto standard for Python-based data analysis, and fluency in Pandas will do wonders for your productivity and frankly your resume. It is one of the fastest ways of getting from zero to answer. Having been written in C, it has increased speed when performing calculations. The Pandas module is a high performance, highly efficient, and high-level data analysis library. It allows us to work with large sets of data called DataFrames.

Note NumPy is a fundamental package for scientific computing in Python. Built from the C language, it uses multidimensional arrays and can perform calculations at high-rate speeds.

The Pandas library is useful in so many ways that you can do any of the following and more:

- Calculate statistics and answer questions about the data like average, median, max, and min of each column

- Finding correlations between columns

- Tracking the distribution of one or more columns

- Visualizing the data with the help of matplotlib, using plot bars, histograms, etc.

- Cleaning and filtering data, whether it's missing or incomplete, just by applying a user-defined function (*UDF*) or built-in function

- Transforming tabular data into Python to work with

- Exporting the data into a CSV, other file, or database

- Feature engineer new columns that can be applied to your analysis

No matter what you need to do with data, Pandas is your end-all-be-all analysis library.

Key Terms

The following are key terms we'll be using throughout this section. Be sure to look over them and reference them when necessary:

- Series ➤ One-dimensional labeled array capable of holding data of any type

- DataFrame ➤ Spreadsheet

- Axis ➤ Column or row, axis = 0 by row; axis = 1 by column

- Record ➤ A single row

- dtype ➤ Data type for DataFrame or series object

- Time Series ➤ Series object that uses time intervals, like tracking weather by the hour

Installing Pandas

To install Pandas, make sure your virtual environment is activated first, then write the following command into the terminal:

```
$ pip install pandas
```

After running the command, it should install a few packages that Pandas requires. If you'd like to check and make sure you downloaded the proper library, just write out the list command.

Importing Pandas

To follow along with the rest of this lesson, let's open and continue from our previous notebook file "*Week_10*" and simply add a markdown cell at the bottom that says, "**Pandas**."

Importing Pandas is simple; however, there is an industry standard when you import the library:

```
# importing the pandas library
import pandas as pd          # industry standard name of pd when importing
```

Go ahead and run the cell. We import Pandas as pd because it's shorter and easier to reference.

Creating a DataFrame

The central object of study in Pandas is the DataFrame, which is a tabular data structure with rows and columns like an Excel spreadsheet. You can create a DataFrame from a Python dictionary or a file that has tabular data, like a CSV file. Let's create our own from a dictionary:

```
1| # using the from_dict method to convert a dictionary into a Pandas
    DataFrame
2| import random
```

```
 4| random.seed(3)      # generate same random numbers every time, number
    used doesn't matter
 6| names = [ "Jess", "Jordan", "Sandy", "Ted", "Barney", "Tyler",
    "Rebecca" ]
 7| ages = [ random.randint(18, 35) for x in range( len(names) )]
 9| people = { "names" : names, "ages" : ages }
11| df = pd.DataFrame.from_dict(people)
12| print(df)
```

Go ahead and run the cell. We import the *random* module so that we may create random ages for our people on line 7. Using the seed method on line 4 will give us both the same random numbers to work with. You could pass any number as the argument into seed; however, if you use a number other than 3, you'll get a different output than this book.

Note   Random numbers aren't truly random; they follow a specific algorithm to return a number.

After we generate a list of names and random ages for each person, we create a dictionary called "*people.*" The magic truly happens on line 11, where we use Pandas to create the DataFrame that we'll be working with. When it's created, it uses the keys as the column names, and the values match up with the corresponding index, such that *names[0]* and *ages[0]* will be a single record. You should output a table that looks like Table 10-1.

Table 10-1. *DataFrame created from fake data*

	ages	names
0	25	Jess
1	35	Jordan
2	22	Sandy
3	29	Ted
4	33	Barney
5	20	Tyler
6	18	Rebecca

Accessing Data

There are a few different ways that we can access the data within a DataFrame. You have the option to choose by the column or by the record. Let's look at how to do both.

Indexing by Column

Accessing data by a column is the same as accessing data from a dictionary with the key. Within the first set of brackets, you put the column name that you would like to access. If you'd like to access a specific record within that column, you use a second set of brackets with the index:

```
1| # directly selecting a column in Pandas
2| print( df["ages"] )
3| print( df["ages"][3] )     # select the value of "ages" in the fourth
                                row (0-index based)
5| # print( df[4] )   doesn't work, 4 is not a column name
```

Go ahead and run the cell. On line 2 we output the entire *ages* column of data. The second statement allows us to access the value at a specific cell. Be careful though, putting the index number in the first set of brackets will create an error, as the first set is only meant for column names and "*4*" is not a column.

Indexing by Record

When you need to access an entire record, you must use **loc**. This allows us to specify the record location via the index. Let's access the entire first record, then the name within that record:

```
# directly selecting a record in Pandas using .loc
print( df.loc[0] )
print( df.loc[0]["names"] )       # selecting the value at record 0 in the
                                    "names" column
```

Go ahead and run the cell. We can see that we're able to output the entire record. In the case of using **loc**, you must specify the record index location first, then the column name.

Slicing a DataFrame

When you want to access a specific number of records, you must slice the DataFrame. Slicing in Pandas works the exact same way as a Python list does, using **start**, **stop**, and **step** within a set of brackets. Let's access the records from index 2 up to 5:

```
# slicing a DataFrame to grab specific records
print( df[2:5] )
```

Go ahead and run the cell. This will output the records at index **2**, **3**, and **4**. Again, be careful when slicing as leaving off the colon would result in trying to access a column name.

Built-in Methods

These are methods that are frequently used to make your life easier when using Pandas. It is possible to spend a whole week simply exploring the built-in functions supported by DataFrames in Pandas. However, we will simply highlight a few that will be useful, to give you an idea of what's possible out of the box with Pandas.

head( )

When you work with large sets of data, you'll often want to view a couple records to get an idea of what you're looking at. To see the top records in the DataFrame, along with the column names, you use the **head()** method:

```
# accessing the top 5 records using .head( )
df.head(5)
```

Go ahead and run the cell. This will output the top five records. The argument passed into the method is arbitrary and will show as many records as you want from the top.

tail( )

To view a given number of records from the bottom, you would use the **tail()** method:

```
# accessing the bottom 3 records using .tail( )
df.tail(3)
```

Go ahead and run the cell. This will output the bottom three records for us to view.

keys( )

Sometimes you'll need the column names. Whether you're making a modular script or analyzing the data you're working with, using the **keys( )** method will help:

```
# accessing the column headers (keys) using the .keys( ) method
headers = df.keys( )
print(headers)
```

Go ahead and run the cell. This will output a list of the header names in our DataFrame.

.shape

The shape of a DataFrame describes the number of records by the number of columns. It's always important to check the shape to ensure you're working with the proper amount of data:

```
# checking the shape, which is the number of records and columns
print( df.shape )
```

Go ahead and run the cell. We'll get a **(7, 2)** tuple returned, representing records and columns.

describe( )

The **describe** method will give you a base analysis for all numerical data. You'll be able to view *min, max, 25%, 50%, mean*, etc., on all columns just by calling this method on the DataFrame. This information is helpful to start your analysis but generally won't answer those questions you're looking for. Instead, we can use this method as a guideline of where to start:

```
# checking the general statistics of the DataFrame using .describe( ),
only works on numerical columns
df.describe( )
```

Go ahead and run the cell. Remember that it'll only give back information on numerical column types, which is why we only see an output for the *ages* column.

sort_values( )

When you need to sort a DataFrame based on column information, you use this method. You can pass in one or multiple columns to be sorted by. When passing multiple, you must pass them in as a list of column names, in which the first name will take precedence:

```
# sort based on a given column, but keep the DataFrame in tact using
sort_values( )
df = df.sort_values("ages")
df.head(5)
```

Go ahead and run the cell. In this cell, we've re-declared the value of our df variable to our newly sorted DataFrame. This way we can view all the people sorted by age. You may also pass in an argument to sort in descending order.

Filtration

Let's look at how to filter DataFrames for information that meets a specific condition.

Conditionals

Rather than filtering out information, we can create a boolean data type column that represents the condition we're checking. Let's take our current DataFrame and write a condition that shows those who are 21 or older and can drink:

```
# using a conditional to create a true/false column to work with
can_drink = df["ages"] > 21
print(can_drink)
```

Go ahead and run the cell. When you want to create a column based on a boolean data type, you need to write out the condition based on the entire column. Here, we created a *can_drink* variable that is storing the entire *ages* column values. They are true-false values because of our condition that we created. We could potentially use this to create another column to work with.

Subsetting

When you need to filter out records but retain the information within the DataFrame you need to use a concept called subsetting. We'll use the same condition as earlier, except this time we'll use it to filter out records rather than create a true-false representation:

```
# using subsetting to filter out records and keep DataFrame intact
df[ df["ages"] > 21 ]
```

Go ahead and run the cell. The output results in only those records whose ages are equal to or above the age of 21. We took the condition from above and wrapped it within brackets while accessing the *df* variable. Although it may look weird, the syntax representation is the following:

>>> *dataframe_variable [conditional statement to filter records with]*

You could also write the following for the same exact result:

>>> *df[can_drink]*

Remember that can_drink is a representation of true-false values, which means that the preceding statement will filter out all records that have the value of false.

Column Transformations

Rarely, if ever, will the columns in the original raw DataFrame imported from CSV or a database be the ones you need for your analysis. You will spend lots of time constantly transforming columns or groups of columns using general computational operations to produce new ones that are functions of the old ones. Pandas has full support for this and does it efficiently.

Generating a New Column with Data

To create a new column within a DataFrame, you use the same syntax as if you were adding a new key-value pair into a dictionary. Let's create a column of fake data that represents how long the people within our DataFrame have been customers with our company:

```
1| # generating a new column of fake data for each record in the DataFrame
to represent customer tenure
2| random.seed(321)
4| tenure = [ random.randint(0, 10) for x in range( len(df) )]
6| df["tenure"] = tenure          # same as adding a new key-value pair in a
   dictionary
7| df.head( )
```

Go ahead and run the cell. The output will result in a new column created with random numbers for their tenure. We were able to add the column and its values on line 6. In Table 10-2, you'll find the updated DataFrame, sorted by age.

Table 10-2. *Adding a new column to the DataFrame*

	ages	names	tenure
6	18	Rebecca	4
5	20	Tyler	6
2	22	Sandy	2
0	25	Jess	5
3	29	Ted	8
4	33	Barney	7
1	35	Jordan	5

apply( )

Adding new columns based on current data is known as "**feature engineering**." It makes up a good portion of a data analysts' job. Often, you won't be able to answer the questions you have from the data you collect. Instead, you need to create your own data that is useful to answering questions. For this example, let's try to answer the following question: "*What age group does each customer belong to?*". You could look at the persons' age and assume their age group; however, we want to make it easier than that. In order to answer this question easily, we'll need to feature engineer a new column that represents each customer's age group. We can do this by using the **apply** method on the DataFrame. The apply method takes in each record, applies the function passed, and sets the value returned as the new column data. Let's check it out:

```
# feature engineering a new column from known data using a UDF
def ageGroup(age):
     return "Teenager" if age < 21 else "Adult"
df["age_group"] = df["ages"].apply(ageGroup)
df.head(10)
```

Go ahead and run the cell. Using the apply method, we're able to create a new column that easily answers our question. When adding the new *age_group* column, we applied the *ageGroup* function based on the values in the *ages* column. It then iterated over each record in the DataFrame and set the return value of either "**Teenager**" or "**Adult**" as the value for the new *age_group* column. The apply method makes it easy for us to add new data with our own UDF. Take a look at Table 10-3.

Table 10-3. *Feature engineering an age_group column*

	ages	names	tenure	age_group
6	18	Rebecca	4	Teenager
5	20	Tyler	6	Teenager
2	22	Sandy	2	Adult
0	25	Jess	5	Adult
3	29	Ted	8	Adult
4	33	Barney	7	Adult
1	35	Jordan	5	Adult

Note   When you need to apply a value based on multiple columns, you must set the axis = 1.

Aggregations

The raw data plus transformations is generally only half the story. Your objective is to extract actual insights and actionable conclusions from the data, and that means reducing it from potentially billions of rows to a summary of statistics via aggregation functions. This section assumes some knowledge of SQL and the *groupby* function. If you're not familiar with how *groupby* works in SQL, visit w3schools[3] for reference material.

---

[3]www.w3schools.com/sql/sql_groupby.asp

groupby( )

In order to condense the information down to a summary of statistics, we'll need to use the **groupby** method that Pandas has. Whenever you group information together, you need to use an aggregate function to let the program know how to group the information together. For now, let's **count** how many records of each age group there are within our DataFrame:

```
# grouping the records together to count how many records in each group
df.groupby("age_group", as_index=False).count( ).head( )
```

Go ahead and run the cell. When the information is grouped together using the *count* method, the program will simply add up the number of records that belong in each category. We'll have two categories: adult with five records, and teenager with two records. The first argument of our *groupby* method is the column we want to group on, and the second is to make sure we don't reset the index to become the age group column. If it were set to *True,* then the resulting DataFrame would use *age_group* as the unique identifier for each record.

mean( )

Instead of counting how many records there are in each category, let's go ahead and find the averages of each column by using the mean method. We'll group based on the same column:

```
# grouping the data to see averages of all columns
df.groupby("age_group", as_index=False).mean( ).head( )
```

Go ahead and run the cell. Using the mean method, we'll be able to get the averages for all numerical columns. The output should result in a DataFrame that looks like Table 10-4.

Table 10-4. *Grouping by age_group and averaging data*

	age_group	ages	tenure
0	Adult	28.8	5.4
1	Teenager	19.0	5.0

Just by averaging the information, we can see that adults tend to have a longer tenure. Notice that the names column was dropped. This is because groupby only keeps numerical data, as it wouldn't be able to average out a string.

groupby( ) with Multiple Columns

When you need to group by multiple columns, the arguments must be passed in as a list. The first item in the list will be the main column that the DataFrame is grouped by. In our case, let's check how many adults have a tenure of five years:

```
# grouping information by their age group, then by their tenure
df.groupby( [ "age_group", "tenure" ], as_index=False).count( ).head(10)
```

Go ahead and run the cell. To answer the question, we needed to group by *age_group* first, in order to condense the information into adults and teenagers. Next, we needed to group the data further based on the *tenure*. This would allow us to see how many adults there are for each length of tenure. As we don't have much data, the answer is only two. We arrive at this conclusion because we used the *count* method while grouping. All other tenures for each age group have only one customer.

Adding a Record

To add a record into the DataFrame, you'll need to access the next index and assign a value as a list structure. In our case, the next index would be **7**. Let's add an identical row that already exists in our DataFrame, so we can see how to remove duplicate information in the next cell:

```
# adding a record to the bottom of the DataFrame
df.loc[7] = [ 25, "Jess", 2, "Adult" ]    # add a record
df.head(10)
```

Go ahead and run the cell. This will add a new record at the bottom with the same data as our record in index **0**. You won't need to add new records too often, but it helps to know how to do it when the time comes.

drop_duplicates( )

Way too often will you see data with duplicate information, or just duplicate IDs. It's imperative that you remove all duplicate records as it will skew your data, resulting in incorrect answers. You can remove duplicate records based on a single column or an entire record being identical. In our case, let's remove duplicates based on similar names, which will remove the record we just added into our DataFrame:

```
# removing duplicates based on same names
df = df.drop_duplicates( subset="names" )
df.head(10)
```

Go ahead and run the cell. This will remove the second record with the name "**Jess**." By passing the column name into the subset parameter, we can remove all duplicates with the same name.

Note   Omitting the subset argument will remove only duplicate records that have identical values in all columns.

Pandas Joins

Often, you will have to combine data from several different sources to obtain the actual dataset you need for your exploration or modeling. Pandas draws heavily on SQL in its design for joins. This section assumes some knowledge of *SQL* and *SQL joins*. If you're not familiar with how *joins* work in SQL, visit w3schools[4] for reference material.

---

[4]www.w3schools.com/sql/sql_join.asp

Creating a Second DataFrame

Let's create a secondary DataFrame to represent our customers posting ratings about our company. We'll create ratings for three users so we can see both inner joins and outer joins:

```
# creating another fake DataFrame to work with, having same names and a
  new ratings column
ratings = {
        "names" : [ "Jess", "Tyler", "Ted" ],
        "ratings" : [ 10, 9, 6 ]
}
ratings = df.from_dict(ratings)
ratings.head( )
```

Go ahead and run the cell. Now that we've created a second DataFrame, we can join the two DataFrames together, much like joining two tables together in SQL.

Inner Join

Anytime you perform a join, you need a unique column to join the data with. In our case, we can use the *names* column to join the ratings DataFrame with our original DataFrame. Let's perform an inner join on these two datasets so that we can connect users with their ratings:

```
# performing an inner join with our df and ratings DataFrames based on
  names, get data that matches
matched_ratings = df.merge(ratings, on="names", how="inner")
matched_ratings.head( )
```

Go ahead and run the cell. We'll get an output that looks like Table 10-5:

Table 10-5. *Joining DataFrames to view customer ratings and ages together*

	ages	names	tenure	age_group	ratings
0	20	Tyler	6	Teenager	9
1	25	Jess	5	Adult	10
2	29	Ted	8	Adult	6

Using the *merge* method, we were able to perform a join. By specifying the *how* parameter to "**inner**," we were able to return a DataFrame with only those records who posted a rating. We could do a lot more with this data now than before. We could calculate average age of customers who gave us a rating, average rating per age group, etc. Joins will always help to connect separate DataFrames together, which helps especially when working with databases.

Outer Join

If we want to return all the records, but connect the ratings for people who gave one, we would need to perform an outer join. This would allow us to keep all records from our original DataFrame while adding the *ratings* column. We need to specify the *how* parameter to "**outer**":

```
# performing an outer join with our df and ratings DataFrames based on
  names, get all data
all_ratings = df.merge(ratings, on="names", how="outer")
all_ratings.head( )
```

Go ahead and run the cell. We'll get a DataFrame of all seven records this time; however, those that didn't give a rating were given a **NaN** for a value. This stands for "*Not a Number.*" Once we combine this information, we could then find out the average age of those who gave a rating and those who didn't. From a marketing perspective, this would be helpful to know who the target demographic should be.

Dataset Pipeline

A dataset pipeline is a specific process in which we take our data and clean it for our model, which will be able to make predictions. This can be a lengthy process if the dataset that you use is unclean. A dataset that is not clean will have duplicates records, null values everywhere, or unfiltered information that leads to incorrect predictions. Here is the general process:

1. **Performing Exploratory Analysis**

    - In this step you want to get to know your data very well. Take notes for what you see at a glance or what you may want to clean or add. You essentially want to get a feel for what your data has to offer. Make note of the number of columns, the data types, outliers, null values, and columns that aren't necessary. This is generally when you want to plot out each column of data and speculate correlations, non-informational features, etc.

2. **Data Cleaning**

    - Improper cleaning can lead to poor predictions and bad datasets. Here, you'll want to remove unwanted observations like duplicates, fix structural errors like columns that have the same name but are typos, handle missing data, and filter outlier information. This is key for the next step.

3. **Feature Engineering**

    - Creating new information that isn't depicted by the dataset is important. You can use your own expertise if you have knowledge of the subject, and you can isolate data which allows your algorithms to focus more on the important observations. Here you can feature engineer columns into a group, add dummy variables, remove unused features, etc. This is where you want to expand on the dataset with your own knowledge if you believe data is either missing or could be created from the information within the dataset.

Now that you know the process in which to clean a dataset, this will come in handy for the first exercise at the end of the day.

```
                       TUESDAY EXERCISES
```

1. **Loading a Dataset**: Go to www.Kaggle.com, click "*Datasets*" in the top
   bar menu. Choose a dataset that you like, and download it into the "*python_
   bootcamp*" folder. Then, load the dataset into a Pandas DataFrame using the
   read_csv method, and display the top five records.

2. **Dataset Analysis**: This is an open-ended exercise. Run some analysis on the
   dataset you chose from exercise #1. Try to answer questions like these:

   a. *How many records are there?*

   b. *What are the data types of each column?*

   c. *Are there duplicate records or columns?*

   d. *Is there missing data?*

   e. *Is there a correlation between two or more columns?*

Today's focus was on learning the all-important Pandas library and how to work
with DataFrames. We used some minor real-life examples, but for the most part,
today was just about understanding what you could do in Pandas. For Friday's
project, we'll use Pandas to help us analyze sporting statistics.

Wednesday: Data Visualization

Data visualization is one of the most powerful tools an analyst has for two main reasons.
Firstly, it is unrivalled in its ability to guide the analyst's hand in determining "what
to look at next." Often, a visual is revealing of patterns in the data that are not easily
discernable by just looking at DataFrames. Secondly, they are an analyst's greatest
communication tool. Professional analysts need to present their results to groups of
people responsible for acting based on what the data says. Visuals can tell your story
much better than raw numbers.

Like how yesterday's lesson began, we need to install a library into our virtual environment. To follow along with today's lesson, cd into the "*python_bootcamp*" folder and activate the environment. We'll begin today within the terminal.

Types of Charts

Knowing which chart to use is important in presenting your data properly. We'll go over several charts today; however, these are some of the common charts you'll want to know:

- **Line Chart**: Exploring data over time

- **Bar Chart**: Comparing categories of data and tracks changes over time

- **Pie Chart**: Explores parts of a whole, that is, fractions

- **Scatter Plot**: Like line charts, tracks correlations between two categories

- **Histogram**: Unrelated from bar charts, shows distribution of variables

- **Candlestick Chart**: Used a lot in financial sector, that is, can compare a stock over a period

- **Box Chart**: Looks identical to candlestick charts, and compares minimum, 1st, median, 3rd quartiles, and max values

Depending on what you need to accomplish in conceptualizing your data, you will be able to choose a specific type of chart to portray your data.

Installing Matplotlib

To install *matplotlib*, make sure your virtual environment is activated first, then write the following command into the terminal:

```
$ pip install matplotlib
```

After running the command, it should install a few packages that *matplotlib* requires. If you'd like to check and make sure you downloaded the proper library, just write out the list command.

Importing Matplotlib

To follow along with the rest of this lesson, let's open and continue from our previous notebook file *"Week_10"* and simply add a markdown cell at the bottom that says, "**Matplotlib**."

Like Pandas, matplotlib has an industry standard name when you import the library:

```
# importing the matplotlib library from matplotlib import
pyplot as plt            # industry standard name of plt when importing
```

Go ahead and run the cell. We import *pyplot as plt* so that we can reference the many charts that matplotlib has to offer.

Line Plot

Let's start with the most basic chart we can create, the line plot:

```
1| # creating a line plot using x and y coords
3| x, y = [ 1600, 1700, 1800, 1900, 2000 ] , [ 0.2, 0.5, 1.1, 2.2, 7.7 ]
5| plt.plot(x, y)       # creates the line
7| plt.title("World Population Over Time")
8| plt.xlabel("Year")
9| plt.ylabel("Population (billions)")
11| plt.show( )
```

Go ahead and run the cell. To start, we create our *x* and *y* coordinates for plotting. The *plot()* method allows us to plot a single line; it just needs the coordinates passed in. Lines 7, 8, and 9 are all for customizing the chart and its appearance. Lastly, we use the *show()* method to render the chart. You should output a chart like Figure 10-1.

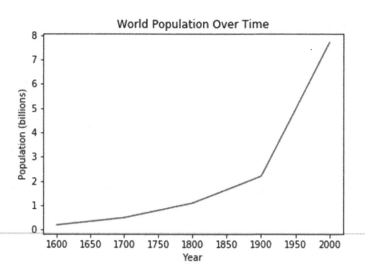

Figure 10-1. *Single line plot of population data*

When you want to add more lines to the chart, you simply apply as many plot() methods as necessary. Let's add some more customization to each plot line this time:

```
1| # creating a line plot with multiple lines
3| x1, y1 = [ 1600, 1700, 1800, 1900, 2000 ] , [ 0.2, 0.5, 1.1, 2.2, 7.7 ]
4| x2, y2 = [ 1600, 1700, 1800, 1900, 2000 ] , [ 1, 1, 2, 3, 4 ]
6| plt.plot(x1, y1, "rx-", label="Actual")      # create a red solid line
                                                 with x dots
7| plt.plot(x2, y2, "bo--", label="Fake")      # create a blue dashed line
                                                 with circle dots
9| plt.title("World Population Over Time")
10| plt.xlabel("Year")
11| plt.ylabel("Population (billions)")
12| plt.legend( )    # shows labels in best corner
14| plt.show( )
```

Go ahead and run the cell. By adding a second set of coordinates, we're able to plot a second line using the *plot()* method on line 7. We also specified how the lines should render using shorthand syntax. For the third argument in the plot method, we can pass a string that represents the color, symbols for dots, and the line style. Finally, we added a label to each line for making it easy to read the multiline chart, and we're able to show it by calling the *legend()* method. The output should look like Figure 10-2.

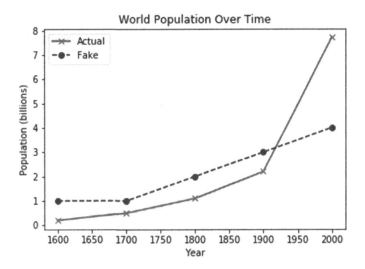

Figure 10-2. *Multiline plot of population data*

Bar Plot

When you need to plot categorical data, a bar plot is a much better choice. Let's create some fake data for the number of people that chose their favorite movie category and plot it:

```
1| # creating a bar plot using x and y coords
3| num_people, categories = [ 4, 8, 3, 6, 2 ] , [ "Comedy", "Action",
    "Thriller", "Romance", "Horror" ]
5| plt.bar(categories, num_people)
7| plt.title("Favorite Movie Category", fontsize=24)
8| plt.xlabel("Category", fontsize=16)
9| plt.ylabel("# of People", fontsize=16)
10| plt.xticks(fontname="Fantasy")
11| plt.yticks(fontname="Fantasy")
13| plt.show( )
```

Go ahead and run the cell. After creating our data to work with, we create our plot on line 5. Using the *bar()* method, we're able to create the bar plot. The numerical data must always be set up on the y axis, which is why we have our *categories* in the x axis.

We've also added several new customizations to the chart. We can adjust the font size, font to be displayed, and even adjust how large the tick marks appear. You should render a chart like Figure 10-3.

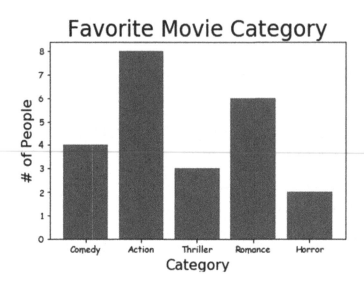

Figure 10-3. *Bar plot of movie categories data*

Box Plot

Box plots are useful in situations where you need to compare a single statistic either over time or against categories. They are like candlestick charts in their design, where you can view the min, max, 25% quartile, 75% quartile, and median, which can be useful for displaying data over time. In the case of stocks, currency would be the y axis data and time would be the x axis data. For our example, let's create two separate groups and display the heights for each:

```
1| # creating a box plot - showing height data for male-female
3| males, females = [ 72, 68, 65, 77, 73, 71, 69 ] , [ 60, 65, 68, 61,
   63, 64 ]
4| heights = [ males, females ]
6| plt.figure(figsize=(15, 8))      # makes chart bigger
7| plt.boxplot(heights)            # takes in list of data, each box is
                                    its' own array, heights contains two
                                    lists
```

```
9| plt.xticks( [ 1, 2 ] , [ "Male" , "Female " ] )          # sets number
                                                              of ticks and
                                                              labels on
                                                              x-axis
10| plt.title("Height by Gender", fontsize=22)
11| plt.ylabel("Height (inches)", fontsize=14)
12| plt.xlabel("Gender", fontsize=14)
14| plt.show( )
```

Go ahead and run the cell. In order to plot the data in separate categories, we need to have a list of lists. On line 4, we declare our data which is holding a list of heights for both *males* and *females*. When we go to plot our data, it will separate each list into its own box. You'll notice the figure is much larger than usual; we declare a new figure size on line 6. To render the chart though, we use the *boxplot()* method on line 7 and pass *heights* in as our data. One of the more important lines is number 9, however, where we define the number of categories to appear on the x axis. We order them as *"Male"* then *"Female"* because that is the order in which they're declared on line 4. The chart should render like Figure 10-4.

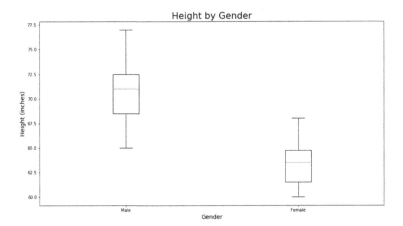

Figure 10-4. *Box plot of height data*

Scatter Plot

If you're familiar with clusters, then you'll know the importance of scatter plots. These types of plots help to distinguish groups apart from each other by plotting a dot for each set of data. Using two characteristics, like height and width of a flower, we can classify which species a flower belongs to. Let's create some fake data and plot the points:

```
 1| # creating a scatter plot to represent height-weight distribution
 2| from random import randint
 3| random.seed(2)
 5| height = [ randint(58, 78) for x in range(20) ]      # 20 records
                                                            between 4'10"
                                                            and 6'6"
 6| weight = [ randint(90, 250) for x in range(20) ]     # 20 records
                                                            between 90lbs.
                                                            and 250lbs.
 8| plt.scatter(weight, height)
10| plt.title("Height-Weight Distribution")
11| plt.xlabel("Weight (lbs)")
12| plt.ylabel("Height (inches)")
14| plt.show( )
```

Go ahead and run the cell. To create some fake data, we use the *randint* method from the *random* module. Here, we're able to create 20 records for both the *height* and *weight* lists. To plot the data, we use the *scatter()* method and add some characteristics to the plot. You should get an output like Figure 10-5.

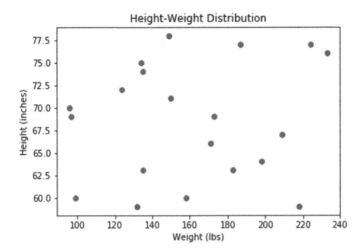

Figure 10-5. *Scatter plot of height-weight data*

Histogram

While line plots are great for visualizing trends in time series data, histograms are the king of visualizing distributions. Often, the distribution of a variable is what you're interested in, and a visualization provides a lot more information than a group of summary statistics. First, let's see how we can create a histogram:

```
1| # creating a histogram to show age data for a fake population
2| import numpy as np        # import the numpy module to generate data
3| np.random.seed(5)
5| ages = [ np.random.normal(loc=40, scale=10) for x in
   range(1000) ]    # ages distributed around 40
7| plt.hist(ages, bins=45)          # bins is the number of bars
9| plt.title("Ages per Population")
10| plt.xlabel("Age")
11| plt.ylabel("# of People")
13| plt.show( )
```

Go ahead and run the cell. We've mentioned the *NumPy* module previously. It's used in data science to perform extremely fast numerical calculations. Pandas' DataFrames are built on top of *NumPy* arrays. For the purpose of this cell, however, you just need to know that we're using it to create random numbers that are centralized around a given

289

number. The number we specify is passed into the *loc* argument on line 5. The *scale* argument is how wide we want the random numbers to be apart. Of course, it will still create numbers outside of that range, but it is primarily creating 1000 random numbers centralized around the age of 40.

To create the histogram, we use the *hist()* method and pass in the proper data. Histograms allow us to see how many times a specific piece of data appeared. In our example, the age of 40 appears more than 60 times. The y axis represents the frequency of the x axis value. The *bins* argument specifies how many bars you see on the chart. You may be thinking: the more bins the better right? Wrong, there's always a fine line between too many and too little; often you'll just have to test out the proper number. We complete this chart by adding customization. The result should look like Figure 10-6.

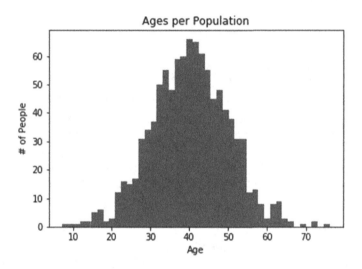

Figure 10-6. *Histogram of centrally distributed age data*

Although the data is fake, we can deduce a lot of information from the chart. We can see outliers that may exist, where the general age range sits, and much more.

Importance of Histogram Distribution

To see why histograms are so important with understanding central distribution, we'll need to create some more fake data. We'll then plot both datasets and see how they stack up:

```
# showing the importance of histogram's display central distribution
florida = [ np.random.normal(loc=60, scale=15) for x in range(1000) ]
         # assume numpy is imported
california = [ np.random.normal(loc=35, scale=5) for x in range(1000) ]
# chart 1
plt.hist(florida, bins=45, color="r", alpha=0.4)          # alpha is
                                                             opacity,
                                                             making it see
                                                             through

plt.show( )
# chart 2
plt.hist(california, bins=45, color="b", alpha=0.4)       # alpha is opacity,
                                                             making it see
                                                             through

plt.show( )
# chart 3
plt.hist(florida, bins=45, color="r", alpha=0.4)          # alpha is
                                                             opacity,
                                                             making it see
                                                             through
plt.hist(california, bins=45, color="b", alpha=0.4)       # alpha is opacity,
                                                             making it see
                                                             through

plt.show( )
```

Go ahead and run the cell. We're able to output three different histograms within this cell because of the three *show* methods being called. When you look at the first two histograms, they look identical. It's tough to see, without looking further into the charts, that the data is completely different. Therefore, to view the data properly, we output the third histogram with both datasets overlapping as seen in Figure 10-7. We're now able to clearly see the difference in central distribution of each dataset. This is important when it comes to analyzing data. We set *alpha* to **0.4** because it allows us to set the opacity. The higher the number, the more solid the data becomes.

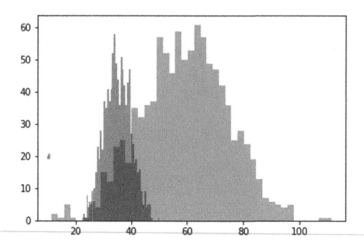

Figure 10-7. *Histogram distribution plotting importance*

Note   When rendering several charts, *matplotlib* understands how to separate each plot by resetting the chart to empty after the show method is run, until then all information being plotted will be included in one chart.

Saving the Chart

Being able to render these charts is wonderful; however, at times you need to use them within a presentation. Luckily for us, *matplotlib* comes with a method that can save the charts we create to a file. The **savefig()** method supports many different file extensions; the most common *".jpg"* is what we'll use. Let's render a simple plot line chart to the local folder:

```
1| # using savefig method to save the chart as a jpg to the local folder
3| x, y = [ 1600, 1700, 1800, 1900, 2000 ] , [ 0.2, 0.5, 1.1, 2.2, 7.7 ]
5| plt.plot(x, y, "bo-")        # creates a blue solid line with circle
   dots
7| plt.title("World Population Over Time")
8| plt.xlabel("Year")
9| plt.ylabel("Population (billions)")
11| plt.savefig("population.jpg")
```

Go ahead and run the cell. You'll notice a new image file in the *"python_bootcamp"* folder called *"population.jpg"* now. If you don't specify a URL path, it'll save the image in the local folder where the Jupyter Notebook file is located.

Note   You can save the chart in other formats like PDF or PNG.

Flattening Multidimensional Data

Generally, in data analysis you want to avoid 3D plotting wherever possible. It's not because the information you want to convey isn't contained within the result, but sometimes it is simply easier to express a point by other means. One of the best ways to represent a third dimension is to use color instead of depth.

For instance, imagine that you have three datasets that you need to plot: height, weight, and age. You could render a 3D model, but that would be excessive. Instead, you can render the height and weight like we have before on a scatter plot and color each dot to represent the age. The third dimension of color is now easily readable rather than trying to depict the data using the z axis (*depth*). Let's create this exact scatter plot together in the following:

```
1| # creating a scatter plot to represent height-weight distribution
2| from random import randint
3| random.seed(2)

5| height = [ randint(58, 78) for x in range(20) ]
6| weight = [ randint(90, 250) for x in range(20) ]
7| age = [ randint(18, 65) for x in range(20) ]        # 20 records
                                                        between 18
                                                        and 65 years
                                                        old
9| plt.scatter(weight, height, c=age)          # sets the age list to
                                                be shown by color

11| plt.title("Height-Weight Distribution")
12| plt.xlabel("Weight (lbs)")
13| plt.ylabel("Height (inches)")
14| plt.colorbar(label="Age")          # adds color bar to right side
16| plt.show( )
```

Go ahead and run the cell. By adding the *c* argument which represents color, into the scatter plot, we can easily represent three datasets in a 2D manner as seen in Figure 10-8. The color bar on the right side is created via line 14, where we also create the label for it. In some cases, you do need to use the z axis, like representing spatial data. However, when possible, simply using color as the third dimension is easier to not only create but to read as well.

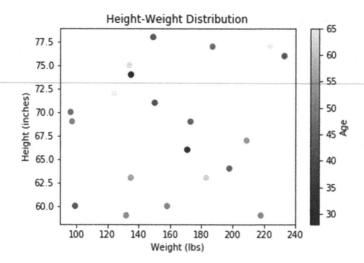

Figure 10-8. *Rendering a 3D plot using color as the third dimension*

WEDNESDAY EXERCISES

1. **Three Line Plot**: Create three random lists of data that have 20 numbers between 1 and 10. Then create a line plot with three lines, one for each list. Give each line their own color, dot symbol, and line style.

2. **User Information**: Create a program that asks any number of users to give a rating between 1 and 5 stars and plots a bar chart of the data when no more users would like to answer. Use the following text as an example of what to ask:

```
>>> What would you rate this movie (1-5)?       4
>>> Is there another user that would like to review (y/n)?     y
>>> What would you rate this movie (1-5)?       5
>>> Is there another user that would like to review (y/n)?     n
*** bar plot renders with two categories and two ratings ***
```

Today we learned the importance of data visualization and how to create custom charts to show off our data properly. There's a wide range of plots to choose from when using matplotlib, and each have their own pros and cons which you need to consider when choosing the type of plot. In the end, if you can't properly show the data to those making the business decisions, then all the data you've collected is wasted.

Thursday: Web Scraping

You may have heard the term "*web scraping*" previously. In most languages like Python, web scraping is comprised of two parts: sending out a request and parsing the data. We'll need to use the **requests** module for the first part and a library called **Beautiful Soup** for the second part. In a nutshell, the script you write to request data and parse it is called a "*scraper.*" For today's lesson, we'll be collecting some data using these two libraries.

Like yesterday's lesson, we need to install a library into our virtual environment. To follow along with today's lesson, cd into the "*python_bootcamp*" folder, and activate the environment. We'll begin today within the terminal.

Installing Beautiful Soup

To install *Beautiful Soup*, make sure your virtual environment is activated first, then write the following command into the terminal:

```
$ pip install bs4
```

After running the command, it should install a few packages that *Beautiful Soup* requires.

Importing Beautiful Soup

To follow along with the rest of this lesson, let's open and continue from our previous notebook file "*Week_10*" and simply add a markdown cell at the bottom that says, "**Web Scraping.**"

We need to import *requests* and the *BeautifulSoup* class that is within the *bs4* library:

```
# importing the beautiful soup and requests library
from bs4 import BeautifulSoup
import requests
```

Go ahead and run the cell. We'll use the requests module to send out a request to a given URL. When the URL endpoint is not an API that gives back properly formatted data but rather a web page that renders HTML and CSS, the response that we get back is the code for that web page. In order to parse through this code, we pass it into the *BeautifulSoup* object, which makes it easy to manipulate and traverse through the code.

Requesting Page Content

To begin scraping data, let's send a request to a simple web page that contains only a poem:

```
# performing a request and outputting the status code
page = requests.get("http://www.arthurleej.com/e-love.html")
print(page)
```

Go ahead and run the cell. We'll get an output of "**<Response [200]>**". This lets us know that the request to the web page was a success. In order to see what we received back as a response though, we need to access the *content* attribute of the *page* variable:

```
# outputting the request response content
print(page.content)
```

Go ahead and run the cell. This will output a large string of all the code that was used to write this web page, including tags, styles, scripts, etc. As the book stated earlier, this URL renders a web page, so the response we get back is a string of all the code. The next step is to turn the response into an object that we can work with and parse through the data.

Parsing the Response with Beautiful Soup

The Beautiful Soup library comes with many attributes and methods that make parsing the code easier for ourselves. Using this library, we can make the code easy to view, scrape, and traverse through. We'll need to create a *BeautifulSoup* object to work with by passing the page content into it, along with the type of parser we want to use. In our case, we're working with HTML code, so we'll need to use the HTML parser:

```
# turning the response into a BeautifulSoup object to extract data
soup = BeautifulSoup(page.content, "html.parser")
print( soup.prettify( ) )
```

Go ahead and run the cell. The **prettify()** method will create a well-formatted output for us to view. This makes it easier for us to see the actual code that is written. The *soup* object knew how to parse the content properly because of the parser that we specified. Beautiful Soup works with other languages, but we'll be working with HTML for this book. Now that we've turned the content into an object we can use, let's learn how to extract the data from the code.

Scraping Data

There are many methods to extract data using Beautiful Soup. The following sections will cover a few of the main methods in doing so. Basic HTML knowledge is assumed for this section.

.find( )

To find a specific element within the code, we can use the **find()** method. The argument we pass is the tag that we want to search for, but it will only find the first instance and return it. Meaning that if there are four bold element tags within our code, and we use this method to find a bold tag, it will respond back with only the first bold element tag found. Let's try it out:

```
# using the find method to scrape the text within the first bold tag
title = soup.find("b")
print(title)
print( title.get_text( ) )          # extracts all text within element
```

Go ahead and run the cell. If you look at the code using the inspector tab in your web browser's console tools, you'll be able to see that the first bold tag within the code is the title of the poem. The first print statement results in "**Love**" and the second is simply the text within the element. We were able to extract the text by using the **get_text()** method.

.find_all( )

To find all instances of a given element, we use the **find_all()** method. This will give us back a list of all tags found within the code. Let's find all bold tags within the code and extract the text:

```
# get all text within the bold element tag then output each
poem_text = soup.find_all("b")
for text in poem_text:
    print( text.get_text( ) )
```

Go ahead and run the cell. If you were to look at the code using your inspector tools, you would notice that all the text is within bold tags. The result is an output of the entire poem.

Finding Elements by Attributes

All HTML elements have attributes associated with them, whether it's a style, id, class, etc., you can use Beautiful Soup to find elements with a specific attribute value. Let's request a response from my personal Github page and find the element that shows my username:

```
1| # finding an element by specific attribute key-values
3| page = requests.get("https://github.com/Connor-SM")
4| soup = BeautifulSoup(page.content, "html.parser")
6| username = soup.find( "span", attrs={ "class" : "vcard-username" }
   )         # find first span with this class
8| print(username)       # will show that element has class of vcard-
                          username among others
9| print( username.get_text( ) )
```

Go ahead and run the cell. We send a request to *Github* and parse the content into a *BeautifulSoup* object to work with. On line 6, we search for a span tag element that has an attribute of class, whose value is "*vcard-username.*" This will output the entire span tag, including text, attributes, and the syntax on line 8. Lastly, we extract the text on line 9 to output the username associated with this page.

Note   Finding elements by attributes also works with the *find_all* method. You can also include multiple key-value pairs to look for within the *attrs* argument.

DOM Traversal

This section will cover how to extract information by traversing through the **DOM** hierarchy. The DOM, short for **Document Object Model**, is a concept in web design that describes the relationships and structure between elements on a browser. All elements on a web page belong to one of three relationships:

1. *Parent-Child*

2. *Sibling*

3. *Grandparent-Grandchild*

This concept is important to understand when you are web scraping because you may need to access the children of a specific element. The children are in reference to all elements within another element. Take the following HTML code, for instance:

```
<body>
    <div>
        <h1>Title</h1>
        <h3>Sub-title</h3>
        <p>Text</p>
    </div>
</body>
```

In this example, the *<div>* element is the parent of the *h1*, *h3*, and *p* elements. Those three elements are known as the children. If we wanted to extract all the text from within this *<div>* element, we could access the children elements.

Note   In the preceding example, the h1, h3, and p elements are all siblings. The body would be the parent of the div element and the grandparent of the h1, h3, and p elements.

As the DOM is a web design concept, it's covered briefly in this book. If you would like more information on the subject or basic HTML knowledge, be sure to visit the *w3schools*[5] resource.

Accessing the Children Attribute

Lucky for us, when Beautiful Soup converts the page content into an object, it keeps track of the children for all elements. This allows us to traverse through the DOM and parse data as we see fit. Let's grab the poem from earlier and convert the response into a *BeautifulSoup* object:

---

[5]www.w3schools.com/js/js_htmldom.asp

```
# traversing through the DOM using Beautiful Soup - using the children
attribute
page = requests.get("http://www.arthurleej.com/e-love.html")
soup = BeautifulSoup(page.content, "html.parser")
print(soup.children)        # outputs an iterator object
```

Go ahead and run the cell. The children elements within the soup object are stored within an iterator. For the following exercise, let's extract the *title* element from the web page.

Understanding the Types of Children

Before we begin, we first need to understand the types of children within the *BeautifulSoup* object. Let's convert the iterator into a list of elements that we can loop over:

```
# understanding the children within the soup object
for child in list( soup.children ):
    print( type( child ) )
```

Go ahead and run the cell. As a result, we'll get four children but only three different types:

- **<class 'bs4.element.Doctype'>**

    – A *Doctype* object is in reference to the Docstring that defines the HTML version used.

- **<class 'bs4.element.NavigableString'>**

    – A string corresponds to a bit of text within a tag. Beautiful Soup uses the *NavigableString* class to contain these bits of text. So far, we've used the *get_text()* method to extract text; however, you can use the following to extract data as well:

    >>> *tag.string*

    Which results in *NavigableString* type.

- **<class 'bs4.element.Tag'>**

  - A *Tag* object corresponds to an XML or HTML tag in the original document. When we access the elements and their text, we'll be accessing the original tags to do so.

If you were to output each of these objects, you'd find that all the code, aside from the *Doctype*, appear in the *Tag* object.

Accessing the Tag Object

If we want to access the text within the *title* tag, we need to traverse into its parent first, which happens to be the *head* tag. Now that we know the elements that we're looking for reside in the *Tag* object, we need to save that object to a variable and output the sections within it:

```
# accessing the .Tag object which holds the html - trying to access the
title tag
html = list( soup.children )[2]
for section in html:
    print("\n\n Start of new section")
    print(section)
```

Go ahead and run the cell. When you output each section within our HTML variable, you'll realize that there's an empty section at the first index, before the location of the head element. We output the print statement for each new section, in case an empty string occupies an index.

Accessing the Head Element Tag

Now that we know the *head* element is at index *1* of the *HTML* children, we can perform the same execution to access each child within the *head*:

```
# accessing the head element using the children attribute
head = list( html.children )[1]
for item in head:
    print("\n\n New Tag")
    print(item)
```

Go ahead and run the cell. When you output each tag within the *head*, you'll notice the *title* tag that we've been searching for resides at index *1*.

Note   Remember that each object stored in these variables is an iterator and can be type converted into lists.

Scraping the Title Text

The final step is to extract the text from the *title* tag:

```
# scraping the title text
title = list( head )[1]
print(title.string)     # .string is used to extract text as well
print( type(title.string) )       # results in NavigableString
print( title.get_text( ) )
```

Go ahead and run the cell. We've just traversed through the *DOM* in order to scrape the text from our *title* element.

Note   The ability to access an object's children elements allows us to create modular or automated web scrapers that can perform a various number of tasks. As most sites follow a similar style on their web pages, creating a script that would extract information on a single page would allow us to do so on many other pages if we knew the proper pattern. For instance, the online statistical database for baseball called *baseball-reference* holds data for all baseball players throughout the history of the MLB. Each player has a unique identifier on the web site's URL. If you wrote a parsing script that would extract information for one player, you would be able to write a loop to extract information from all players in the database.

THURSDAY EXERCISES

1. **Word Count**: Write a program that counts how many words are in the following link: `www.york.ac.uk/teaching/cws/wws/webpage1.html`. Use the requests module and Beautiful Soup library to extract all text.

2. **Question #2**: Using the following link, extract every stadium name out of the table: `https://en.wikipedia.org/wiki/List_of_current_National_Football_League_stadiums`. There should be 32 total names.

Today we learned how to collect information via a web scraper. Using the requests module, we can receive a response of code that renders a given web page. We can then turn this response into an object to easily parse and extract data via the Beautiful Soup library. In tomorrow's lesson, we'll use all the libraries that we learned throughout this week in order to analyze information that we scrape off the Web.

Friday: Web Site Analysis

Today's project will include the *requests* module, *Beautiful Soup*, and *matplotlib* libraries. The goal for this project is to create a script that will accept a web site to scrape and display the top words used within the site. We'll plot the results within a nicely formatted bar plot, making it easier to understand for those looking at the data.

To follow along with today's lesson, cd into the *"python_bootcamp"* folder, and activate the environment. We'll continue from our previous notebook file *"Week_10"* and add a markdown cell at the bottom that says, **"Friday Project: Website Analysis."**

Final Design

As we do each week, we need to lay out a design of what the final program should look like, as well as how it should function. For testing purposes, we'll use Microsoft's home page. Eventually, we'll want the final output to look like Figure 10-9.

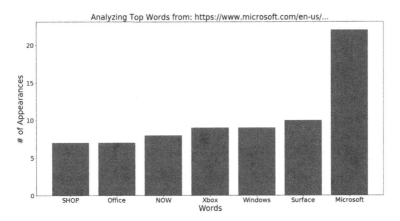

Figure 10-9. *Analyzing Microsoft's most frequent words on their home page*

We're going to make the program continually ask the users if they'd like to scrape a web site, followed by accepting the users' input for the site they'd like to analyze. After that, we can perform our web site; filter out all information that isn't useful like article words, newline characters, etc.; and finally be able to create the bar plot. The program output should look like the following:

```
>>> Would you like to scrape a website (y/n)? y
>>> Enter a website to analyze: https://www.microsoft.com/en-us/
>>> The top word is: Microsoft
>>> *** show bar plot ***
>>> Would you like to scrape a website (y/n)? n
>>> Thanks for analyzing! Come back again!
```

In order to get the output working properly, we need to create an outline of the steps the program will require. Feel free to take a second to try and write them out yourself. The program that we create will need to perform the following steps:

1. Ask users if they'd like to web scrape a site.

    - If the user says yes

      1. Accept input from users about the site they would like to scrape.

      2. Send a request to the web site.

      3. Parse all text from page content within the request response.

4. Filter out all non-text elements, such as scripts, comments, etc.

5. Filter out all article words and useless characters like newlines and tabs.

6. Loop over all remaining text and count the frequency of each word.

7. Keep the top seven words and display the most used word.

8. Create a bar plot of the top seven words.

- If the user says no

   1. Exit the program and display a thank you message.

2. Continue to ask the users if they'd like to scrape a site until they say no.

Importing Libraries

We need to start off by importing all the libraries that we'll be using throughout this project. Let's put all the imports in their own cell so that we only need to run the import once rather than importing them each time we run the code for the program:

```
1| # import all necessary libraries
2| import requests
3| import matplotlib.pyplot as plt
4| from bs4 import BeautifulSoup
5| from bs4.element import Comment
6| from IPython.display import clear_output
```

Go ahead and run the cell. The only new import that you haven't seen before is the import on line 5. To analyze only words that appear on the page, we'll need to filter out all text within the comments somewhere in the program. Using the *Comment* class later will allow us to recognize if the text is within a comment or not, so that we can filter it out properly.

Creating the Main Loop

Let's write all the following code in the next cell, so that we don't have to rerun all the imports. We'll need to create a main loop, so that we can continue to ask the users if they'd like to scrape a web site. When they do, we'll simply print the site they entered for now:

```
1| # main loop should ask if user wants to scrape, then what site to
   scrape
2| while input("Would you like to scrape a website (y/n)? ") == "y":
3|   try:
4|           clear_output( )
6|           site = input("Enter a website to analyze: ")
8|           print(site)        # remove after runs properly
9|   except:
10|           print("Something went wrong, please try again.")
12| print("Thanks for analyzing! Come back again!")
```

Go ahead and run the cell. This gives us our basic loop structure of asking the users for input about the site they would like to scrape. If they choose not to scrape, then we output a thank you message. We want to wrap the main portion of this loop in a *try-except* clause because we can't expect the user to always input a valid URL. If the user doesn't put in a valid URL, an error could occur. Now, we don't have to worry about the error, and the program will continually ask the users if they'd like to scrape another web site.

Note   Anytime you restart the notebook, you'll need to run the import cell again.

Scraping the Web Site

Now that we've accepted input from the user, we need to scrape the web site. It would be best to separate this code from the main loop, so let's put it inside of its own function:

```
1| # request site and return top 7 most used words
2| def scrape(site):
3|   page = requests.get(site)
```

```
 5|   soup = BeautifulSoup(page.content, "html.parser")
 7|   print( soup.prettify( ) )     # remove after runs properly
 9|   # main loop should...    □□□
14|            site = input("Enter a website...       □□□
16|            scrape(site)
17|   except:    □□□
```

Go ahead and run the cell. After we ask the user to input a web site, we call the *scrape* function on line 16 with the *site* variable as the argument. The program will then request the content from the site and parse it with BeautifulSoup. For testing purposes, we use the *prettify()* method to output the response that we get back. If you look through the output, you'll notice there's a lot of text inside of element tags that don't show up on the web site. Tags like *scripts* and *comments* include text that we do not want to include in our analysis, so we'll need to filter them out eventually. Once they are filtered out, we'll be left with the actual text that appears on the home page of the web site. Remove the code on line 7 once the cell runs properly.

Note   To follow along with the book, use the Microsoft URL: `www.microsoft.com/en-us/`.

Scrape All Text

Now that we're receiving a response, we can begin to parse all the text within the page content:

```
 1|   # request site and return top 7 most used words
 2|   def scrape(site):
 3|     page = requests.get(site)
 5|     soup = BeautifulSoup(page.content, "html.parser")
 7|     text = soup.find_all(text=True)     # will get all text within the
       document
 9|     print(text)     # remove after runs properly
11|   # main loop should...    □□□
```

Go ahead and run the cell. We use the find_all method from our BeautifulSoup object in order to grab every piece of text contained within the page. Notice this gives us back a list that contains newline characters, tab characters, scripts, comments, and the actual text that we need within the proper text elements like *h1*, *p*, etc. The next step is to filter out those unnecessary elements. Remove line 9 once the cell runs properly; this is used for testing purposes only.

Filtering Elements

Although we're parsing the text from the page content, much of the text is within elements that we don't want to include in our analysis. Let's take the script tag, for instance. The *script* tag is used to write JavaScript within the web page. If we were to include this in our analysis, it would lead to improper results. The same goes for HTML comments, which look like the following:

```
<!-- this is an HTML comment -->
```

Any text within an HTML comment is not seen on the web page. It's the same concept as a Python comment. They're used for programmers and not read by compilers. Knowing that we only want to perform an analysis on words that appear on the page, we must filter out these unnecessary elements:

```
 1| # filter out all elements that do not contain text that appears on site
 2| def filterTags(element):
 3|   if element.parent.name in [ "style", "script", "head", "title",
      "meta", "[document]" ]:
 4|         return False
 6|   if isinstance(element, Comment):
 7|         return False
 9|   return True
17| text = soup.find_all(text=True)...      □□□
19|   visible_text = filter(filterTags, text)
21|   for text in visible_text:
22|         print(text)        # remove after runs properly
24| # main loop should...    □□□
```

Go ahead and run the cell. After we parse all the text from the page content on line 17, we filter out the unnecessary elements on line 19. The filter method is used to loop over every item within our *text* variable and apply the *filterTags* function to know if the item should be included. We basically want to return *True* if the item is not a comment or element tag that shouldn't be included. Line 3 is where we check to see if the text is within an element that we do not want to include. All the strings included in the list on line 3 are HTML elements. Comments are slightly different though because they are not elements. To know if an item is a comment, we need to use Beautiful Soup's *Comment* object.

Note   When Beautiful Soup parses the page content, it recognizes HTML as one of four objects: Tag, NavigableString, BeautifulSoup, and Comment.

On line 6, we check to see if the item is an instance of the *Comment* object. If it is, we return *False* so that we can filter it out. If the item is not a comment or its parent is a valid element, then we return *True*. We then loop over the variable to output each item on line 21. We're now left with only the words that appear on the web page. You'll notice that there is a lot of white space between each word, which is the next step. Remove line 22 after the cell runs properly, as it is only used for testing purposes.

Filtering Waste

The next step is to filter out any escaping characters (*newlines, tabs*); article words, such as a, an, the, etc.; and any other words we deem useless. When we perform the analysis on a site, we want to see the topmost descriptive words. Knowing that a site's top word is "*the*" does not depict any information about the site. For example, when scraping a news site, we would expect to see keywords about the top story of the day. To perform this filter, we'll need to create another function that will handle removing what we call "*waste*":

```
1| filter article words and hidden characters
2| def filterWaste(word):
3|   bad_words = ( "the", "a", "in", "of", "to", "you", "\xa0", "and",
     "at", "on", "for", "from", "is", "that", "his",
4|                  "are", "be", "-", "as", "&", "they", "with", "how",
                    "was", "her", "him", "i", "has", "|" )
```

```
6|  if word.lower( ) in bad_words:
7|          return False
8|  else:
9|          return True
11| # filter out all elements that do not...    □□□
31| for text in visible_text:    □□□
32|          words = text.replace("\n", "").replace("\t", "").split("
")       # replace all hidden chars
34|          words = list( filter(filterWaste, words) )
36|          for word in words:
37|                  print(word, end=" ")       # remove after runs properly
39| # main loop should...    □□□
```

Go ahead and run the cell. We start this process on line 31 by looping over each item in visible_text and replacing all newline and tab characters with empty strings. Then we run a filter on that item with our *filterWaste* function to see if we need to remove it from the list on line 34. Within the *filterWaste* function, we define a set of words or characters that we want to filter out called *bad_words*. After converting the item to lowercase, we check to see if it exists within *bad_words*; if it does, we return *False*; otherwise, we return *True* to keep it within the list. On line 37 we output each word after we perform the filter. The words contained in this output are descriptive and informative enough to tell us what the web site is mainly talking about. Remove line 37 once the cell runs properly, as this is used for testing purposes only.

Note   You can add more words or characters to the *bad_words* data collection if you'd like. This is to simply get us by for the time being. There is a library called *NLTK* which has a large list of article words and characters that you can use for larger projects when necessary.

Count Word Frequency

After we've filtered out all the waste and elements, we're left with the proper words to run our analysis on. The next step is to count the number of times a given word appears. A dictionary would be best practice to keep track of the count for each word because we can use the word as the key and the frequency as the value:

```
29|    visible_text = filter(filterTags, text)...      □□□
31|    word_count = { }
33|    for text in visible_text:      □□□
38|        for word in words:      □□□
39|            if word != "":           # if it doesn't equal an empty
                                        string
40|                if word in word_count:
41|                    word_count[ word ] += 1
42|                else:
43|                    word_count[ word ] = 1
45|    print(word_count)      # remove after runs properly
53| # main loop should...      □□□
```

Go ahead and run the cell. On line 31 we create our dictionary to keep track of the word count. As we loop over each word in our *words* list, we first check to see if it's an empty string because we converted all escaping characters to empty strings and certainly don't want to include them in the count. On line 40, we check to see if the word has already been added to the dictionary, in which case we would add one to the value (*line 41*). If it hasn't been added to the dictionary yet, then we simply add a key of the word and a value of **1**. We output the result on line 45 to see the word and its frequency. Now we can view all the words and the times they occurred; however, we want to plot the top words, so we'll need to sort the dictionary next. Remove line 45 after the cell runs properly.

Sort Dictionary by Word Frequency

In order to output or return the top seven words, we'll need to sort the dictionary by
the value:

```
43|                                     word_count[ word ] = 1          □□□
45|    word_count = sorted(word_count.items( ), key=lambda kv: kv[1],
       reverse=True)   # sort on value
47|    print( word_count[ :7 ] )       # remove after runs properly
49| # main loop should...    □□□
```

Go ahead and run the cell. To understand what's going on here, first we need to
clarify what the output of *.items()* becomes:

```
>>> d = { "word" : 1, "hello" : 2 }
>>> result = d.items( )
>>> print(result)
dict_items( [ ("word", 1), ("count", 2) ] )
```

The result is a couple tuples within a list. Normally, using the *sorted* function on a
dictionary would result in a list sorted by the key; however, when we use the *lambda*
function to sort based on value by changing the *key* argument, it's really taking in each
of these tuples and sorting based on index 1, which is the value, which represents the
frequency of the word. Remember that the *sorted* function returns a list. When we run
line 45, it results in a list of tuples sorted from highest to lowest value because of the
argument "*reverse=True*". Lastly, we output the top seven words by slicing. Remove line
47 after the cell runs properly.

Displaying the Top Word

Now that we're getting the top seven words, let's output the most used word for good
measure:

```
45|    word_count = sorted...      □□□
47|    return word_count[ :7 ]
49| # main loop should...    □□□
54|            site = input("Enter a website...       □□□
```

```
56|              top_words = scrape(site)
58|              top_word = top_words[0]     # tuple of (word, count)
60|              print("The top word is: { }".format( top_word[0] ))        #
don't remove
61|    except:        □□□
```

Go ahead and run the cell. We start by returning the top seven words from the *scrape* function rather than printing them out. This will return the list of tuples back to our main loop on line 56 and save them into the *top_words* variable. After that, we assign the first tuple into our *top_word* variable because it represents the most frequent word used on the page. Lastly, we output the top word on line 60 by accessing the zero index of the tuple that contains the word and frequency count.

Graphing the Results

The last step in our program that we need to execute is graphing the results within a bar plot:

```
1| # graph results of top 7 words
2| def displayResults(words, site):
3|   count = [ item[ 1 ] for item in words ][ : : -1 ]        # reverses
                                                                order
4|   word = [ item[ 0 ] for item in words ][ : : -1 ]         # gets word out
                                                                of reverses
                                                                order

6|   plt.figure( figsize=(20, 10) )        # define how large the figure
                                             appears

8|   plt.bar(word, count)

10|  plt.title("Analyzing Top Words from: { }...".format( site[ :50 ] ),
     fontname="Sans Serif", fontsize=24)
11|  plt.xlabel("Words", fontsize=24)
12|  plt.ylabel("# of Appearances", fontsize=24)
13|  plt.xticks(fontname="Sans Serif", fontsize=20)
14|  plt.yticks(fontname="Sans Serif", fontsize=20)
```

```
16|  plt.show( )
77|          print("The top word is...      □□□
79|          displayResults(top_words, site)      # call to graph
80|  except:      □□□
```

Go ahead and run the cell. We'll get the final output that we we've been programming toward throughout this entire lesson. The graph will show the top seven words and their frequency in a nicely formatted bar plot by calling the *displayResults* function on line 79. We pass in the arguments of *top_words* and *site* in order to give the graph its data and title. On lines 3 and 4, we separate the values and words into their respective lists using comprehension. We then reverse them using the slice at the end; otherwise, it would show the graph from highest to lowest. The bar graph is plotted on line 8 by passing this data into the *bar* method. Lastly, we add a title, labels, and some styles.

Final Output

The program is now complete and can be used to analyze the top words for any web site. Note that some sites can and do block the request, in which case the exception will be executed. You can find all the code for this week, as well as this project in the Github repository.

Today we learned how to create a program that would scrape any site input by the user. It was important to see how we could use several of these data analysis libraries together to create a useful tool. Now we can use this web tool to analyze news sites and see trending information. Of course, this is a simple web scraper but with proper modifications could become a more useful tool.

Weekly Summary

There are many Python libraries that are useful for data analysis. Throughout this week, we covered some of the most widely used modules and libraries in the industry. This week has prepared you to begin learning more about analysis and how to implement these libraries further to improve your skills. Having covered **virtual environments**, you'll know how to work with Python libraries and manage your packages. Using the

requests module, we were able to call APIs and parse page content. This module allows our programs to communicate with other software in order to improve user experience. One of the most important libraries this week, however, is the **Pandas** data analysis library. It's used by data analysts and scientists in almost every field. It gives you the power to use Python and SQL together; it's extremely efficient and makes working with databases and files much easier. It's truly the end all, be all library for analysis. Data analysis wouldn't be complete, however, without visualization. Using **matplotlib** we were able to cover a variety of plots that we could use and how to effectively showcase our data. It's important to remember that data without proper visualization will never produce quality results. The last library we covered was for web scraping with **Beautiful Soup**, an important library to help make sense of other languages within Python, where we were able to parse information and text from a page request. Lastly, we coupled three of these four lessons within a program to create a web scraping analysis tool. To further your learning on this topic, you can use `www.elitedatascience.com` or learn about the data science libraries, such as *NLTK* and *SK-Learn*.

Challenge Question Solution

As we learned in the lesson on Wednesday, it's difficult and time-consuming to try and implement a 3D visualization of data. The question this week asked how we could simplify this while expressing a 3-dimensional graph. Having covered the answer toward the end of the lesson on Wednesday, we found that we can use **color** as a third dimension. This allows us to keep a graph within 2-dimensional space but have three dimensions. This is important to keep in mind when trying to simplify data for those who make decisions based on visualizations.

Weekly Challenges

To test out your skills, try these challenges:

1. **User Input**: As we saw in our Friday project, there were many article words or characters that we wanted to filter out. Unfortunately, we can't keep track of all of them for each site. For this challenge, implement a block of code that asks the users what additional words or characters they would like to filter out so that they may alter the words shown.

2. **Saving the Plot**: Implement a block of code that asks the users if they would like to save the file. If they do, be sure to ask the users what they would like to call the image and save it with that name.

3. **Pandas Implementation**: Rather than using a dictionary to track the words from the web site scrape in our project, implement Pandas into the code to track the information. You should be able to perform a head or tail function to see the top or bottom most frequently used words.

4. **Saving the Data**: After implementing Pandas to save the unique words and their frequency, output the information to a CSV for each site. The name of the file should represent the web site name, for example, *"microsoft_frequent_words.csv"*.

Post-Course: What to Do Now?

Often, when a student finishes a class or a reader finishes a book, they're left wondering where to go next? It's a broad question, especially when you're new to this field. If you've been programming for a long time, this is probably easy for you, as you most likely read this book to pick up or switch to Python. For the rest of you, it's much tougher, especially if this is the first book you've read on programming.

My answer is generally the same to each person that asks… what interests you? Your answer will affect my advice for you. What follows is a list of resources, video channels, and other books to read based on the category that interests you. Each section has been separated by the types of jobs you can receive with knowledge of Python.

When you embark on becoming a programmer, remember to give back to the community. As a developer, we use resources like Quora or Stack Overflow to help get answers to our problems. Be the type of person that answers respectfully and helpfully. Remember those that helped you out did so on their free time. Without the continued help throughout our community, we would not learn and continue to improve.

Back-End Development with Python

When you become a developer, there are many roles you can apply for. Back-end development is made for those of us who don't want to worry about the design, interfaces, or anything front end related but rather focus on the algorithms, speed, and mechanics of the software itself. If you find passion in Python and back-end concepts like SQL, servers, requests, and APIs, then this is a great place for you to start.

319

© Connor P. Milliken 2020
C. P. Milliken, *Python Projects for Beginners*, https://doi.org/10.1007/978-1-4842-5355-7

Full-Stack Development with Python

Full-stack development encompasses front end, back end, server side, and web dev all in one. There's a lot to learn when you want to become a full-stack engineer. If you're eager to learn more about how to build full-scale web sites, software as a service, networking, and more... then this path would help.

Data Analysis with Python

We only began to scratch the surface of what you can do with Python in data analytical roles. If you found that you enjoyed Week 10 within the book, then this would certainly be a great next step for you.

Data Science with Python

We never touched upon this subject, merely pointed out certain concepts in Week 10. Data science encompasses many different fields of study: machine learning, artificial intelligence, computer systems, web scraping, forms of data analysis, and much more. If you think you'd be interested in learning more about these topics, this is the right step for you.

Resources

Table 1 shows general resources. These are resources just to get you started on the right path. There are many more valuable resources out there for each of these categories.

Table 1. *Resources*

Name	Type	Category
Beginning Django *By Daniel Rubio (Apress, 2017)*	Book	Full Stack
Beginning Python, 3rd ed. *By Magnus Lie Hetland (Apress, 2017)*	Book	General
The New and Improved Flask Mega Tutorial *By Miguel Grinberg (Self-published, 2017)*	Book	Full Stack
HTML and CSS: Design and Build Websites *By Jon Duckett (John Wiley & Sons, 2011)*	Book	Front End
Deep Learning with Python *Francis Chollet (Manning Publications, 2017)*	Book	Data Science
Practical SQL *By Anthony DeBarros (No Starch Press, 2018)*	Book	Back End
Python for Data Analysis *By Wes McKinney (O'Reilly Media, 2012)*	Book	Data Analysis
Python Machine Learning *By Sebastian Raschka (Packt Publishing, 2015)*	Book	Data Science
Python Crash Course ***By Eric Matthes (No Starch Press, 2015)***	Book	General
Quora www.quora.com/	Web	General
Stack Overflow https://stackoverflow.com/	Web	General
Code Wars www.codewars.com/	Web	Back End
Hacker Rank www.hackerrank.com/	Web	General ·
w3schools www.w3schools.com/	Web	General

(continued)

Table 1. (*continued*)

Name	Type	Category
Geeks for Geeks www.geeksforgeeks.org/	Web	Back End
Elite Data Science https://elitedatascience.com/	Web	Data Science
Socratica www.youtube.com/user/SocraticaStudios	YouTube	General
Traversy Media www.youtube.com/user/TechGuyWeb	YouTube	Full Stack
Sentdex www.youtube.com/sentdex	YouTube	Data Science
Siraj Raval www.youtube.com/channel/ UCWN3xxRkmTPmbKwht9FuE5A	YouTube	Data Science
Pretty Printed www.youtube.com/channel/UC- QDfvrRIDB6FObIO4I4HkQ	YouTube	Full Stack
Programming with Mosh www.youtube.com/user/programmingwithmosh	YouTube	Full Stack
DesignCourse www.youtube.com/user/DesignCourse	YouTube	Front End
Computerphile www.youtube.com/user/Computerphile	YouTube	Back End

Final Message

To my readers, I just want to thank you from the bottom of my heart for taking the time to read this book. A lot of work, time, effort, and sweat went into the creation of each of these lessons, and I hope that you enjoyed reading them, as much as I have enjoyed writing them. It's truly been an honor to contribute to the world of technology, and I'm forever grateful for the opportunity to help you in your pursuit of knowledge. If I can give you one last piece of advice, it's to always keep learning and don't give up. I didn't enjoy programming for a long time, but then it became a passion of mine. With hard work and effort, you can accomplish anything.

Index

A

Algorithmic complexity
  Big O Notation, 234–236
  Bubble Sort, 239
  dictionaries *vs* list, 238
  hash tables, 236, 237
  insertion sort, 240
Anaconda, 6
  defined, 8
  installation, 6–8
Application programming
      interface (API), 259
Attributes
  declaration, 156
  global *vs.* instance, 159, 160
  __init__() method, 157–158
  instances, 157
  self keyword, 158

B

Big O Notation, 234–236
Binary search
  final design, 209–211
  program setup
    loop to repeat steps, 214–215
    middle index, 212, 213
    output, 216
    return false, 215
    sort the list, 211–212

value greater, 213
    value less, 214
Blackjack game
  addCard method, 177, 178
  build, deck, 175
  calcHand method, 180, 181
  calculate winner, 183
  code, 184
  dealer's turn, 182, 183
  game class, create, 174–175
  game loop, 185
  necessary functions, import, 174
  player class, create, 176, 177
  player's turn, 181, 182
  pop method, 175
  pullCard method, 176
  showHand method, 178, 179
Branching statements/conditionals
  elif statements
    checking multiple conditions, 59
    within conditionals, 60
    working, 58
  else statements
    code, 62, 63
    working, 62
  if statements
    checking user input, 54
    code, 53
    comparison operators, 54
    vs elif statements, 60

© Connor P. Milliken 2020
C. P. Milliken, *Python Projects for Beginners*, https://doi.org/10.1007/978-1-4842-5355-7